SCIENCE FICTION IN THE CINEMA   by John Baxter
Above: *The Incredible Shrinking Man*

In the same series
produced by THE TANTIVY PRESS
and edited by Peter Cowie:

SCIENCE FICTION IN THE CINEMA

by JOHN BAXTER

THE INTERNATIONAL FILM GUIDE SERIES
A. S. BARNES & CO., NEW YORK
A. ZWEMMER LIMITED, LONDON

Acknowledgements

THE AUTHOR wishes to acknowledge the assistance of the following individuals and organisations: The British Film Institute; The Danish Film Archive; Ceskoslovensky Filmexport (Dr. Edward Hais); National Library of Australia (Mr. Charles Gilbert); National Film Board of Canada; Sydney Film Festival (Mr. David Stratton); Paramount Pictures (Mr. Jim Sayle); Universal Pictures (Mr. George Cansdell); Ron West, Charles Higham, Ian Klava, Ian Dunlop, Joan Saint, Anne Hirsch and Barrie Pattison's All Electric Lounge Room Wall.

Portions of this book originally appeared in a different form in *Film Digest* magazine, and are reprinted by permission of the Editorial Board.

In the case of American films mentioned in this book, all dates, spelling etc. are based on the *Catalogue of Copyright Entries: Motion Pictures 1912–1939* (Library of Congress, Washington, D.C., 1951).

In the compilation of the filmography, the author is indebted to Carlos Clarens's *Horror Movies* (Secker and Warburg: 1967), *Monthly Film Bulletin,* Barrie Pattison, Ian Klava and Alan Dodd.

This book is for JOSEPHINE.
Un siège d'honneur, belle orchidée.

COVER STILLS
Front: *Barbarella* (courtesy of Paramount)
Back: *The Space Children* (also Paramount)

Contents

Above: Zeman's AN INVENTION FOR DESTRUCTION
Below: Richard Carlson in his RIDERS TO THE STARS

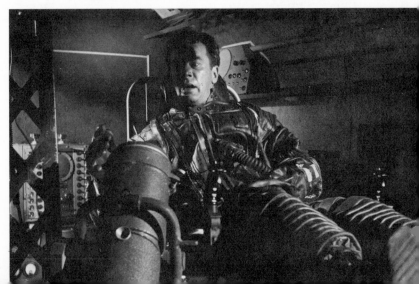

1. What Science Fiction Films Where?

Throughout the history of science fiction it has been an article of faith among its readers that filmed sf was an abomination, that it degraded the field and provided nothing of interest to the serious mind.

After seeing a few sf films one accepted this view with alacrity. The plots one saw unrolling on the screen had little relation to those used in the books and magazines of science fiction which one read, while the recreation of fantastic situations fell far short of that possible in the mind of the interested sf reader. If one went to sf films after that, it was to mock rather than to watch.

A similar lack of interest was shown by film buffs, who found as much to scorn in the films' plots as did science fiction fans. Yet neither side spared a thought for the faceless crowd surrounding them, the devoted audience which filled theatres for even the most trivial and transparent piece of space opera. If anybody was aware that science fiction film was a popular part of the commercial cinema, he quickly put the idea aside.

Whatever we may think of science fiction films, the field remains a lively and popular form of entertainment, but unlike the Western it has never achieved a sufficiently large audience to rate serious study. Filmgoers reject it because its visual conventions are often crude and unformed. Science fiction readers likewise reject it because its plots are tawdry. But in a sense sf films are neither science fiction nor films; to understand why, one must analyse both fields and the vexed relations between them.

Pragmatic, idealistic, sustained by the mystique of technology and a belief in the desirability of mathematical order in human affairs, science fiction's concern is not with individuals but with movements and ideas. Generally its characters have no function except as symbols in the writer's chessboard development of his premise. It is not that people are unimportant in the science fiction writer's scheme of things, but rather that they are useless in developing the idea or concept which he is putting forward. As Kingsley

Amis has said, in sf the "hero" is often the plot itself.[1]

Contrast with this utilitarian field the fantasy and illusion of film. Even the greatest of cinema artists cannot do more than approximate in symbols the intellectual development of an abstract premise on which science fiction depends so much for its effects, while the lack of a set of symbols common to sf writer and film-maker renders the work of one totally alien to the other.

Science fiction film, then, is an intellectual impossibility. Yet some thousands of films have been made which are advertised and viewed as science fiction, and which the public accepts as a field of expression differing quantitatively alone from the stories available to them in sf novels and magazines. What are these films if not science fiction?

The answer to this question is as difficult as that to the query, "What *is* science fiction?" In terms of audience response sf literature and sf cinema have little common ground. The audience for science fiction film is not a science fiction audience, but merely part of the great mass audience of the cinema generally. Similarly the film-makers creating sf films are not sf devotees but artists working in a sub-section of the mass cinema. Their preoccupation and attitudes are, like those of their audience, remote from those of sf readers. Contact is tangential, a genuine coincidence of outlook rare in the extreme.

Science fiction and film critics have both summed up the difference in attitude between sf writers and sf film-makers. Discussing sf films in the early Fifties Penelope Houston commented, "Perhaps a more significant implication is to be found in the whole attitude to science itself (*in these films*). The old-style wicked scientist, part alchemist, part witch doctor, who spent his time manufacturing death rays, turning men into apes or apes into men, has become a somewhat *démodé* figure. Human agency now counts for little, and the rocket, the atomic weapon, the electronic gadget, the cybernetic brain machine—expressions of science considered almost as an abstraction—have taken charge. One may conjecture that superstition, the exposed nerve of society on which the horror

8

film played in its time, is now bound up for most of us with this alarming apparatus."[2]

From the other side of the fence distinguished science fiction critic Damon Knight expressed similar misgivings in discussing Richard Matheson's novel *The Shrinking Man* and Frank Robinson's *The Power*. "Why did the movies buy this bad book (*The Shrinking Man*)?" he asks. "Because it has a Creature in it—the aforesaid Black Widow Spider. But this only leads up to another question; how did it happen that the big science fiction movie boom turned itself into a Creature cycle? . . . . . To answer by indirection, let's look again at *The Power*. (*The book's superman villain*) is not a man but a symbol; he's danger walking faceless down a dark street; danger, lurking invisible somewhere in the mechanical hum of the city. (*He*) is the wise guy that wants to kill you. He's the man with the keen eyes who uses words you can't understand, who juggles with dangerous things that you can't even see. He's the man who invented the V2 and The Bomb. The scientist, Professor, Egghead. . . . It's anti-science fiction; a turning away, not only from the standard props of science fiction . . . but from the habits of thought and belief which underlie science itself—the assumption that things can be put into categories . . . ; that things can be measured . . . ; the assumption of cause and effect."[3]

Both writers are noting the same phenomenon, but with totally different responses. To Miss Houston the horror in sf film is an expression of a universal human tendency—"superstition, the exposed nerve of society"—but to Mr. Knight, the horror is a betrayal on the part of artists, both writers and film-makers, of their role as creators of visionary literature. In his statement he reaffirms the basic tenets of science fiction, the belief in order and the duty of humankind to observe it. To one, superstition is natural, to the other it is anathema. The gulf is profound and unbridgable—it is the same gulf that exists between the cinema and science fiction.

In considering these films, however, both writers have agreed on one thing; the basis that sf films have in superstition and horror. Knight observes that books like *The Shrinking Man* and *The Power*

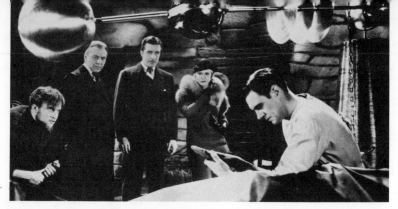

Artificial life: Colin Clive (foreground) in FRANKENSTEIN

are "anti-science fiction." By implication the films based on them are also anti-science, and in fact both works when filmed did exhibit the tendencies which the critics underlined. Science fiction supports logic and order, sf film illogic and chaos. Its roots lie not in the visionary literature of the Nineteenth Century, to which science fiction owes most of its origins, but in older forms and attitudes, the medieval fantasy world, the era of the masque, the morality play and the Grand Guignol.

Like the horror film, which shares some of sf film's ritual nature, science fiction cinema relies heavily on a set of elements handed down from generation to generation. These elements provide the building blocks from which the writer and director may construct a story acceptable to the vast public devoted to this field. In the horror film these elements are Germanic phenomena like artificial life (*Frankenstein*, *Der Golem*), dismemberment (*The Hands of Orlac*, *Mad Love*, *The Beast with Five Fingers*), Beauty and the Beast (almost all horror films), masks and waxworks (*Waxworks*, *Mystery of the Wax Museum*, *House of Wax*); the list is finite but extensive. Armed with an intimate knowledge of these building blocks, producers of horror films have supplied the market with a stream of fascinating but largely interchangable stories, distinguishable one from another only by subtle differences in visual style and approach.

Science fiction film works on a similar principle but, because it does not have the benefit of a rich tradition of European material on which to draw, its fund of concepts is limited. Those it has fall generally into two categories, the loss of individuality and the threat of knowledge.

The loss of personal individuality is probably the most common plot situation in sf film. It is at the root of countless hypnotism stories from Fritz Lang's *Dr. Mabuse der Spieler* through Forties American serials of brain transfer, right up to modern productions like *Privilege* and *Fahrenheit 451*. The threat can be manifested in many ways; social control, as in *Metropolis* and *Things To Come,* psychological control, as in *Donovan's Brain;* direct electrical domination of the mind, as in *Batman.*

It is not difficult to see a direct relationship between the fear of science to which Damon Knight refers and the sf film-makers' habit of contrasting humanistic protagonists with forces that attempt unsuccessfully to overwhelm the individual mind, but the fear and distrust of science reaches its most obvious form in films devoted to the second theme, the threat of knowledge. Probably no line is more common to sf cinema than, "There are some things Man is not meant to know." A thousand actors have delivered it to unheeding mad scientists, just as many chastened heroes mumbled it over the smoking ruins of invading spaceships and experimental research laboratories. It expresses the universal fear all men have of the unknown and inexplicable, a fear science fiction rejects but which has firmly entrenched itself in the sf cinema.

This belief in the dangerous nature of knowledge has motivated all the mad scientist plots since *Paris Qui Dort,* where an amiable but misguided tinkerer freezes Paris into immobility for a few days until his niece and a young adventurer sort it all out, their success illustrating yet another sf cinema belief, that love can protect, solve and illuminate more than any other force. The same pattern can be seen in the whole Creature cycle of the Fifties, where some trivial action, often nothing more overt than the mounting of an expedition to farthest Swaziland, brings to life a monstrous throwback that ravages the countryside until tamed by the intervention of man or, more often, God. Having ruined New York, London or Tokyo, the creature retires majestically to the sea, leaving man to repent of his hubris. No medieval morality play could dramatise more meaningfully nor in such readily acceptable images the desirability of remaining firmly in the grip of our simpler emotions, sustained only by faith in a benign creator.

If sf film's sources lie remote from science fiction, its visual style is likewise drawn from other areas, primarily the semi-visual world of the comic strip. Like the *bande-dessinée*, sf film offers simple plots and one-dimensional characters in settings so familiar as to have the quality of ritual. It relies on a set of visual conventions and a symbolic language, bypassing intellect to make a direct appeal to the senses. Written sf is usually radical in politics and philosophy; sf cinema, like the comic strips, endorses the political and moral climate of its day. "In aesthetic terms," a recent history of the comic strip points out, "the strips' achievement is the development of a form of narrative art using its own unique conventions and techniques."[4] This phrase is equally appropriate to the sf film.

But science fiction is more than a comic strip that moves, and the "form of narrative art" which the field has developed is of such complexity that one book can do little more than glance at it. In addition its ingenuity in exploring old themes and developing new ones makes sf film an inexhaustible area for the historian and devotee of cinema. The use of set symbols and patterns of construction does not hamper the great sf film-makers. In order to dramatise the inhumanity of the technological universe and man's domination by the machine, Fritz Lang in *Metropolis* harnesses his hero to a grotesquely enlarged gauge, the hands of which reduce him remorselessly to exhaustion. Searching for a similar response, John Frankenheimer in *Seven Days in May* shows Martin Balsam bobbing across a harbour in a tiny boat while above him looms the vast flank of an aircraft carrier. In both cases a sense of man oppressed by an unfeeling technology is tellingly conveyed.

There is no stock situation, no matter how over-used, which does not come newly to life in the hands of an imaginative director. The aged *cliché* of innocent childhood menaced by brute force can be Frankenstein's monster kneeling beside a studio lake to watch a little girl picking flowers, or a child stumbling terrified out of the desert to scream wild-eyed about "Them! Them! *Them!*". Only the most obvious similarities can be noted between Ishiro Honda's stolid creatures shambling knee-deep through Tokyo and Eugene Lourié's tortured Rhedosaurus enmeshed in a burning roller coaster in *The Beast from 20,000 Fathoms;* and who would ever confuse the palatial flying saucer of *Forbidden Planet* with Klaatu's ascetic vehicle in *The Day the Earth Stood Still?* It is variations like this engineered by inspired creators that have made science fiction film one of the most fascinating fields in the complex mosaic of contemporary cinema.

These are the aesthetics of science fiction film, and it is with this aspect of the field that we are mainly concerned here. The social significance of sf film is a good deal harder to analyse, especially when one is still so close to the period which produced it in its greatest bulk. We have long recognised that the horror film is a palimpsest of national psychoses from which it is possible to deduce much of interest about cultural motivation, but the true significance of the sf film has yet to be explored fully.

But whatever its sociological importance, sf cinema is basically a sensuous medium. It is the poetry of the atomic age, a shorthand evocation of the pressures that are making us what we are and will be. It is also heir to a strange hieratic beauty and a cultural humour which one imagined technology had robbed us of. Just as the pop music of the Forties seems more redolent of that age's anxieties and attitudes than its rather self-conscious literature, so phenomena like sf film may one day be seen to represent more completely than any other art form the *angst* of this decade.

13

2. First Contact

O N OCTOBER 24, 1895, two Englishmen applied to patent a new invention. Herbert George Wells was twenty-nine, a young author who had only recently given up teaching to write professionally. Robert Paul was about the same age, but with a wider background in his own specialty, manufacturing scientific instruments. Together they made application for a patent on a device to duplicate the effects Wells had described in his novel *The Time Machine* published the previous year.

As Paul and Wells conceived it, the Time Machine was the first audiovisual mixed media art form, a chamber fitted with movable floors and walls, vents for injecting currents of air, and screens on which could be shown scenes from all periods of time by means of motion picture film and slides. Audiences could be given the illusion of moving back or forward in time, of seeing in close-up or at a distance life in eras long before or after their own. It was a sophisticated and showmanlike idea.

"After the last scene is presented," Paul wrote, ". . . the spectators should be given the sensation of voyaging backwards from the last epoch to the present, or the present epoch may be supposed to have been accidentally passed and a past scene represented on the machine coming to a standstill, after which the impression of travelling forward again to the present epoch may be given, and the re-arrival notified by the representation on the screen of the place at which the exhibition is held. . . ."[5]

The plan might have worked had either man possessed the money to develop it. However, Wells moved on to eminence as a writer and Paul to frustration and obscurity as a pioneer of the cinema. For both, the splendid dream of a Time Machine which worked was soon forgotten, but a vital contact had been made. For the first time the imagination and mythopoetry of science fiction had encountered the pragmatism of technology. The relationship, though chronically strained, exists to this day.

The idea developed by Paul and Wells was the most meaningful of all early attempts to combine sf and cinema. Nothing to compare with it in imagination or ambition was to occur until the Forties, when cinematic technique finally offered us the all-enveloping realism of three dimensions, wide-screen and sophisticated sound systems. The Time Machine marked the beginning of the basic sf film style, the attempt to recreate in visual terms the effects of an imagined situation. All film-makers attempting sf film for the next half century were to develop this essentially arid area.

The years between 1895 and 1930 are dotted with films which, by the loose plot-oriented definitions of the field, qualify as sf. Georges Méliès in 1902 produced what is probably the first example of sf film, A Trip to the Moon (Le Voyage dans la Lune), a sixteen minute production in thirty tableaux representing a rough approximation of Verne's From the Earth to the Moon and Wells's First Men in the Moon. As in Verne's book the astronauts are fired from a huge gun, but where he had them falling into orbit around the moon and never landing, Méliès takes from Wells the landing, an encounter with a race of "Selenites," a last minute escape to Earth and the erection of a commemorative statue in the town square.

It is easy to laugh at Méliès's music hall depiction of space flight, but A Trip to the Moon differs little from the polished products of today's sf film producers. The chorus line of Folies Bergère poules who load the projectile into the space gun serve roughly the same purpose as the sexy heroines of Fifties space opera, and the "Selenites" with pop-eyes and prickly cardboard carapaces display as much imagination on the part of their designer as more modern bug eyed monsters. But, as Georges Sadoul says, "Méliès explored every device of the theatre in order to exploit it for the cinema."[6] A Trip to the Moon, whatever the form in which it is presented, is basically a theatrical performance.

More cinematic merit exists in Méliès's second excursion into sf, his 1904 production An Impossible Voyage (Le Voyage à Travers l'Impossible), in which a high-speed train takes off from the summit of the Jungfrau, travels through space, freezes, falls into the sea, then returns safely to dry land. It is interesting to compare Méliès's

15

approach to this plot with that of Robert Paul in a similar film made in 1905, *The ? Motorist*. Paul's motoring couple rises into space as a result of exceeding the speed limit, and encounters a number of planetary bodies before returning to earth. However, where Méliès deluges us with trick effects of dubious skill, Paul confines himself to less ambitious but better conceived visions. The film is a far cry from its maker's concept of a Time Machine that would show the beginning and end of the world, but his image of the young couple motoring gravely around the rings of Saturn is nothing to be ashamed of.

By 1905 the era of Méliès was over. Cinema audiences were taking a greater interest in content, looking for realism and drama in a world where the pace of life had become faster and more violent. The films of Ferdinand Zecca had begun to exert an influence which was to culminate in the rich invention of Louis Feuillade, many of whose serials utilise sf elements like television culled from Verne and the early American science romances. Divisions were becoming apparent in the approach of film-makers working in the area of fantasy, by far the bulk of them, in France at least, tending towards the ornate and symbolic. Science fiction was becoming a vehicle for cinematic experiment and social comment, a role it was to play for decades.

In England, however, the writing of Wells, Shiel and other pioneers of science fiction was being reflected in the cinema. Charles Urban produced in 1909 probably the first film which deserves to be considered as true science fiction. Originally released as *The Airship Destroyer*, it has been variously screened as *Aerial Warfare*, *Aerial Torpedo* and *Battle in the Clouds*. Although running less than twenty minutes the film includes a variety of surprisingly realistic effects, most of them achieved through clever model work. Beginning with a bombing attack on London by a fleet of—unaccountably—moored dirigibles, *The Airship Destroyer* shows towns and railroads destroyed by explosions and some primitive tanks wrecked. The inventor of an aerial torpedo sees his girl friend's house also blown up, but manages to rescue her and bring his invention into action. The torpedoes, radio controlled but apparently powered by a rather smoky solid fuel, are launched with remarkable effect and the war is ended.

The success of *The Airship Destroyer* led to others in the same mould. *The Aerial Anarchists* (1911) again showed airships destroying London, effects heightened in this case by an early use of tinting to suggest St. Paul's in flames. Like Urban's film this ran only fifteen minutes, as did *The Pirates of 1920* (1911), although this film exhibited more imagination as to plot. A young navy officer is on board a ship attacked by aerial pirates. Finding a photograph of the hero's sweetheart, the pirate captain conceives an overpowering desire for the girl and kidnaps her. Only the intervention of the navy and the girl's valour in threatening to blow up the pirate airship save her from the standard Fate Worse Than Death.

All these films depended for impact, as had Méliès's stagey efforts, on the accuracy of their special effects. Little attempt was made to heighten tension or atmosphere by cutting, lighting or intensification of the narrative. As in many modern sf films, it was considered enough to show the wonders of technology, its mystique remaining unevoked. In Europe, however, a different spirit obtained. French and German directors were beginning to concern themselves with the bizarre and grotesque, exhibiting the interest in mental disturbance and deformity which was to result in one of the cinema's richest periods. The spirit which produced the great horror films and resulted indirectly in much of the American film's quality was stirring in the studios of Berlin and Paris.

This was the time of expressionism in art, of Klein and Kokoscha. Painting had become a matter of shapes, textures and colours rather than the literal depiction of reality. The transfer of information by direct physical stimulation was becoming more common, and while the Bauhaus had not yet been formed, a belief in new directions for architecture and design was already apparent in the work of German pioneers. Art and architecture in Germany symbolised the national predilection for the violent and tyrannical, features reflected in its national cinema, then the most inventive in the world.

In France, too, a similar urge towards experiment and iconoclasm was apparent. Film-makers like L'Herbier, Dulac and Gance had established a dialogue with the more advanced artists and visual theorists, resulting in films which combined extravagant subject matter with complex film language. Neither in Germany nor France was science fiction recognised by the cinema as a form to be utilised in the expression of ideas. Fantasy, however, was considered a reasonable means of excusing the combination of *avant-garde* visual and intellectual matter, and it was as a branch of fantasy that science fiction was incorporated into the films of this period.

The French influence on sf cinema was occasional and remote, confined mainly to a development of themes such as hypnotism which were later to dominate periods of sf film. Abel Gance's *The Madness of Dr. Tube (La folie du Dr. Tube*, 1915) used distorting lenses and trick camera effects to show the insanity of a scientist experimenting with breaking up light waves. Visually the film is unusual, but it leans so heavily on symbolism for effect that its release was suppressed for some time. *The Inhuman One (L'Inhumaine*, 1925), an extravagant melodrama of a man-killing opera star who is revived after her death by the machines of a scientist admirer, utilised the talents of painter Fernand Léger to create a *mise en scène* derived mainly from the geometrical artificiality of cubism. Visually advanced, both films nevertheless proved thin in content, without the saving intensity which rescues from obscurity the better American product of the Fifties.

This visual experiment had not affected so markedly the sf cinema of other countries. England continued in the tradition of its airship dramas with a version of *First Men in the Moon* (1919) in which a triangle love story was introduced for greater effect. Unfortunately this did not divert attention from the lunar scenes, described by an observer as "inadequate." In Denmark, Forest Holger-Madsen directed *Heaven Ship (Himmelskibet*, 1917), a faintly ridiculous romance in which a group of Earthmen journeys to Mars in a spaceship closely resembling Lindbergh's "The Spirit

Méliès's drawing of the Selenites for A TRIP TO THE
MOON (above left); Olaf Föns in HOMUNCULUS
(above right); the spaceship of HEAVEN SHIP (below)

of St. Louis." Mars is pictured as a well-mown garden planet, its inhabitants placid and peaceful. As in many early science fantasies, a plea for international peace and understanding led to a loss of intensity and imagination.

Russia, too, flirted with science fictional concepts, stimulated by the fiction of Alexei Tolstoy, whose novels *Aelita* and *The Hyperloid of Engineer Garin* were well ahead of overseas developments. (Both were written in the mid-Twenties, but *Amazing Stories,* the first true American sf magazine, did not commence until 1926.) *Aelita,* in which a group of Russian astronauts foments a revolt on Mars, was filmed in 1924, with expressionist sets by Alexandra Exter of the Tairov Theatre. The design, with its strong compositions and startlingly grotesque costumes for the enslaved Martians, their heads bound in geometrical metal masks, obscured the fact that Tolstoy's stories depended excessively on revolutionary doctrine for their impetus.

The Death Ray (Luch Smerti, 1925) bears a strong resemblance to Tolstoy's *The Hyperloid of Engineer Garin,* and although the film was produced a little before this story was published, the plot device of an engineer whose invention is coveted by anti-revolutionary powers is common to both. Leo Kuleshov, one of the Soviet's greatest directors of the period, used this melodrama set in an unnamed Western country as a means of dramatising to the Russian people the sophistication of Soviet film-making, then equal to the world's best. The film science fictional content is minimal, consisting of the laser-like ray that the hero employs to thwart Fascist bombing raids on his home city, but *The Death Ray's* degree of commitment was to remain unchallenged until the polemical onslaughts of *On the Beach* near to our time. Sf film had not yet decided to acquire a conscience.

In the U.S.A. cinema remained remote from the new work in science fiction then being carried on in the magazines. In 1916 D. W. Griffith wrote and produced *The Flying Torpedo* for Triangle but the film has since been lost. The only material resembling true sf in the cinema took the form of prehistoric romances and comedies, a still prolific field which began with Griffith's *Man's Genesis* (1912). In a scruffy past inhabited by mechanical dinosaurs of canvas and timber, "Weak Hands" conquers "Brute Force" by using his brain to invent the axe. Chaplin parodied this film cleverly in *His Prehistoric Past* (1914), playing "Weak Chin" who was pitted against Mack Swain's "King Lowbrow." Frank Butler's *Flying Elephants* (1927), in which Laurel and Hardy play knock-about cavemen, was the last gasp of the cycle. In 1925 *The Lost World* took the idea seriously and almost by accident discovered its immense dramatic potential.

Experiments in sf film carried on in England, America, Denmark and France are only marginally reflected in the sf cinema of to-day, but the work then being done in Germany has left an indelible mark on modern film. Under the high pressure of German artistic and social revolution a rich new art was in gestation. *The Cabinet of Dr. Caligari* (1919) re-made cinema design, but preceding it in 1916 was Otto Rippert's *Homunculus*, a serial in six one-hour parts describing the life of an artificial man without a soul, and paving the way for sf film's most complex topics. There is a direct connection between *Homunculus, Frankenstein* and *Creature from the Black Lagoon*. In fact, this progression, which really began with Wegener's *Der Golem* (1915), provides the clearest example of the influence which links German cinema with that of the U.S.A.

Rippert's film is the first in which science and scientists are characterised as intrinsically dangerous. Homunculus is created by a scientist who wishes to make a creature of pure reason and will, but like the Golem, Frankenstein's monster and the creatures that came after, Homunculus cannot come to terms with his lack of a "soul." Driven from country to country by the knowledge of his inhumanity, he turns by an undescribed but quite naturally accepted process into a tyrant. Becoming dictator of a nation he systematically destroys it by fomenting revolution within and crushing the rebellion totally from above, as the leader of Metropolis was to do in Lang's film ten years later. Finally an outraged universe sends a bolt of lightning to destroy him. Danish actor Olaf Föns played

Homunculus like a stocky Judex, his melodramatic clothing and acting style making him into a figure of national admiration, and Robert A. Dietrich's settings, similar to those he created for the remakes of *The Student of Prague* and *Der Golem,* provided a basis on which *The Cabinet of Dr. Caligari* was built.

Homunculus seems a primer of almost every sf film element. The experimental *ergo* dangerous *ergo* evil formation of the "mad scientist" stereotype is apparent in Rippert's drawing of Professor Hansen, the creature's inventor, and the progression from Homunculus to more modern creatures is equally clear. Additionally, however, we can see the curious and again illogical imputation of superior physical strength to the manufactured creature, as if pure reason implied a natural mental and physical tyranny. Finally there is the divine destruction of the godless man, the obligatory blast of heat and light that destroys him with the element that created him. Countless deaths by fire, lightning, electricity and other similar causes can be traced directly to the climax of *Homunculus.*

Rippert's film has thankfully survived in European archives but the vast majority of early sf classics have long since rotted away. No evidence exists of the preservation of Hans Werkmeister's *Algol* (1920), an interstellar romance set on the star of the same name and featuring settings by poet-architect Paul Scheerbart which, from the stills available, seem truly remarkable. A contemporary critic has left some tantalising descriptions. "One scene," he writes, "represents a stellar landscape of abrupt and fantastic contours, a convulsed, volcanic world, revealing matter in a struggle with space and time. There are surfaces of snow and silver, spines and crevasses, rounded tumuli of primeval stuff, sharp crags rising like outstretched arms to the stars. A female figure, like a triumphant spirit, and invested with veils of different darknesses, lifts out of the stone. Above her, there is spanned arch upon arch of a borealis and swarm upon swarm of stars. . . ."[7]

Algol was the product of a dying movement. Its gross overdecoration and symbolic subject matter place it with the voluptuous fan-

On the Eiffel Tower: Clair's PARIS QUI DORT

tasies of L'Herbier and Delluc in France, part of an impulse which had its mainspring in graphic art and design. The cinema, an art of movement and action, could not gain by such an association, and film-makers soon realised this. The lavish romances of France in the Twenties faded as did A. Merritt's decadent fantasies, their literary equivalent. German directors like Rippert had set the scene for a new kind of film in which national predilections could be expressed in science fiction form, and while the influence of *Homunculus* spread into all areas of the cinema it remained strongest and purest in the sf film.

Outside Germany a similar process was apparent. American directors were toying with scientific fantasy as written sf began to increase in popularity, the comic strips providing a convenient point of departure, while in France René Clair was to touch briefly on the field in his exploration of comedy before moving on to more bitter topics. His *Paris Qui Dort* (1923) is an early precursor of modern science fiction film, exhibiting a number of the same pre-occupations as modern works in the field.

A young man (Albert Préjean) has taken the job of night watchman on top of the Eiffel Tower. One morning he wakes to find that his relief has not arrived, and that the lift is stuck at ground level. Walking to the bottom via twisting metal staircases he discovers Paris frozen into immobility, all the clocks having stopped at 3:25 the previous night. He finds a thief and the policeman chasing him both frozen, takes the watch that the thief holds, then puts it back. The other people untouched by the freeze behave in a similarity irresponsible way, holding drunken parties, fighting over who is to have the one girl left, and generally loafing along. A radio message takes them on to a scientist's house from which the experimenter has turned on a ray which paralyses the whole city, but even after the effects have been reversed the group retains its problems, their social situations, poverty or tangled love-lives unchanged by the brief hiatus. All of them return to their previous existence except the young watchman who disappears up the Eiffel Tower with the scientist's daughter, hanging up after him a sign indicating that the Tower is closed until morning.

Most notable of all the themes in *Paris Qui Dort* is the now familiar assumption that science and human nature are essentially evil, or at least mischievous. Clair also gives us one of the first "mad scientists," though admittedly a benign one. His invention, used without thought or planning, causes a disaster, just as do most sf film gadgets, up to and including the atom bomb. The scientist is shown as comic, vague and unrealistic, in contrast to his pert daughter, the first of a thousand heroines in similar situations. The hero is tough, lower class, ignorant. The tendency of the group to run amok when relieved of authority's pressure is also typical, presaging the orgies of every End Of The World film.

Setting the story of the Eiffel Tower was one of Clair's best ideas. The tracery of metal is a perfect sf background, and evokes the incidental poetry of the urban world. One of the best scenes shows the girl walking in a filmy back-lit gown along a railing-less ledge with Paris spread out in the background. The humour varies, but is often sharply witty; a man arriving back to find his wife asleep with a lover, the thief companionably breaking into houses on request, the industrialist paying his night club bill into the hands of an inanimate waiter. Even today *Paris Qui Dort* is a film of wit and charm.

But it was in Germany that the pace was quickening. Having absorbed the visual advances of Rippert and Wiene, other directors were looking for means to exercise the vastly increased cinematic vocabulary now at their disposal. The country was ready for a physical expression of the national myth, some tangible character or attitude that would catch their imagination and focus their hopes as Homunculus had done. It was the process that was to produce Germany's triumphs in architecture and engineering, then rot into Nazism, but at the time both its threat and its promise were veiled. With a surge of pure imagination German film-makers leapt into the dark, groping for a dream they could barely apprehend. The result was *Metropolis*.

3. Utopischefilme

M ETROPOLIS IS A FILM capable of wide interpretation. To Siegfried Kracauer parts of it are "humanly a shocking failure,"[8] but Fritz Lang, who rejects Kracauer's entire thesis, has said that all his films show "the desire to keep an individual an individual."[9] Bardèche and Brasillach, despite their pro-German bias, find it "disconcertingly childish,"[10] yet Raymond Durgnat is impressed by its "nameless, fatalistic suspense."[11] Each decade has found things to praise and criticise in *Metropolis,* but in the cinema's one unalterable standard, technique, the film rates high. From the day of its release in early 1927 to the present, *Metropolis* has proved a rich source of technical innovation, and its influence on the spectacle film, especially in the Thirties and Forties in Hollywood, is substantial.

Fritz Lang's talent was a supercharged version of the skill which produced the early French and American serials. Although trained as an architect his real flair was for the graphic arts. Travelling round the world before the First World War he supported himself drawing cartoons, post-cards and caricatures, and when he first took up writing after having been wounded in combat, he turned automatically to the detective story and the fantastic romance, his knowledge of which he carried into film writing and direction. Like the serial makers Lang combined a brisk and simple visual style with a shrewd knowledge of popular fiction, but added a genius for the film medium and a set of ingenious variations on classic fantasy themes that marked his films as peculiarly individual.

His first major films were variations on the serial concept, often planned as a set of interlocking features to be screened on successive nights, but budget problems usually meant that the series were reduced to four hours in length and released in two parts only. *The Spiders (Die Spinnen,* 1919) was planned as four films, but released as two, telling the story of a power group using buried Inca gold to take over the world. *The Hindu Tombstone (Das Indische Grabmal,* 1920) was in two parts, as were *Doctor Mabuse, the Gambler (Doctor Mabuse, der Spieler,* 1922) and *Der Nibelungen* (1923/24). As in the case of American serials, newspaper influences were common. Popular film stories were serialised in the papers, and the stories and films often drew on topical events for plots. Like the Bond films of the Sixties, real situations provided a departure point into fantasy. If the comic book was the key literary influence on the American fantasy film, the newspaper occupied a similar position in Germany's fantasy thrillers.

The influence is noticable in *Doctor Mabuse, der Spieler,* one of Lang's finest films and a masterpiece which today still retains its original ferocity. Borrowing equally from Feuillade and contemporary events, Lang and scenarist Thea von Harbou—then wife of

26

actor Rudolf Klein-Rogge, who played Mabuse, but later Frau Lang—put together a brisk thriller similar in theme to *Die Spinnen*. Mabuse, financial wizard, master criminal and genius of disguise, leads his band of hoods, drug addicts and dupes on a rampage of evil until stopped by an energetic D.A. and the jaded socialite who has agreed to help him. Aside from the hypnotism and telepathy Mabuse uses to control his victims the film has little science fiction, but in its sense of detachment it recalls much written sf. The scene where a disguised Mabuse manipulates the stock market from boom to slump and back again under the cold eye of a huge clock foreshadows his *Metropolis* vision of Mankind as a mob that the strong can turn to their own ends.

Throughout his career Lang toyed with science fiction. All his Mabuse films have sf elements, including *Das Testament des Dr. Mabuse* (1932), the Mabuse-influenced *Spione* (1927) and the later *Die Tausend Augen des Dr. Mabuse* (1960). Later, in his American career, Lang planned a version of the Jekyll and Hyde story, and also *Man without a Country*, an anti-Nazi drama in which spies search for a ray that destroys human sight, but neither was produced. Visually inventive, armed with an intimate knowledge of his art, Lang was the ideal man to interpret the energy and intellectual pretension of science fiction, but only one of his films has ever adequately done this, the brilliant *Metropolis*.

Visiting America in 1924 to study Hollywood production methods, Lang was impressed by the nocturnal fantasy of New York's skyline seen from the sea, and decided to incorporate the sight into his next film. This story, re-told in every note on *Metropolis*, has the effect of accentuating the architectural aspect of the film at the expense of other qualities. Undoubtedly Lang's architectural training is apparent in the massive sets and the careful integration of characters into the grinding machinery of the city, but the real merits of *Metropolis* are more personal and emotional. Widely characterised as unfeeling and Germanically dour, *Metropolis* in reality is a film of immense fantasy, a sensuous voyage into a manufactured universe happily alien both to Lang's time and our own.

In a montage of chugging machines and sprawling cityscapes Lang introduces Metropolis, a city of the future governed by John Fredersen (Alfred Abel), an ascetic and benign Mabuse who occupies an office of awesome responsibility high in the city's towers. While Fredersen struggles with his problems, dictating decisions to a team of expectant aides, his teenage son Freder (Gustav Froehlich) competes with other youths in the stadium or relaxes in a rooftop garden, watched over by a venerable chamberlain who supplies scantily clad girls for his approval. Freder is in the garden when it is invaded by a group of ragged children and their ethereal nurse Maria (Brigitte Helm). Indicating the awed Freder, his courtesans and companions, Maria explains, "These are your brothers," but before he can respond the interlopers are forced back by huge doors.

Intrigued, Freder asks his father to explain about Maria, the children and the workers who live in the city far below, but John Fredersen is too concerned with the problems of state. Lang superbly directs the scene where Freder invades his father's office, the older man gesturing impatiently for silence as his son interrupts him in the middle of a calculation, the whole office hanging in silence as he frowns, produces the right figure, then turns to see what the boy wants while his team of secretaries retreats to put the decisions into effect. When John Fredersen is evasive about Maria and her charges, Freder persuades an equerry to gain him access to the lower levels of the city where he is assured Maria can be found.

Mingling with the workers in their anonymous coveralls, Freder investigates with fascination and horror the catacombs of Metropolis, with their monstrous machines and trudging crumpled inhabitants. Festooned over vast machines, exhausted men labour at dreary, reiterative tasks, juggling levers or releasing valves in endless repetition. Finally one collapses, a gauge explodes and a machine blows up. Thea von Harbou conjures up a baroque dream of technology gone mad, showing the giant machine as an effigy of Moloch into which human sacrifices are flung. Retreating from the vision Freder finds a worker collapsing as he tends a huge dial,

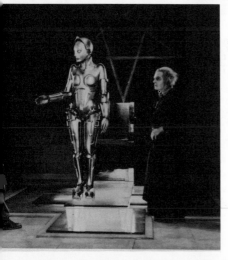

METROPOLIS:
*above left, the model
work; above right, the
erotic night club dance
of Maria's double;
and left, the robot
woman without her
synthetic flesh.*

matching its clock-like hands with lights that flick on and off around its perimeter. Helpfully taking over from the exhausted man Freder is quickly reduced to a state of collapse, and himself nearly causes another explosion.

Eventually he finds Maria, who in a subterranean church preaches to the workers about the importance of mediation between labour and management. She tells the story of the Tower of Babel, and in a strikingly directed insert Lang shows Babel as a tilted wedding cake of stone seething with slaves bent like the workers of Metropolis into complete subservience. The audience responds with child-like faith, but none of them is aware that John Fredersen and the evil scientist Rotwang (Rudolf Klein-Rogge) are spying on the meeting. When Fredersen instructs Rotwang to wipe out Maria and the incipient revolt, the scientist fixes on an ingenious means of doing so.

"We have made machines out of men," he says. "Now I will make men out of machines—a robot indistinguishable from a real woman." The result is a glittering miracle of oiled precision, a creature at once feminine and mechanical. Covered in synthetic flesh, she is the double of Maria, and it is as Maria that she performs an erotic semi-nude dance at a huge night-club, exciting the watchers to a frenzy of desire. With her at their head the workers revolt, smashing the mechanical heart of the city and flooding the lower levels. However the real Maria escapes, saves the children from drowning, and is finally able, with Freder's help, to convince his father that he must co-operate with the workers. Fredersen, with his son as intermediary, gingerly makes up with a hairy foreman and the bargain is sealed, at least for the fade-out, though one can legitimately doubt whether the moral that "the heart must mediate between the brain and the hands" is really strong enough to sustain a lasting *entente*.

Intellectual objections, however, do not vitiate the quality of *Metropolis*. Like all filmed science fiction its plot ideas are not meant to be taken seriously, the real values lying in its visual and narrative power. The Moloch image, so often criticised by writers on the film, is admittedly a specious one by any intellectual standard, but in terms of execution it is a splendid visual poem given remarkable point in those prints where Lang's original titles remain. The jagged impressionistic lettering jumping together from disarranged letters flung into the frame from outside marks the title as a divider between what precedes and follows the episode. It is not meant to be either real or meaningful, any more than the casino episode in *Dr. Mabuse der Spieler* with its fold-away merry-go-round gaming table and peek-a-boo nudes is meant to be accepted literally. Both are flamboyant gestures by a film-making team that prized above everything the fire of imagination.

The creation of the robot Maria is another exercise in pure fantasy, though because of its superficial logic critics seldom revile it to the same extent as Moloch. Lang returns to the medieval world of *The Golem* for this scene, showing Rotwang's house as a gingerbread cottage lurking comically among the roots of the skyscrapers. Over the door is the five-pointed star of the pentagram, symbol of demonic intervention, and Rotwang is played by Klein-Rogge as a classic wizard, complete with remote control doors and the means of making artificial life. Universal's designers working on *The Bride of Frankenstein* copied the metal-banded machine with which Rotwang vivifies his creation, but one doubts than an American could have conveyed with Lang's skill the miraculous beauty of the robot, its shimmering body with stylised breasts and domed head, the exquisitely inhuman face of a Mycaenean death mask.

Accustomed as we have become to the misty sensuousness of von Sternberg, Lang's violent eroticism seems on the surface overbearing and crude, the fantasy of von Harbou's script a case of imagination totally out of control. Hollywood, with its *penchant* for the flattering angle and the discreet diffuser, makes us forget that before the growth of the studios sexuality was a matter of direct presentation rather than suggestion, that fantasy in the silent period more often showed the violent energy of *The Thief of Bagdad* than the subtlety of *The Blue Bird*. *Metropolis's* more direct ancestors are the films of Griffith, specifically *Intolerance* whose historical sequences closely parallel in style Lang's film. Both directors used architecture as a source of spectacle, both showed individual characters as members of a faceless mob, both introduced female nudity as a minor element of their set-ups, but in doing so made no attempt at subtlety.

This direct approach, with sexuality used as an incidental element in set dressing, characterises *Metropolis*, and especially the use of the robot Maria. Only in her dance does Brigitte Helm have the opportunity to shine as a sex symbol, and it is one she seizes eagerly. Clad in a handful of sequins and beads, she drives her audience into a frenzy of lust with a performance of calculated Oriental eroticism. At its peak she mounts an ornamental dais supported by grotesque life-sized human figures on top of which is a hideous statue of a seven-headed monster. As she displays herself provocatively on this horror, flourishing a wine cup, the men surge up and grope despairingly for her, the unattainable symbol of human desire.

Brigitte Helm is the real focus of *Metropolis*, and her playing dominates the film, despite the difficult double role. Aside from the occasional simper Maria is a believable Twenties heroine, the bland playing of some scenes providing an adequate contrast to the terror of others, such as that in which Rotwang searches for her in the caves under Metropolis, chasing her from niche to niche with the beam of a flashlight until she is pinned helpless in its glare. Her best sequences, however, are those as the robot; her awakening in Rotwang's laboratory, the dance, and perhaps her most terrifying scene, that in which the workers burn her at the stake, only to see her change in the flames from a woman to robot, the hideously beautiful mask glaring out at them with implacable, immortal hatred.

Klein-Rogge's wild-eyed Rotwang is one of the cinema's most interesting villains, a scientist/magician with his roots deep in German Gothic. Significantly most of his wonders can be interpreted either as science or magic—a television eye, the automatic doors of his laboratory, his ability to create an artificial human—while the pentacle that decorates his home and workshop hints at a deal with the devil. Sf film-makers have not drawn heavily on Rotwang as a pattern for future mad scientists, mainly because of his eccentricity, but fragments of his appearance survive today. The mutilated and black-gloved right hand, recalling the severed hands of Paul Leni's *Waxworks* and Robert Wiene's *The Hands of Orlac*, reappears later in *Son of Frankenstein* and *Dr. Strangelove or How I Learned To Stop Worrying and Love the Bomb*, as well as a number of less distinguished horror and fantasy films.

The real influence of *Metropolis* lies, however, in its technical innovation, since absorbed by all branches of the world cinema. American producers quickly copied its impressive set design and process work, and many later American films, especially *Just Imagine* (1930), show *Metropolis* touches. The clever special effects, a combination of model work, forced perspective and the "Shuftan Process," in which models and mirrors placed close to the lens give the impression of whole structures built in the distance, still represent one of the finest combinations of reality and fantasy in the cinema. Although these techniques, or variations on them, were developed by American technicians as early as 1908[12] the use of them in *Metropolis* is arguably the most skilled in cinema history.

Shot over a period of nine months this film was one of the most expensive ever produced by Ufa, but its popularity ensured a substantial profit. Although still in circulation today, it is some time since the complete two hour version of *Metropolis* has been shown, most modern prints running about ninety minutes. Many lack the brief but impressive sequence in which Freder races with other gilded youths in a stadium of Olympic proportions, while the pleasure garden sequence and Brigitte Helm's erotic dance often suffer censor cuts. One of the most unfortunate deletions is the remarkable title design; enterprising effects include that for the "Moloch" episode mentioned earlier, the word "Babel" dripping blood and a roll-up title for the first shot of workers descending into the earth so that we appear to sink underground with them.

In passing, it is interesting to compare Lang's film with the Thea von Harbou novel on which it is based.[13] Heavily written and decorated with a wealth of religious imagery, the novel often reads like a deistic tract. After an opening in the cathedral of Metropolis, with Freder forgetting his misery playing the organ, it launches into an elaborate comparison between the machines of the city and a variety of gods, both pagan and Christian. One mechanism is compared with Ganesha, another with the Juggernaut, a third arrangement of objects seen to resemble the scene at the crucifixion of Christ. In the film, all these parallels are combined with great economy into the "Moloch" episode.

Unfortunately other more valuable points are lost in translation from book to film. The difficult question of why Fredersen engineers with Rotwang the destruction of Metropolis is explained in the book as a gesture by Fredersen to give his son a reason for living. "The city is to go to ruin," he says to Freder, "that you may build it up again." One is not surprised that Lang did not retain this unlikely motivation. Nor did he leave in one of the book's most important plot points, though in this case the reasons are more personal. In the book, Fredersen's dead wife Hel was once the wife of Rotwang, but was stolen by the former to the scientist's rage and sorrow. Inasmuch as Lang later married the divorced wife of the actor playing Rotwang, this change may have had a diplomatic basis.

Metropolis was the end of a fashion in German film. With most major talents already committed to the American cinema through its many European subsidiaries, films with an aggressively German tone became rarer. *Metropolis* had its influence on the American epic but sf film was still too small a field to use Lang's techniques. In Europe, sf film was still a rarity, and did not become common until the Thirties when the rise of German nationalism was reflected in a series of well-conceived scientific romances expressing in concrete terms the nation's pride in its technology. Both Lang's two-part *Nibelungen* and *Metropolis* had suggested this new nationalism, but aside from one further scientific adventure Lang was not to participate in the movement he founded. Seeing the Nazi menace, he fled to the U.S.A. and a new career.

The last sf film produced by Lang himself after another Mabuse-style thriller *The Spy (Spione, 1928)*, was *Woman in the Moon (Die Frau im Mond, 1928)*. Also known as *The Girl in the Moon* and *By Rocket to the Moon,* this film is one of the most elusive of sf features, the original rocket ship models, film negative and all available prints having been destroyed by Hitler in the Thirties because of the similarity between Lang's space ship and the prototype rocket weapons then being perfected in Germany. Both Hermann Oberth and Willy Ley, leading members of the Rocket Society that Lang approached for expert advice, worked as technical advisers on the film, and their suggestions for a workable moon rocket are interestingly prophetic. Oberth later worked for the Nazis on rocket experiments, while Ley came to the U.S.A. as a science writer and propulsion expert.

Since the war, prints have been struck from the surviving material and *Die Frau im Mond* is once again available. Unfortunately the film is an inadequate successor to *Metropolis,* the Lang/von Harbou script lacking the symbolic fire of the earlier film. While the mechanics of the rocket launching are remarkably convincing, both plot and scientific accuracy decline after a landing is made on the moon. Perpetuating Wells's erroneous theory that the moon has a breathable atmosphere in the lower areas of the landscape and in subterranean valleys, it had the mismatched party clambering over a landscape little different from that of the Alps, picking up raw diamonds and chunks of gold that lie conveniently at hand on the surface. Questions of reduced gravity, longer day and night, extremes of temperature—the party usually wears ordinary street gear—are ignored, and the film, aside from its setting, suggests a routine thriller which might have been set anywhere on earth.

A prophetic picture: WOMAN IN THE MOON

After *Die Frau im Mond* interplanetary romances vanished for a time from the cinema, the quickening pace of international politics encouraging a more direct response to reality. In America films became overtly escapist, and Hollywood offered its audiences situations and settings that, while overlaid with an aggressive optimism, remained recognisable. This was the era of the musical, the gay romance, the melodrama of high life and low necklines. European films too reflected this escapist mood, though in Germany the cinema was able to employ science fiction to exalt the sophistication of its technologists. Ufa especially made use of its technical resources and extensive capital to produce some extravagant scientific romances.

F. P. 1. Antwortet Nicht (F. P. 1. Fails to Reply, 1933) starred Hans Albers as the inventor of a floating platform in mid-Atlantic from which aircraft could operate. Albers, matinee idol and romantic lead, was not especially convincing as the aviator/inventor, but the Ufa technical team created some exciting scenes of the platform's construction. Günther Rittau, who had executed the process photography for *Metropolis*, again used the Shuftan process to good effect, and the scenes of huge tri-motor airliners lumbering down to land on the metal surface of F. P. 1 are far more impressive than the routine thriller plot in which scenarist Curt Siodmak involves his characters as opponents try to wreck the project.

Like many European films of the time *F. P. 1 Antwortet Nicht* was made in two other versions, a French one with Charles Boyer as the star and an English version with Conrad Veidt. A similar

F.P.I. ANTWORTET NICHT: tension in mid-Atlantic

Beneath the Atlantic: DER TUNNEL

situation exists in the case of *Der Tunnel* (1933), directed by Curtis Bernhardt in a German and French version, though the issue is often confused by the fact that in 1934 Maurice Elvey directed *Transatlantic Tunnel*, an English copy with a new cast. The German film, by far the most impressive of the three, is a compelling picture of an attempt to drive a tunnel under the Atlantic, and its sets are among the most remarkable ever created for a science fiction film. The natural disasters—flooding, volcanic eruption—are magnificently staged. Their realism may be gauged from the fact that during one sequence the film's associate producer, August Lautenbacher, was killed when the tunnel collapsed. Elvey's remake, while efficient, lacks the imagination of the original, and today possesses an unearned reputation.

Hans Albers again appeared in *Gold* (1934), another Ufa scientific romance made in German and French versions. Set mostly in an underwater laboratory crammed with Otto Hunte's extravagant sets, it dealt with a scientist who had discovered the secret of turning lead into gold and the attempts of a young atomic physicist to prevent the inventor from wrecking the world's economy. Rittau's process photography and Hunte's sets make much of the climax, with the huge machine flashing lightning from enormous condensers, and this part of the film still survives as the last reel of Curt Siodmak's *The Magnetic Monster* (1953), which incorporates the footage originally shot by German director Karl Hartl. Aside from these scenes, *Gold* is largely routine, although in cost and shooting time it far exceeded *Metropolis*.

In more ways than one, films like *Gold* were the end of an era. If *Metropolis* concluded the days of symbolism and allegory for the German cinema, *Gold* and *The Tunnel* also ended the period during which German film-makers explored the implications of Lang's technocratic fantasy. By the middle Thirties, however, German film had been transplanted to America, with the finest technicians of the silent period working happily in Hollywood. The new German cinema, devoted to commercial extravaganzas, escapist comedies and a few laudatory works of militarism and patriotism, no longer exhibited the dark energy of Lang, Rippert and Wiene. German film was never to recover from the combined effect of Hollywood and Nazism, though in other countries the old influences, for better or worse, continued to flourish in unfamiliar ground.

4. The Doctor Will See You Now

BY THE LATE 1920s, Hollywood's wholesale takeover of the German film industry was almost complete, with a large number of the country's greatest talents either working in America or about to do so. Directors Lubitsch, Curtiz, Leni and Murnau, stars Negri, Jannings and de Putti, designers Dreier, Fegté, Grot, cameramen Freund and Sparkuhl; these people led a mass exodus which in the space of a few years enriched the American cinema and made it the world's leader. With them they brought, in addition to superior technical skill, the interest in fantasy and horror which is central to the German psyche. It soon became an integral part of Hollywood movie making.

Even before the influx of German film personalities, the visual experiments of Wiene and Rippert had been seen in America and their influence absorbed. *The Wizard* (1927), *The Magician* (1926) and *The Phantom of the Opera* (1925) all contained Germanic elements which occasionally exceeded in grotesquerie the models on which they were based, while most horror or fantasy films of the time relied heavily on European visual effects. In plot, however, such films usually derived from models in the past of English literature rather than the contemporary psychological and psychosexual preoccupations of the German cinema. Variations on the Faust legend were common, but aside from the legendary 1910 Edison version of *Frankenstein*, no American film had examined the idea of manufacturing human life which motivated German films like *Homonculus, Alraune, The Golem* and, to a lesser extent, *Metropolis,* nor had they used the classic myths of the vampire, or of Jack the Ripper, so skilfully evoked in *Waxworks* and *Pandora's Box.*

The reasons for this gap in transference were, in the case of the Homonculus/Alraune legend, reasonably clear. To the German film-makers the idea of man challenging God and making artificial life was one which reflected the prevailing mood of the country. In addition, the imputation of evil intentions to the creatures so manufactured was one which German audiences could accept without argument. As Kracauer has pointed out, the view of man as a creature in whom good and evil war continually is a key one in the German mind. Robert Wiene's audiences did not find it hard to accept his 1925 adaptation of Maurice Renard's *The Hands of Orlac,* in which a maimed concert pianist inherits, along with the hands of an executed murderer, his homicidal capabilities. Despite the physiological nonsense of this idea it expressed a view held by the country as a whole, that man was a vehicle for good or evil, a vessel to be filled and emptied as a ruling power dictated.

American audiences were more pragmatic and sceptical, and it was not until 1931, when the German born Carl Laemmle at Universal made *Frankenstein,* that this dark stream of German fantasy touched the United States. Sensing the American desire to see some logical reason for basically fantastic events, Laemmle dressed the story in quasi-medical trappings, with considerable success at the box-office. In adapting Mary Shelley's novel, Robert Florey, who was originally to have directed the film instead of James Whale, carefully respected his model but nevertheless inserted a situation not present in the original. When the film's Dr. Frankenstein manufactures an artificial man from dead bodies, he accidentally transfers into the skull of his creation the brain of a madman. The monster then inherits, as did Orlac, the powers of the donor, and it is this mad brain that sends the creature out to ravage mankind. Despite

Conrad Veidt and Alexandra Sorina in
Wiene's THE HANDS OF ORLAC

its gimcrack logic, a superficially plausible justification was given for the acts of the monster, and the American public accepted it eagerly.

Frankenstein and its many sequels are only tangentially sf. Visually and intellectually their antecedents are Wegener's two versions of *The Golem* and the horror films of Leni, with their skilful blending of grue and humour. *The Hands of Orlac* is, however, very close to sf film, in its central concept of organ transplantation, its pessimistic mood and bland visual style. As a result, it has had a number of American re-makes. In contrast to most horror films of the time Wiene's is slow-paced, pale and grey, relying on long shots of dusty interiors, measured acting by Conrad Veidt, and a mood more characteristic of the sick room than the haunted house. While *Frankenstein* may have been the vehicle by which the German fantasy of dismemberment was transferred to America, the form when it finally took root rejected most of Whale's visual ideas, retaining instead Wiene's limp and unhurried approach. *Frankenstein* and *Dracula* continued to flourish on the traditions of German Gothic, but it was the ideas of *The Hands of Orlac* which Hollywood adopted whole-heartedly and which provided the basis of the sf genre.

American audiences have a fascination with doctors, and films with medical subjects have always been popular. Gertrude Atherton's best seller *Black Oxen*, dealing with rejuvenation by X-ray, was filmed in 1923 by Frank Lloyd, while most new medical advances from gland transplant to rhinoplasty were immortalised on film. Allied with the grisly interest in dismemberment inherited from the German cinema, this medical predilection produced a string of films during the Thirties and Forties in which mad doctors, either for revenge or distorted ideas of progress, worked their dreadful will on mankind.

Key actor and symbol of the fashion was Boris Karloff. Each decade has its stock menace, an expert in fantasy and grim humour who becomes Hollywood's resident monster and mad scientist. In the Twenties it was Lon Chaney, in the Fifties Vincent Price, but Karloff

Bela Lugosi and Boris Karloff in Hillyer's THE INVISIBLE RAY

dominated the Thirties and Forties with a series of superior performances calling for that combination of sensitivity and menace that only he could project. His commanding height and saturnine face, his skilful body and hand movements, perhaps most of all his deep, slightly lisping voice summed up the combination of command and menace which the public demanded in its mad doctors.

After playing a gallery of tortured grotesques—Frankenstein's monster, the mummy Imhotep in Karl Freund's classic version of *The Mummy* (1932), a murderer mutilated by Bela Lugosi in *The Raven*—Karloff finally achieved dominance in *The Invisible Ray* (1936). This smooth Lambert Hillyer drama allowed Karloff one of the first roles in which Jack Pierce's make-up was not the real star. Karloff is Janos Rukh, an experimental physicist living with his frustrated wife (Frances Drake) and blind mother (Violet Kemble Cooper) in a crumbling observatory set high in the Carpathians. Using a special attachment to his telescope he demonstrates to a group of scientists, including a sceptical Bela Lugosi, that centuries ago a meteorite landed in Africa containing a super-powerful element, Radium X. Despite their disbelief, Karloff finds the element, but is infected by its radiation. Able to kill at a touch and project death rays from his eyes, he hunts down the people who refused to help him, until his mother deprives him of his vital drugs and he is consumed by his disease.

Beginning in what seems a ludicrous variation on the horror film, with an observatory set like the traditional castle on a mountain top, guests arriving in the middle of a thunderstorm to gulp neat brandy and complain about the creepy surroundings, *The Invisible Ray* soon becomes a tight and visually inventive sf thriller with an interesting visual surface, glossy and metallic. Searching for Radium X in Africa, Karloff is lowered into a volcanic fissure clad in silvery radiation suit and cylindrical metal helmet. Hillyer uses soft focus to give the studio jungle an eerie quality, and plays with light and shadow to the same effect in the scenes where Karloff discovers that his touch can kill, leaving ghostly, phosphorescent hand prints on the bodies of his victims. Back in Paris he glares from under his soft felt hat at six statues above a church and dissolves them one at a time for each victim he kills, the images crumbling to dust at his glance.

The climax is beautifully handled; the victims shivering in evening dress, momentarily expecting their nemesis, hail beating against a clock face, then Karloff peering through the window. Before he can kill his wife, his mother smashes the drug phials which keep him alive, and the doomed scientist throws himself out of the window, to dissolve in a puff of flame before he hits the ground. The film is full of cautionary lines, some directed towards scientific scepticism— "Every scientific advance began in the mind of a man called 'mad'"— but most the reverse, including the first recorded use of the classic, "There are some things Man is not meant to know." Although

44

scientifically specious—it even resurrects the myth that a murderer's face is imprinted on his victim's retina—*The Invisible Ray* presages the sf films of the next decade. Pale, grey, relying more on detail than suggestion for its effects, it set the mood for a whole genre of quasi-scientific fantasies.

Karloff's next film was Michael Curtiz's *The Walking Dead* (1936), with his status reduced to that of Edmund Gwenn's experimental animal. Electrocuted for a crime he did not commit, Karloff is resurrected by Gwenn and sent out to avenge himself. In the oddly named *The Man Who Changed His Mind* (1936), Karloff reversed roles, playing a mad scientist who switches the brains of his enemies with those of twisted cripples. *The Man They Could Not Hang* (1939), directed by the talented Nick Grinde and one of the best of this series, had Karloff surviving the electric chair by using techniques in the development of which he killed a student, thus earning the death sentence for murder. Intent on revenge he lures the judge, jury and hostile witnesses to a booby-trapped house in which trap-doors, electrified grilles and other devices dispose of his victims one by one. Briskly directed, *The Man They Could Not Hang* is a notably evil drama presented with Grinde's characteristic panache and cynicism.

After the feeble *Black Friday,* directed by Arthur Lubin, with Karloff again switching brains between college academic and condemned criminal, the actor made two further films with Grinde, *The Man with Nine Lives* and *Before I Hang* (1940), but neither had the pace of *The Man They Could Not Hang*. The first used the idea of deep-freezing to save people with incurable diseases until cures are found, while the second offered a stew of immunology *clichés* culminating in Karloff going mad when a rejuvenation serum he has developed turns out to have been derived from the blood of a murderer. As in *The Hands of Orlac* and the fantasies made in America subsequent to it, the supernatural belief in crime and especially murder as a physical disease, transmittable from person to person, occupies an important place. Science fictional in design and surface, all these films derive in plot from far older and darker

The stylish THE MASK OF FU MANCHU

originals.

Plots of the period leaned more on necromancy than science, while scientific laboratories more often than not resembled the dens of alchemists. The medicinal powers of ape blood, expounded by Bela Lugosi in *Murders in the Rue Morgue* (1932) and Boris Karloff in *The Ape* (1940), were a popular subject for scriptwriters of the period, but no other animal was ever considered as a potential experimental subject, though a possible exception is Charles Brabin's stylish *The Mask of Fu Manchu* (1932), in which Karloff as Fu subdues a victim with serum derived from reptile venom. In Michael Curtiz's *Doctor X* (1932), Preston Foster flirted briefly with "synthetic flesh," a porridge-like substance which, when smeared on the skin, became animate and gave the wearer great physical strength, but in *The Return of Doctor X* (1939), blood was again the vehicle of evil, and Humphrey Bogart with a startling white streak through his hair became a scientific vampire who, resurrected from the dead by yet another "mad doctor," was forced to steal living blood in order to survive.

In terms of cinema, the quality of these films varied in direct proportion to the skill of their directors, and predictably the Curtiz film is far more memorable than William Nigh's flaccid *The Ape*. Directorial skill accounted also for the impact of two films by Erle C. Kenton, *The Island of Lost Souls* (1932) and *House of Dracula* (1945), though Kenton, usually a technician of routine competence, did little else in his career that was remarkable. As in the case of James Whale, only the special ambience of fantasy film seems to have been capable of arousing a latent skill.

Writing of H. G. Wells's *The Island of Doctor Moreau*, Aubrey Beardsley remarked that it was "certainly a horrible affair, and very well set forth." The book is one of Wells's smoothest works, a grim romance largely free of preaching. Intended as a reasoned examination of vivisection and its socio-religious significance, the book has a traveller arrive by accident on a remote tropic island to find there the fugitive Doctor Moreau. Despite being hounded out of Europe for his work with the vivisection of dogs, Moreau has continued his experiments to combine the qualities of man and beast in one animal. His island, it emerges, is peopled by half-human results of his researches, ape-men and dog-men who have formed a weird society based on their fear of Moreau and his "House of Pain."

In scripting *The Island of Lost Souls*, Waldemar Young and Philip Wylie took substantial liberties with the plot and characters. Wells's benign white-haired Moreau became an obese and foppish tyrant played with great glee and much cracking of a stock whip by Charles Laughton, while the horror of vivisection and blood-soaked bandaged bundles writhing with pain in shadowy laboratories were replaced by the presumably intentional comedy of actors in crepe hair and leopard skin. However, by shooting the film's exteriors on Catalina Island off the California coast, Kenton escaped from the tedium of the studio jungle, offering instead sunlit walls, paths and clearings choked with realistic greenery and a mood of sinister fantasy in keeping with the eccentric story. Through this phantom world the beast men glide, gathering to chant the Law that is their religion. "Not to chase other men . . . not to go on all fours . . . not to eat flesh or fish. That is the Law—*are we not men?*" Despite Wells's repudiation of the film, it is one of the cleverest Hollywood adaptations of his work.

Almost forgotten today, Kenton's *House of Dracula* (1945) is in its way as bizarre a variation on an original as the Wells film. Gothic shadows replaced by the pale surface of sf, *House of Dracula* attempts a scientific approach to the ancient legends. A doctor (Onslow Stevens) sets out to gather together and cure the three classic "creatures," Count Dracula, Matthew Talbot (the Wolf Man) and Frankenstein's monster. In a cliff-top house by the sea he entertains Dracula (John Carradine) and Talbot (Lon Chaney Jr.) while in a cellar his staff works at extracting curative drugs from a special flower which grows only in the foggy dungeon. One of Atwill's helpers is a beautiful nurse with a hunch back, and the doctor has promised to free her of this affliction by using the drug, which can soften and make flexible the living bone. Working on the dubious theory that Talbot's problem is due to pressure on the brain and that the softening drug will cure it, Atwill successfully treats him, but the effect fades and most of the cast die in a grim climax.

Burdened with a silly plot (though one which fits in with the theory that Americans like their fantasy explained in logical terms) *House of Dracula* is of variable interest only, and it is hard to sit straight-faced through scenes such as that in which two characters, exploring the doctor's cellar, "discover" Frankenstein's monster (Glenn Strange) sprawled in a pool of mud where he has settled since the last of the series. The idea of a scientific reason and cure for vampirism and lycanthropy is, however, of some interest, as is the steamy cellar, with the precious plants growing in their glass cases, tended by the twisted nurse, her beautiful face and long hair providing an odd conflict with her distorted body.

Aside from the shadowy grotesques of Curtiz and Kenton, medical sf reached its highest point in *The Lady and the Monster*, George Sherman's 1943 adaptation of the Curt Siodmak novel *Donovan's*

Brain which has since had a number of television and film reincarnations. With Erich von Stroheim contributing a rich portrait of the mad doctor and John Alton's low-key lighting, the film is one of the Forties' most diverting horror films. After financial wizard W. H. Donovan has been killed in an aircraft accident near von Stroheim's desert laboratory, the doctor removes the undamaged brain and keeps it alive in a murky glass tank, from which it learns to take over the minds of others. Sherman's style, slow, detached, inclined to stand back for long shots of lofty Spanish-revival interiors clogged with shadows, gives the trivial plot a Forties ambience that makes it comparable to *The Uninvited* as an exercise in horror. The scene where the brain comes to life in the night-time laboratory and enters the mind of hero Richard Arlen is deservedly a classic of camerawork and direction; is every way, the film far outclasses Felix Feist's 1953 version, best of the re-makes.

Hollywood fantasy and sf was marked by its tendency to re-make subjects, a reflection of the ritualised nature of the field in which the use of traditional elements takes priority over the imaginative creation of new ones. As in the case of the comic strip, familiarity combined with brisk narrative is the aim, and Hollywood was seldom backward in finding new ways to present traditional material. This urge to re-work popular subjects accounts for the popularity in the Thirties and Forties of two key themes, but it is also significant that both allowed extensive opportunity for the exercise of special effects. It is not enough to understand what is happening; audiences must actually *see* it, even if tiny or invisible. This requirement made the twin themes of invisibility and miniaturisation among the most popular Hollywood was to produce.

There were miniaturisation effects in Roy del Ruth's *Wolf's Clothing* (1925) and in the early part of *The Bride of Frankenstein* (1935), with Ernest Thesiger admiring a collection of homonculi kept in glass bottles, but the first genuine exercise of the idea came in Tod Browning's *The Devil Doll* (1936). An adaptation of A. Merritt's *Burn, Witch, Burn!*, it shows Lionel Barrymore as a convicted scientist who, obtaining the secret of miniaturisation from a

Miniaturised people: Schoedsack's DOCTOR CYCLOPS

fellow inmate of Devil's Island, escapes to use it as a means of revenge. Dressed as an old lady toymaker, he plants two tiny creatures in the homes of his enemies, then telepathically instructs them to attack. The woman, cuddled by a little girl who thinks she is a doll, wriggles away from her owner to creep along the edge of the bed and stab a man with a poisoned needle, while on the Christmas tree a man, held in place by a floppy bow under his arms, stirs and struggles out to make a similar assault. Competent matte work and excellent out-of-proportion sets make this a remarkable scientific fantasy.

In *Doctor Cyclops* (1940), by *King Kong*'s Ernest B. Schoedsack, Albert Dekker is the bald and bullet-headed Doctor Thorkel who maintains an experimental laboratory in the Peruvian mountains, using a local radio-active deposit to reduce human beings in size. A group of scientists whom he has shrunk to the size of mice eventually lure him to his death down the mineshaft from which he draws his power, but not before they have endured a variety of terrors. Aside from the variable colour, the film's major distinction is in Tom Kilpatrick's cold-blooded script which ingeniously pursues the Ulysses/Cyclops parallel, including the death of Thorkel as a direct result of the prisoners having smashed his thick glasses, thus effectively rendering him blind. An excellent film, *Doctor Cyclops* is, however, feeble beside Jack Arnold's *The Incredible Shrinking Man*, in which the theme is not merely used as an excuse for the exercise of special effects but is squeezed of its intrinsic horror.

The horror of invisibility has seldom been adequately conveyed on the screen, and despite the unpleasantness that one would normally expect to feel at disembodiment, invisible heroes and heroines have on the whole taken it with good humour, even relishing it as a means of revenging themselves on others. Claude Rains in the original James Whale version of Wells's *The Invisible Man* went mad as a result of the invisibility drug he imbibed, but his madness was that of the megalomaniac rather than the conventional homicidal mania of the vampire or manufactured creature. As in the case of Homonculus his idea was to take over the world, or at least throw it into chaos with a campaign of murder and terrorism. Whale, a cultured English stage designer and producer imported to Hollywood in the early sound era, brought to this film as he did to his other grotesques, *Frankenstein, The Bride of Frankenstein* and *The Old Dark House,* a mood of black comedy, and in his examination of the idea managed to reflect Wells's own amusement with it.

John P. Fulton's special effects are still as good today as they were at the time, perhaps because in the necessary optical work Hollywood was the most sophisticated of the world's cinema centres. Wires are seldom used, and the intricate double exposure and negative juggling is unobtrusive and smooth. To this, Whale adds his special approach, the shooting of Claude Rains removing the bandages from an invisible face proving extremely skilled.

Using Wells's chosen setting, the English countryside, Whale recalls a gallery of rustic types, including choleric squires, phlegmatic policemen and a shrewd farmer who, hearing heavy breathing in his barn, informs the law that its quarry is hiding there. Confident of escape, Rains bursts out, only to be betrayed by his own footprints in the snow and cut down. Wry, biting in its clever dialogue, *The Invisible Man* is one of the best Wells adaptations, and Boris Karloff may well have regretted his decision in declining to play the part because of its radio orientation.

Invisibility cropped up again in *The Invisible Man Returns* (1940), briskly directed by Joe May with a characteristic German edge. Joseph H. Lewis's *The Invisible Ghost,* Edward L. Marin's *The Invisible Agent* (1942) and Ford Beebe's *The Invisible Man's Revenge* (1944) seem indistinguishable from one another now, with the trick being used by a variety of heroes to revenge wronged relatives, fight the Nazis or unravel mysteries of dubious importance. A better variation was *The Invisible Woman* (1940), directed with sly wit by A. Edward Sutherland, an old hand at comedy, and having access to the talents of an ageing John Barrymore. At the end of his career and with his mind severely impaired by alcohol, Barrymore is a tragic figure, but his ad libs still have a hint of the old panache.

Virginia Bruce is a fashion model made invisible by eccentric scientist Barrymore, after which she returns to play havoc in the store where she works and improve conditions for the models, including young Maria Montez in a bit part. The polished script scores a variety of points, mainly sexual, with Miss Bruce living in a permanent state of embarrassment as her status changes from visible to invisible and back again. Barrymore, obviously horrified by the plot, is ruffled, vague and bemused, peering thoughtfully at his machinery with the look of an Oxford don confronted by the interior of a cyclotron and poking at buttons with a "Maybe *this* one?" expression. Only Sutherland's direction prevents his role from revealing completely the great actor's mental and physical decline.

Hollywood in the Thirties is one of the cinema's richest areas, but its science fiction and science fantasy films are generally undistinguished. The Germanic influence resulted in some classic horror films, but it was not until the Forties that audiences became sufficiently interested in technology to accept the less horrific sf product. By the war, sf magazine fiction was well established, and the success of comic strip characters like Buck Rogers and Flash Gordon in the film serials had built up an acceptance of space adventure. For a decade, the serial was to dominate the field, until the boom of the Fifties revived the need for adventure and off-beat plots that had motivated the original rise of sf literature.

Only one film of the Thirties offered anything that was genuinely new and imaginative in sf, and this, though directed by an American, was made in England. Flawed, faded today, *Things To Come* still has an impact that makes it a classic of the field.

5. William Cameron Menzies and 'Things To Come'

WHEN H. G. WELLS was asked to write an introduction to the collection of his scientific romances printed in 1933[15] he was faintly disparaging of them. Discounting *The Time Machine, The Invisible Man* and *The War of the Worlds* as aiming "only at the same amount of conviction as one gets in a good gripping dream," he directed his readers' attention to the harsher realities of the time. "The world in the presence of cataclysmal realities has no need for fresh cataclysmal fantasies," he said tersely. "That game is over. Who wants the invented humours of Mr. Parham in Whitehall, when day by day we can watch Mr. Hitler in Germany?"

Wells, then sixty-eight, was expressing his irritation with a world that, despite the flood of pamphlets, polemical novels and cautionary works he had lavished upon it, took cursory notice only of his technocratic theories. Even though most of his scientific romances had been written in the early 1900s at the beginning of his career,

NATIONAL
BULLETIN
JUNE 1970

OUR OPERATIONS AGAINST
THE HILL PEOPLE HAVE
BEEN SUCCESSFUL.

FURTHER HOSTILITIES
WILL BRING A VICTORIOUS PEACE

LONG LIVE
THE CHIEF

they remained far more popular than his works on world history and social revolution. Like most sf writers Wells believed that rule by science and scientists offered the best chance of a sane world, and was understandably upset when humanity disagreed.

It was probably because of this irritation that, in 1934, Wells accepted Alexander Korda's invitation to adapt for the screen *The Shape of Things To Come,* a book summing up the ideals for which the writer had been fighting since his career began. Always interested in the cinema, partly as an art form but mostly as a medium for the expression of his ideas, Wells in 1929 had written a scenario for a silent film, *The King Who Was a King,*[16] but providentially it was never produced. Even Wells later agreed that this overwritten condemnation of war and international profiteering was "an entirely amateurish effort." Korda however was a good deal more experienced than the producer who had commissioned *The King Who Was a King,* and both men agreed that their film would be a clear expression of Wells's views as well as a box-office success. Consequently Wells put his signature on a penny postcard agreeing to write a draft script, and *Things To Come* was born.

Today, we can afford to be lofty about *Things To Come.* The ideas that seemed revolutionary in 1933 are flat and unreal by the standards of the Sixties. Technocracy then looked an ideal means of government, but we know now that nothing in human society is that simple. Having become aware of the mind and its possibilities, we no longer see as desirable a civilisation based on public service and the pursuit of a mild and undemanding happiness. To us, Wells's whole-wheat-bread Utopia looks as dull and unworkable as anything from the visionary writers of the Sixteenth century.

Nor is *Things To Come* always cinematically remarkable. William Cameron Menzies's design is superb, but his direction is unprofessional. Shots set up to achieve maximum visual effect do not cut together well, with the result that actors frequently appear

Opposite: Menzies's THINGS TO COME: *Raymond Massey in a film of occasional brilliance*

to leap across the room in the middle of a scene. Most disastrous of all is the design of the special effects, ludicrously unreal by modern standards. The model work is clumsy, the process photography of variable quality. Wells scorned *Metropolis,* but in its skilled use of models and mirror shots it often makes *Things To Come* look little better than an amateur production.

Wells soon realised that the task of writing a scenario from *The Shape of Things To Come* was larger than he had anticipated. "The book on which this story rests," he commented, "is essentially an imaginative *discussion* of social and political forces and possibilities, and a film is no place for argument. The conclusions of that book therefore are taken for granted in this film, and a new story has been invented to display them, a story woven first about the life of one man . . . and then in the second part about his grandson . . . . "[17]

When the script of *Things To Come* was published Wells told the story of how it had been written. "This was the first film treatment written by the Author for actual production," he said, "and he found much more difficulty in making it than he did any of its successors. . . . What is before the reader here is the last of several drafts. An earlier treatment was made, discussed, worked upon for a little and discarded. It was a 'prentice effort and the Author owes much to the friendly generosity of Alexander Korda, Lajos Biro and Cameron Menzies, who put all their experience at his disposal during the revision.

"They were greatly excited by the general conception, but they found the draft quite impracticable for production. A second treatment was then written. This, with various modifications, was made into a scenario of the old type. This scenario again was set aside for a second version, and this again was revised and put back into the form of the present treatment. Korda and the Author had agreed upon an innovation in film technique, to discard the elaborate detailed technical scenario altogether and to produce directly from the descriptive treatment here given. We have found this work very well in practice—given a competent director. By this time, however, the Author, now almost through the toils of his apprenticeship, was in a state of fatigue towards the altered, revised and reconstructed text, and, though he had done his best to get it into tolerable film prose, he has an uneasy sense that many oddities and awkwardnesses of expression that crept in during the scenario have become now so familiar to him that he has become blind to them and has been unable to get rid of them. . . . ."[17]

Undoubtedly there are "oddities and awkwardnesses of expression," all of which Korda would have been aware of, but most were allowed to remain in the completed film. Lajos Biro claims to have pointed out to Korda in a memorandum that special effects could not make up for Wells's lack of cinematic thinking, and that the film needed a competent scriptwriter to make something of his ideas. He also noted that, apart from minor details, the whole story could have been just as well set in 1934 as 2054, Wells having failed to include any genuinely realistic technical advances in his scheme for the future. Despite these arguments, Korda continued to defer to Wells, and while it is probably not true, as some writers have claimed, that no word of the script could be changed without the author's approval, the film as it appears today does rest heavily on Wells's shaky foundation.

The team Korda assembled to realise this script was itself a doubtful quantity. William Cameron Menzies, despite his extensive credits as a production designer, had never before directed a major feature film, and in inviting him to Britain to make *Things To Come* after negotiations with Lewis Milestone had broken down, Korda took a gamble which did not quite come off. Menzies frequently required assistance in directing some of the acting scenes, and was not always happy with the script. In addition, many of the actors on the film still considered screen roles little more than pot boilers to feed them until their next stint at the Old Vic, and as a result the playing is often sketchy.

Among the technicians, Ned Mann had built a substantial reputation for special effects on such films as the first *The Thief of Bagdad* (1926) which Menzies had designed. Alexander Korda's brother Vincent was an excellent designer of period sets for the Korda organisation. Georges Périnal had photographed many classics, including Clair's *Le Million* and Korda's *Rembrandt*. René Hubert was a major name in theatrical costume design, and Arthur Bliss a composer of merit, if not genius. The editor, William Hornbeck, was also later to become one of the cinema's foremost craftsmen. Over all these men, however, loomed the presence of H. G. Wells. With Korda's approval he circulated memoranda to all the technicians involved, setting out in detail his exact requirements in the matters of architecture, clothing and decoration. What Menzies thought of this is not recorded.

Faced with these problems, it is to Menzies's credit that he managed to create from the material at hand a coherent and impressive work of art. *Things To Come* is not a masterpiece, but like many flawed films it rises occasionally to a special brilliance. Wells marred it deeply with his simple-minded and often shoddy pamphleteering, but frequently the material is saved by a piece of magic in the design, a clever performance or some neat construction. Almost single-handed Raymond Massey sustains the film with his playing of John and Oswald Cabal, projecting an image that is every science fiction reader's idea of a leader; dedicated, visionary, apolitical.

The film's opening contains the best of Wells and Menzies, traditional British values twisted abruptly into contrast with the realities of war. Although the location is given in a title as "Everytown," Menzies used London's Oxford Circus as a model for the set which acts as a pivot for much of the story. As the film begins, it is Christmas, and the streets are jammed with shoppers hurrying home. Menzies cuts significantly from laughing crowds to newspaper posters forecasting war. The words "War Scare" on a poster and "Merry Christmas" carefully chalked by a pavement artist are contrasted by rhythmic cutting, toys in a shop window followed by the grimly prophetic sign "Christmas Turkeys." Over it all, Bliss provides martial variations on "God Rest Ye Merry Gentlemen."

Later we enter the tranquil home of John Cabal (Raymond

Massey), where he is entertaining his friends Passworthy (Edward Chapman) and Harding (Maurice Braddell). They discuss the war scare, none of them taking it as seriously as Cabal. Harding doesn't care whether there is war or peace providing he can continue with his medical research, while Passworthy speaks strongly for war as a cultural stimulus. But Cabal is adamant. "If we don't end war," he says, "war will end us." However the argument lapses, and the men join in singing "Noël," while Menzies cuts to the children playing with war toys under the Christmas tree.

A moment later the threats of the newspaper posters become reality. Radio announcements of a bomber force crossing the British coast are followed by a sequence showing the city square cleared of crowds by a flood of troops. A loudspeaker directs people to go home, and they panic, jamming the subways. The bombing raid which follows is poorly done, exhibiting inferior model work, but Menzies's final crane shot moves across the square, now heaped with rubble, to linger eloquently on the half-buried body of a child.

The next few reels are an extended montage of battle scenes, showing the treadmill of war. A man leaves his family, enters the army and melts into the marching shadows, never to be seen again. Tanks roll across the hills, men and armies die. Dates like tombstones mark off the years, and though the tanks become more futuristic and the dates more remote, the war is still the same. Again, poor model work vitiates the power of these scenes, Mann's technique proving unequal to the strain Wells places on it.

Much more is said about the futility of war in a brief scene of an air battle in which John Cabal shoots down an enemy fighter pilot (John Clements). As Cabal comforts the dying man, a child wanders up, and rather than see her killed by the poison gas leaking from his plane, Clements gives her his gas mask. As the fumes become thicker, Cabal hands his pistol to the doomed man and takes off. Menzies's use of a low angle for the whole scene and the clever construction of the crashed plane, "built" as much as any piece of architecture, convey a mood of timeless gallantry.

1966 comes. A corpse is spreadeagled on barbed wire. A dissolve—

and all that is left are scraps of cloth and hair. We glimpse a news-paper—cost £4 Sterling—which announces in ill-set type that a "Wandering Sickness" is afflicting Europe; people are warned to avoid stagnant water and bomb craters. As a rolling title explains the disease and its most terrifying symptom, an uncontrollable urge to walk which ends only in death, a crowd of ragged blank-eyed people grope over a hill.

"Everytown" reappears, now a ruined shell. A crooked sign says "Hospital" and from below frame a hand gropes up, clutches, and drags erect a pale, sweating man. Later, a girl lurches out into the square, and people run screaming as she shambles towards them. On top of a shattered cinema a man in furs (Ralph Richardson) orders a guard to shoot the woman, but finally does it himself. Richardson is The Chief, warlord of the area and a symbol of every-thing Wells despised—militarism, capitalism, politics. He wears bulky robes of fur and a tin helmet with black plumes fastened to it, while his wife (Marguretta Scott) is decorated significantly with necklaces of coins.

The Chief is waging a war against the Hill Tribes who have access to shale oil plants, but he cannot fight them effectively without aircraft. His chief engineer (Derrick de Marney) tries to repair the ancient biplanes, but there are no materials. Doctor Harding is also attempting to continue his medical experiments, Wells wryly re-ferring back to his earlier remarks about research by showing how a shortage of chemicals caused by the war makes his work im-possible. As The Chief is demanding that de Marney get the planes into the air, they see a strange black aircraft approaching. It coasts to earth, and a remarkable image shows it framed by two ruined collonades in arresting perspective. The plane is piloted by John Cabal, his black leather clothing and chitinous glass-fronted helmet making him an almost alien creature.

Cabal and The Chief are a study in opposites, Richardson refusing to believe Cabal's claim that he is a representative of a society of scientists, The Airmen, who from their base at Basra are remaking the world. "Who are you?," he demands. "Law and sanity," Cabal says. *"I'm* the law," The Chief thunders. "I said 'Law *and sanity!'* " Cabal replies. Dismissing him as "some sort of aerial bus driver," The Chief locks Cabal up, then attacks the Hill Tribes with considerable success, but while his attention is diverted de Marney escapes, returning with the Airmen. A pacifying gas crushes all resistance, but the invaders find that The Chief has unaccountably died from its effects, a symbolic sacrifice to dedicate the new society. "Dead, and his world dead with him," Cabal says triumphantly over the corpse. "Now begins the rule of the Airmen."

One can discount most of the next reel, consisting as it does of inept model scenes purporting to show a century of scientific progress. The narrative re-emerges in Everytown of 2036, an asceptic city with transparent exterior lift tubes, international tv, artificial sunlight in every home and a variety of similar superficial technological advances. Oswald Cabal, grandson of John Cabal, is the city's leader, though he is hard pressed by a sculptor named Theotocopulous (Cedric Hardwicke) who demands a return to the old days when life was "short and hot and merry." The two men conflict most on the use of the Space Gun, a graduated electric cannon of vast dimensions which, as a means of launching a space craft, is not as scientifically unlikely as some people think. With it Cabal proposes to send two young people, his own daughter and the son of Passworthy IV, on an expedition around the Moon.

Pursued by a mob with Theotocopulous at its head, Cabal and his group reach the Space Gun and manage to fire it just in time. In the final scene of the film, Cabal and Passworthy stand before a huge telescope mirror and watch the ship begin its journey into space. The dialogue of this sequence, used exactly as Wells wrote it, is so rich in the essential spirit of science fiction and so effective a summation of this film's merit that it deserves reproducing in full.

Cabal watches the mirror intently, then cries to Passworthy:

"There—there they go! That faint gleam of light."

"I feel that what we've done is monstrous."

"What they've done is magnificent."

"Will they come back?"

"Yes. And go again and again, until a landing is made and the Moon is conquered. This is only a beginning."

"If they don't come back—my son and your daughter—what of that, Cabal?"

"Then, presently, others will go."

"Oh, God, is there ever to be any age of happiness? Is there never to be any rest?"

"Rest enough for the individual man—too much, and too soon, and we call it Death. But for Man no rest and no ending. He must go on, conquest beyond conquest. First this little planet with its winds and ways, and then all the laws of mind and matter that restrain him. Then the planets about him, and at last out across immensity to the stars. And when he has conquered all the deeps of space and all the mysteries of time, still he will be beginning."

"But . . . we're such little creatures. Poor humanity's so fragile, so weak. Little . . . little animals."

"Little animals. If we're no more than animals we must snatch each little scrap of happiness and live and suffer and pass, mattering no more than all the other animals do or have done." Cabal points to the image of space in the mirror. "It is this—or that: all the universe or nothingness. Which shall it be, Passworthy? Which shall it be?"

Over this dialogue Bliss imposes a soft but powerful melody, building with the intensity of Cabal's speech until the full orchestra and choir surge up at the end with an echo of his final question. I am not uncritical of Bliss's score; despite its many qualities it seems often coarse and shrill, and Wells's claim that "the music is part of the constructive scheme of the film" is seldom borne out. The final scene, however, is a triumph of music and image. The hard-edged side lighting and almost stylised close-ups of Massey's face, his impeccable delivery of what is basically a technocratic credo and Bliss's profoundly moving music combine to give it a unique quality of optimism and dignity.

The most remarkable quality of *Things To Come* is the coherence and consistency of its design. Menzies may not have been a master of direction, but his sense of balance and his mastery of what Eisenstein called "visual counterpoint" has never been better displayed than in this film. Concerned only in the most general way with textures and movements within the frame, Menzies puts his whole effort into the balance of his sets, the conflict between masses, the choreography of matter. His designs fill the frame both vertically and horizontally, giving some sequences an almost three-dimensional character, while use of the low angle sends individual groupings surging out at the audience.

These techniques are most notable in the sequences showing Everytown as a ruin. The tumbled masonry of the ruined cinema with its incongruously jumbled lettering is a perfect example of Menzies's talent for "building" ruins, and he is at his best in the confrontation between Cabal and The Chief in his headquarters, a lofty chamber whose dome has been caved in by bombs. In both cases the set dominates the action, presenting men as creatures imprisoned by their circumstances, and showing Richardson especially as a person who is almost part of the chaos: the ruin *is* the man. Only Cabal, monastic in black leather, and to a lesser extent the cunning and coin-bedecked Marguretta Scott stand out against the rubble, and finally it is Cabal alone who prevails.

It is because Menzies chooses to pursue this interest in the character of Cabal that the final scenes prove so disastrous. Visually Menzies's vision of the far future is feeble, most of the sets leaning heavily on Thirties *moderne*. Just as Richardson is part of his ruined home, so Massey is part of the future Everytown, but with no traditions on which to rely, Menzies has set him in a riot of neon lighting, perspex and white plaster. Although Massey looks imposing and delivers his lines with perfect diction, the sequences collapse from their own weight.

The film's ideas often exhibit a similar paucity of imagination, especially in the future sequences. Philosophically Wells offers little in his script that is new or viable, being content to rely on the views he held throughout his life. In April 1899, he remarked "What seems to be inevitable in the future is rule by an aristocracy of organizers, men who manage railroads and similar vast enterprises."[18] Thirty-seven years later he put forward the same idea in *Things To Come,* but by then whatever relevance it had possessed was gone.

In one of his memos to the staff, Wells unburdened himself on the form of the future. "Things, structures, in general will be great, yes, but they will not be monstrous. Men will not be reduced to servitude and uniformity, they will be released to freedom and variety. All the balderdash one finds in such films as Fritz Lange's [sic] *Metropolis* about 'robot workers' and ultra-skyscrapers etc. should be cleared out of your minds before you work on this film. As a general rule you may take it that whatever Lange did in *Metropolis* is the exact contrary of what we want done here."[17]

Despite his ease with words like "freedom" and "variety," what Wells offers seems a subtle variation on Fascism. "Our revolution didn't abolish death or danger," Oswald Cabal says. "It simply made danger and death worth while." A curious sentiment for someone allegedly devoted to the good of mankind. Later he remarks ringingly, "The best of life is nearest to the edge of death," recalling the traditional exhortation of the sergeant urging his timid men up the beach; "What d'ya wanna do, live forever?" Wells's freedom is the freedom to be dominated by visionaries like Cabal, his variety invested primarily in the number of ways one can suffer in this dangerous and ambitious world of 2036.

Politically and sociologically *Things To Come* is specious, but this does not detract from its substantial merit as a film. One might even excuse many of its excesses as being symptomatic of the time. The depression was just over and England hung suspended between the Crash and the War, floating briefly at the peak of a parabola. Robert Graves and Alan Hodge recall in speaking of that time "the common conviction that a vigorous replanning of the democratic, capitalist system would bring about complete recovery,"[19] and it is this almost mystical faith in the political and economic freedoms that motivates *Things To Come.* Today, armed with Keynesian economics and modern political philosophy, we know that social engineering is not that simple, but to Wells, Menzies and Korda it must have seemed the physical expression of a beautiful dream, a scientific Eden free of even the serpent.

Unfortunately its makers did not even have the satisfaction of appealing to the mass audience. *Things To Come* cost £350,000 to produce, and even after years of release it had not made its costs back. People responded to its fantasy, but the message went over their heads. When it was announced in the first scenes that a bombing force had crossed the coast of England, audiences of the time broke into laughter. Nobody, except perhaps Wells, could know that in only a few years this part of the film would come grimly true.

Like many artists who encountered the sf cinema in the Thirties, Menzies went on in later years to produce other associated films. Part of the reason clearly lies in the fact that the adventurous designer was forced to work in fantasy, horror or sf in those days if he wished to be genuinely experimental, but obviously Menzies had a flair for sf which it pleased him to exercise. Additionally, two of the films were in the abortive 3-D process, a system which, though offering the art director a remarkable opportunity to achieve startling effects of dimension and depth, dictated that his subject should be violent and fantastic, providing the audience with a stream of visual shocks. Despite deficiencies in plot and characterisation, however, all three films are interesting excursions into a personal and intriguing world of fantasy.

The Whip Hand (1952) was the last gasp of the Nazi spy cycle which enjoyed a vigorous vogue from 1940 to 1950. Korea put paid to the fashion for stories of German communities plotting in isolated country towns, Nazi beasts preparing for a violent comeback and the ferretting out of concentration camp commandants in Argentina, but this film's story of a German biologist using a small American town for secret experiments in germ warfare was of sufficient intrinsic interest to justify low-budget production. Menzies, hampered by limited resources, made a competent job of his designs for the town, and managed by a clever use of the studio's facilities to suggest the dusty lassitude of a hamlet hoping to be forgotten by mankind.

Seizing on the fact that the town has dried up due to the death of the fish in a nearby lake, Menzies constructed his designs to suggest decay and emptiness. An abandoned factory and a ruined pier by the lake are cleverly used as settings for a search, with slatted light lancing through the dusty air as the hero hides from his pursuers. The Nazi hideout is a sinister mansion in the middle of a pine forest, Menzies gaining nice effects as the hero looks down from the hill at its courtyard in which mysterious figures dodder about in the wintry sunshine. Inside, these figures—experimental human guinea pigs infected with various virulent diseases—are kept in a sterile area through the glass window of which they peer with hopeless faces, shambling objects swathed in shroud-like sheets. When the Nazi scientist hides out in this room at the climax, the movement with which the patients close in on him and beat him to death has an especially horrible quality of animal revenge for which Menzies has carefully prepared us.

In *The Maze* (1954), 3-D and Menzies's designs are cancelled out by a trivial plot, but the film is still a clever piece of horror/sf. Richard Carlson is a playboy who, on the eve of his marriage, inherits a Scottish castle, his initial visit to which stretches into months. His *fiancée* goes there only to find Carlson immured in a crumbling keep, his privacy protected by a forbidding butler (Michael Pate). Her entreaties for him to leave are unsuccessful, and slowly she begins to uncover the mystery of the castle. In 1750, it eventuates, one of Carlson's ancestors was born a freak: short-circuited at an earlier stage of evolution, he emerged as a giant frog, with a frog's longevity. Still alive after 200 years, his welfare is the responsibility of each successive heir, but Carlson is released from the duty when the creature, crazed by fear, falls from an upper window to his death.

The necessities of 3-D guide Menzies's approach to *The Maze*. Most shots have a small figure moving from foreground to background in a straight line, or light figures shown against a dark ground. The maze in which Carlson and Pate exercise the creature every night is an ideal setting for 3-D effects, and even projected "flat" the images have a remarkable depth. Unfortunately Menzies is not above more trivial ideas: the frog falling onto the camera, envelopes and other impedimenta jammed into the lens at every opportunity. Generally, however, his work is in good taste. His castle, with trees like black spiders, huge doors, odd ramp-like stairs and a bluntly simple stone staircase leading to the forbidden chamber is a splendid creation.

Neither of these films was truly science fiction, but *Invaders from Mars* (1954), in 3-D and colour, is a notable fantasy of alien invasion containing some of Menzies's most assured work. He carries his design philosophy into every sequence, giving even conventional interiors and action scenes a characteristic perspective. The hill on which a little boy (Jimmy Hunt) first sees the landing of a flying saucer is complete with leafless trees, two-rail fence and grey-white sand pits, a beautiful piece of studio recreation which might have been borrowed direct from *Gone with the Wind*. The aliens take over Jimmy's parents by inserting crystals into their brains, but when he flees to the police station, the boy finds that the police chief too has a tell-tale scar at the base of his skull. Reflecting his fear, the police station is an ominously gigantic place, Menzies using out-of-scale furniture and alarmingly featureless walls to accentuate its disturbing quality.

After a struggle, the boy convinces the army that aliens are indeed in residence under his home, and entrances are blasted into the tunnels the Martians have made, looming caverns with walls of bubbled green glass. At the core of the installation, guarded by lofty "mutants" (clad in zip-up green plush boiler suits), they find the Martian intelligence, a disembodied bulbous head in a glass sphere. With the aliens vanquished, the little boy wakes up: it was all a dream. But there is a sound outside and he looks through the window to see a flying saucer landing, just as he imagined.

Despite some nonsensical inventions, Menzies makes *Invaders from Mars* into more than a conventional fantasy by his brilliant design. The alien intelligence is a remarkable throw-back to the spirit of *The Thief of Bagdad* (1940), for which he created a clockwork eight-armed woman programmed to murder those who came near her. The quick intelligence of the Martian's eyes and the weaving of its scaly tentacular arms recall some of this classic's mood. Nor is it easy to forget the shot of the heroine helpless as the Martian machine extends a needle-like probe towards her unprotected neck with a red crystal glinting at its point. Drugged, she rests her forehead on her hand, her face childlike and tranquil as the point draws horrifyingly close. Despite its deficiencies in acting, *Invaders from Mars* is a remarkable exercise in sf cinema.

It was also Menzies's last film as a director. In 1956 he died, a master of design who failed to gain the recognition he deserved. His many remarkable films, both in the field of fantasy and outside it, have earned him a place in the cinema that is uncontested. Unfortunately there are few films to which we can refer confident in the knowledge that they represent his pure vision. Even *Invaders from Mars* was tampered with during and after production. Sequences of army manoeuvres were inserted from stock footage, all the more ludicrous for the fact that limited 3-D material made it necessary to re-use the same shots time after time. The ending was often cut for release, and many scenes between Jimmy Hunt and scientist Arthur Franz were also deleted. In the final ignominy, the film was re-made by W. Lee Wilder and today *Invaders from Mars* is a rarity. No fitting memorial to a great artist, it is nevertheless eccentrically typical of the genius of William Cameron Menzies.

6. A Note on the Serials

THE SERIAL is the cinema's comic strip, and because of the close relationship between sf cinema and the comics, the two fields have interacted to a greater degree than have written sf and the cinema. Sf film has tended to reflect the comic strip approach to sf rather than that of the magazines, and in general it has been via the comics that sf film has absorbed sf trends. Where a science fiction trend was not taken up by the comics—telepathy, for instance, being an effect difficult to render in the strips—it is seldom apparent in sf film, while a popular one—robots are a good example—will be adopted with enthusiasm.

Despite the basic similarity in form between serials and comics, with the enforced fragmentation brought on by the necessity in each case to divide up the action and at the same time retain audience interest, serials have seldom equalled the comic strip's vitality in plot or visual style. With certain notable exceptions the serial field is the worst endowed area of sf film, presenting a drab and arid face that only the uncritical can accept. The tendency for directors, writers and actors to remain in the fantasy field rather than attempt other areas worked against the serials, in which a team of untalented nobodies seemed to churn out year after year the same trivial nonsense.

However, the serial field is far from undistinguished, and has in its time produced its share of masterpieces. The late silent and early sound serials of Hollywood have a tight narrative pace and visual elegance, with directors like George Seitz and B. Reeves Eason showing the flexibility and energy of the serial form. And in the Fifties, with comic strips again accepted by artists as an accurate mirror of the world, film-makers like Franju and Resnais returned to serials for inspiration, and revived the form with their frequent *hommages* to Feuillade. Despite its malnutrition, the serial field has proved a hardy genre with a contribution to make to the cinema, and to science fiction film.

Science fiction in the early serials was usually a matter of detail,

69

used by Feuillade as window dressing—the *art nouveau* tv screens of *Judex*—or by American producers as a catchpenny trick. In *The Black Box* (1915), a Holmesian detective invents, among other gadgets, a means of seeing who is ringing him on the telephone, while *The Secret of the Submarine* (1916) shows the hero and heroine cheating the Japanese of an invention whereby a submarine could extract oxygen from the water and remain submerged indefinitely. Never documented, these inventions usually served to initiate a conventional action plot, and their effect on the form of the serial was limited.

This pattern continued through most of the silent period. The spirit of *Popular Mechanics* and Gernsback's *Electrical Experimenter* hangs over most of the serials, with mysterious electronic "black boxes" being stolen by dacoits, and retrieved only to be stolen again. New sources of power were popular, and serials at one time or another concerned substitutes for coal, a powdered gasoline and various "...iums" and "...ites" that would provide unlimited power if only they could be made available to the world. Obviously derived from an imperfect understanding of radium and its properties, these mysterious elements died out in the late silent period, to be replaced by robots, remote-controlled appliances and the more photogenic results of automation.

The silent serials managed to produce their share of memorable moments, like the "photo-telepathy" of *The Mysteries of Myra* (1916), where the heroine's thoughts could be recorded by placing a special photographic plate against her forehead. In *The Shielding Shadow* (1916) Pathé had a halting try at the invisibility idea, but wires were much in evidence. A primitive robot, known as "Q, The Automaton," made its appearance in *The Master Mystery* (1918), Harry Houdini's disastrous film *début*, but in the end "Q" was revealed as a fraud controlled by the villain. An indication of the low esteem in which sf was held by producers can be gained from the fate of the script written by serial specialist Frank Leon Smith for George B. Seitz's *The Man Who Stole the Moon*. Originally an sf thriller with Martian villains, it was turned by the producers into a comedy based on the by now familiar search for a mysterious power source. To retain the best visual ideas, the Martian villain became a *hero* in a futuristic plane, his alien powers being explained by the fact that he had been until recently a stage magician and hypnotist!

The serials always encouraged specialists who could work within the tight schedules required, and who were prepared to cut corners to bring in the material on time. In the Twenties, George Seitz and Robert F. Hill dominated the field, but in the following decade a new group of men trained in the silents rose to take over what had become, for the smaller studios at least, a highly profitable side-line to feature production. Republic, Columbia and Universal controlled the serial field from its boom in the Thirties until its demise in the early Fifties, and the men they employed as serial directors—Spencer Gordon Bennett, Fred Brannon, B. Reeves "Breezy" Eason, James W. Horne—contributed substantially to the richness of the period's commercial cinema.

If it is hard to praise the Z features of the sf field, doing justice to the serials is harder still. Derived almost exclusively from the comics, with a few characters out of radio and the thriller pulps, they barely paid lip service to the visual conventions of either comics or cinema, depending instead on an unstable union of both. Dialogue was frequently abysmal, more often just silly, acting as bad as one would expect from a field where budgets were pared to the bone and the major part of the talent money went on stunt men. In every other department from music to costumes they depended on the second-rate and the derivative. And yet to anyone who cares about the cinema there is an attraction about the serials that is inescapable.

Part of the charm lies in their necessarily brisk pace. Most serials were released in fifteen two-reel episodes, with the initial episode occasionally running to three reels. Designed for a juvenile audience, they could not depend on holding interest with dialogue or characterisation, nor divert the audience with intricate cutting. Deprived of close-ups, conversations and the possibilities of editing, the serial makers fell back on a flat, detached style in which the frame was filled by disorganised but violent stunts, fights and chases. As close-ups would reveal that stunt-men often replaced actors, a fact usually apparent even in long-shot, loud effects and music were used over stunts to provide the necessary impact, and the need for almost non-stop music led to scores that were reiterative and trite. Today, however, the reasons are unimportant, and we find that the stunt-men with their jammed-on hats, the foolish music and chintzy costumes convey a mood of the past more accurately than any work of social comment.

Serial makers tended to work in pairs, one shooting the dialogue scenes and fights while another operated a second exterior unit for chases. B. Reeves Eason was already a talented second unit director when he came to serials, having managed the charge in Michael Curtiz's magnificent *The Charge of the Light Brigade* (1936). In 1935 he handled second unit for Mascot's *The Phantom Empire* (co-director Otto Brower) and in 1936 for Republic's *Undersea Kingdom* (co-director Joseph Kane), both serials showing his grasp of essential action. *The Phantom Empire* is especially fine, a foolish but memorable combination of four or five traditions conceived as a vehicle for singing cowboy Gene Autry. Clad in impeccable Western gear, Autrey operates a radio station on his Texas ranch and battles various crooks, initially unaware that beneath his land exists a lost civilisation.

Entered through a disused mineshaft, the phantom empire is a weird Metropolis-like city with transparent lift tubes reminiscent of *Things To Come,* lumbering robots as casually constructed as children's cardboard armour and futuristic costumes derived directly from the comics. The entire serial has a mood of subtle menace that is difficult to isolate or explain. Perhaps it is the alienation effect of conflicting traditions, the unintentional poetry of Autry clattering to a halt at the mine entrance with his posse, throwing up his hand to open the doors, then plunging into the dark with its unspecified dangers.

Undersea Kingdom was designed to cash in on the success of *The*

Phantom Empire, and followed a roughly similar plot. The hero was Ray "Crash" Corrigan, a lively naval officer who spent part of the first episode demonstrating his athletic skill in a Navy gym. Lured into accompanying a visionary scientist on an exploratory submarine trip, he is with the party when it discovers Atlantis surviving in an artificial environment somewhere on the ocean bed. Supplied with light and air by means never adequately explained, Atlantis is a thriving military power, but Corrigan and his companions are able to foil its plan to invade Earth. Atlantis, predictably, is an uneasy mixture of the vintage and futuristic, recalling the period's pulp sf and the better comic strips. The Atlanteans use horse-drawn chariots, but nevertheless possess a death ray with which they ravage the surface until prevented. These oddities aside, *Undersea Kingdom,* though inferior to *The Phantom Empire,* is not without merit.

The most famous serials of the Thirties are those produced by Universal from the "Flash Gordon" strip of Alex Raymond and the "Buck Rogers" strip of Dick Calkins. With Larry "Buster" Crabbe as both Flash and Buck, the serials have a continuity which makes them best considered en bloc. Frederick Stephani directed *Flash Gordon* in 1936, Ford Beebe and Robert Hill *Flash Gordon's Trip to Mars* in 1938, Beebe and Ray Taylor *Flash Gordon Conquers the Universe* in 1940, and Beebe and Saul A. Goodkin *Buck Rogers* in 1939. More completely than other sf films, these serials derive from comic strip antecedents, and much of the original fantastic background and narrative vitality survive in the cinema versions.

As in the comic strip, each Flash Gordon serial had the hero with his blonde girl friend Dale Arden and tame scientist Dr. Zarkov battling the sinister tyrant Ming the Merciless who from his planet Mongo was intent on enslaving Earth. After avoiding shark-men, clay-men, fire dragons, prehistoric monsters and a variety of creatures created or controlled by Ming, the friends invariably triumphed. Despite a pretence towards scientific accuracy, the serials drew heavily on the swashbuckling fantasy of the pulps, as well as other older models. In costumes recalling the medieval clothing of

Lang's *Nibelungen* and opposed by spear-carrying enemies in similarly Wagnerian winged helmets and boots, Crabbe was the personification of the epic hero of European mythology, a pure-minded warrior vanquishing by force of virtue the evils that surround him.

Significantly, the menaces concocted to oppose Flash and Buck often derived from the popular sf film theme, loss of individuality. Ming attempts frequently to confine Flash physically and mentally rather than kill him, while the Zuggs of *Buck Rogers* and the Incense of Forgetfulness employed in *Flash Gordon's Trip to Mars* threaten mindlessness or are threatening because of it. Constructed from preformed elements, the Flash Gordon and Buck Rogers serials are classic examples of tinker-toy production, though in this case the models come from other fields as well as from within sf. Bits of old sf features, costumes from earlier serials, lines from the comics themselves, extracts from Nordic, Anglo-Saxon and American mythology, even a ballet sequence from Dimitri Buchowetzki's *The Midnight Sun* are employed to create a jackdaw world of fantasy that is nevertheless coherent and fascinating.

Aside from these excursions into space opera, the serials seldom extended themselves again beyond the mundane world of the sf thriller. Drawing more and more on the comics, faced with manpower and budget problems brought on by the war, the serial makers relied increasingly on the flat action techniques soon to become traditional. Lambert Hillyer's *Batman* (1943) and Spencer Bennett's 1949 sequel *Batman and Robin* show respectively the beginnings of this impoverishment and its eventual result. The Hillyer serial still retains some of the Thirties' fantasy, including a sinister Japanese villain (J. Carroll Naish) who hides out in a sideshow purporting to illustrate the atrocities which bestial Japanese have inflicted on their victims, but in general the trappings are cheap, its nearest antecedents paltry melodramas like Monogram's 1935 *The Mysterious Mr. Wong*, with which it shared many situations, settings and lines of dialogue. The revival of this serial in the Sixties did a grave disservice to the field, drawing attention to a film which, as much through circumstances as any lack of talent on Hillyer's part, is completely atypical.

Sf elements in *Batman* are limited, resting mainly in a weird machine with which Naish saps the mind power of his victims, rendering them automatons. The device, an open-work metal helmet from which smoke billows at every application, is unconvincing, as are the actors on whom it is used. With the draft depriving him of able-bodied extras, Hillyer was forced to use only the aged and 4F, who hobble about in a convincing depiction of mindlessness brought on as much by rheumatism as electronics. The serial's plot shows similar lack of foresight or craftsmanship. After an episode during which the spy ring struggles to obtain a coffin mysteriously dropped off the American coast by a Japanese submarine, it is smuggled into Naish's presence and the lid pried off. Inside is a moribund Japanese Army officer who, before expiry, croaks out a direction to examine a button on his jacket. Reading the message inside, nobody thinks to suggest that there are easier ways of delivering orders, even to a master spy.

Some directors of the period were still able to recall the Thirties, and occasionally to improve on it with a skill that Hillyer never achieved. James W. Horne's *The Spider Returns* (1941), based on the popular radio series, was a tight and inventive thriller serial in which the contest with a conventional masked master killer, The Gargoyle, was used as an excuse on the part of Horne and his cameraman James S. Brown to create some miraculous visual effects. The Spider, in Shadow gear of black cape and soft felt hat, executes some remarkable stunts, including acrobatic somersaults worthy of a master stunt man like Bob Rose or Yakima Canutt. The Gargoyle's electrical gadget with which he can remotely control machines and vehicles is just a device, but Brown's shots of trains slowing to halt in silhouette against evening skies and factories stopping abruptly to the consternation of their owners are weirdly appropriate and visually elegant.

By the middle Forties, Spencer Bennett had been replaced as the serial king by Fred C. Brannon, with whom he directed *The Purple Monster Strikes* (1945). Cursed with a five foot hero whose high fedora and elevator shoes do nothing to disguise his physical drawbacks, the serial is grotesque today, and the plot, with a sneering Martian in ex-Flash Gordon rig arriving on Earth as the vanguard of an invasion, does not invite serious consideration. Much time is occupied in a favourite effect, in which the Martian, having killed a key character, periodically occupies his body with some trite double exposure and mumbo-jumbo with a smoking phial held under his nose. After three characters have been taken over by Martians, thus doubling the effective life of those actors, one is unsure of what is going on, and ceases to care.

Fred Brannon's *King of the Rocket Men* (1949) shares the ineptness of *The Purple Monster Strikes,* with an experimental scientist battling crime in a rocket flying suit he has perfected. A few shots of the Rocket Man, a captive balloon towed briskly across the skyline, are memorable, but the general result is not. Never a competitor of either Bennett or Eason, Brannon's work was the forerunner of the Fifties serials, with their disastrously dull plots and reiterative settings. The cinema serial could never hope to survive into the era of television, a medium wholly suited to the grey style and disordered action of juvenile fantasy.

In the history of sf film, the serials are at most a footnote, but to the cinema they represent the clearest manifestation of that vein of childish primitivism which drew the first *cinéastes* to Méliès. The world of the serials is the world of childhood, with its fascination for passwords, costumes and secrets for their own sake. Much was made of the master criminals with their darkly flamboyant capes and masks, their velvet-draped sanctums with arcane machines to watch the hero and punish inept minions; sophisticated expressions of a child's world, where "cubby houses," gangs and "dressing up" wove the fabric of existence. The fights and chases too were reflections of childish fantasy, designed to be re-enacted in a thousand backyard battles the next day. Despite their minor status as the juvenile auxiliary of sf cinema, the serials' fascination is undeniable, their influence on two generations of film-goers impossible to erase.

7. The World Next Door

FOR THE VICTORIANS, exploration was not only a right but a duty. The urge to know, sustained by an imperial mystique, encouraged both colonialism and scientific research, exploration of territory and of nature, inquiry into the natural and the supernatural. Visionaries were encouraged to expand their ideas, and even the most blatant crackpot could depend on at least a hearing. Qualification was less important than initiative and opportunity; missionaries explored the centre of Africa, botanists climbed mountains and physicists experimented with spiritualism. To the mind of the Nineteenth century Englishman, there was no conflict in this; the world was a huge and mysterious place, and who was to know what lay hidden in its more inaccessible corners?

Out of this single-minded spirit of inquiry sprang a whole new attitude to popular literature. It is no coincidence that the Sherlock Holmes stories, spiritualist novels like *The Land of Mist* and the fantastic adventures of *The Lost World* should have been written by the same man—Sir Arthur Conan Doyle was typically inquisitive and impatient of labels. But he had compatriots and successors—Bram Stoker, horror story and adventure writer, Rider Haggard, author of *She, King Solomon's Mines* and a string of associated romances, A. Hyatt Verrill, Talbot Mundy, Ray Cummings, Edgar Rice Burroughs. From 1890 to 1930 these men created a field somewhere between sf and adventure fiction. Any theory, natural, paranormal or just plain fantastic, was an acceptable theme, any plot feasible if it allowed an excursion into worlds of medieval grandeur or symbolic purity. Largely forgotten today, this field survives only in the Tarzan series and a handful of elements and plots in sf film.

The lost world novel was one of the earlier forms of sf to penetrate into the cinema, despite the daunting scope of the most popular plots. H. Rider Haggard's books invariably involved massive ruins, huge crowd scenes and effects that even the most competent technician would find a challenge, while the monsters suggested by Conan Doyle in *The Lost World* evaded Hollywood until Willis

77

The discovery of Ayesha in the 1935 version of SHE

O'Brien emerged as the genius of model animation. Paradoxically, the *genre* did not have adequate filmic expression until it was long out of date, which may explain why each successive generation has subtly altered the basic models to suit its social and political views.

H. Rider Haggard's novel *She*, published in 1887, is a key work in the field of lost world films. First produced as a film in 1916, it has had five film incarnations, while Haggard's sequel *Ayesha, The Return of She,* has also been filmed. In 1919, French novelist Pierre Benoit published *L'Atlantide (Atlantis),* a romance heavily based on *She,* and this too has been produced a number of times. Both books share a similar situation, the discovery in a remote part of the world—*She* Central Africa, *L'Atlantide* the Sahara—of a lost civilisation ruled by a white queen. In each, a number of men fall in love with the queen, but are destroyed by her icy indifference to them. And in each, the queen is immortal, though successive film-makers have varied on this point as the mood took them. Despite literary similarities, however, the two plots in terms of sf film are quite different, each having a unique set piece which remains constant no matter what liberties are taken with the remainder.

In *She,* film-makers have been fascinated by the source of the queen's immortality, a pure cold flame into which she steps for revivification. In 1899, Méliès created a film version of this effect and in one sense this (despite its length, a mere sixty-five feet) was the first sf film. In 1916, there was a British version of *She,* directed by Will Barker and starring Alice Delysia, and the following year another in America produced by William Fox and directed by Kenean Buel. According to contemporary reports, all made extravagant use of the immortality effect, as did the first version to survive in general circulation, that directed by Leander de Cordova in 1926 with Betty Blythe in the title role. Miss Blythe's long veil, combined with a brisk updraft of air and a spot-light are surprisingly effective at suggesting Haggard's conception, but modern connoisseurs of special effects are not usually impressed.

The most memorable version of *She* is that produced by Merian C. Cooper for RKO in 1935, directed by Irving Pichel and Lansing C. Holden. Cooper, associate of Ernest Schoedsack on *King Kong, The Last Days of Pompeii* and *Doctor Cyclops,* produced an ambitious film with extravagant sets and costumes not always matched by the quality of the dialogue, contributed by Ruth Rose (Cooper's wife) and Dudley Nichols. Unaccountably set in the Arctic instead of Africa, this version had explorers Randolph Scott and Nigel Bruce encountering Helen Gahagan's queen in a lost civilisation of perforated, almost Germanic *décor* and masked guards of indeterminate race. Predictably, the immortality effect roused RKO's effects department to prodigies, and Miss Gahagan's treatment in a filmy gown that seems to dissolve in the light is the film's high point.

In the Sixties, *She* returned in a British re-make directed by Robert Day for Hammer, the traditional "horror" studio, with a statuesque Ursula Andress playing the lead. Inexpensively but ambitiously mounted the film has two interesting twists. One is the accent on horror, predictable from the prolific Hammer team; Christopher Lee as the sinister chamberlain flings victims into a pit of molten lava without a backward glance and is himself horribly disposed of, while the heroine crumbles into old age and dust in an instant. The other new ingredient is probably logical given the Sixties' emerging nations; in an unconvincing sub-plot, the queen's native minions are demanding their freedom, and finally revolt to overthrow the decadent monarchy of She-Who-Must-Be-Obeyed.

Pierre Benoit's novel *L'Atlantide* was published in 1919, and was so successful that in 1920 Belgian ex-actor Jacques Feyder took a unit to Morocco to produce a version of Benoit's book with ageing *Comédie Française* star Stacia Napierkowska as Antinea, queen of lost Atlantis. Fabulously expensive, alarmingly handicapped by the meandering plot and variable acting, Feyder's version was nevertheless a commercial success, and the Benoit story has since been refilmed a number of times, most successfully by G. W. Pabst in 1932. As in the case of *She*, the popularity of *L'Atlantide* as a film subject springs directly from a unique set-piece. Antinea's hall of mummified lovers, a sequence that has interested producers of this subject as much as the immortality flame in *She*. Plots and characters change, but this scene remains constant, an element now firmly part of the sf film-maker's pack of cards.

Like She, Antinea is queen of a lost kingdom, though Benoit is vague as to her immortality. Film-makers have generally preferred to show her as mortal but part of a long line, a queen trained from birth to play a complex and inhuman role. However, Edgar Ulmer's Sixties version offered an ambiguous rite in which Haya Harareet appears to die by serpent strangulation, only to rise again renewed a moment later. In Feyder's film, Antinea is a fetching if plump seductress who holds in her underground city the three foreign legionnaires who are lured there by one of her Arab minions. One of them becomes her lover, dies, and is "galvanised," then displayed in a hall along with dozens of others. When a second prisoner refuses to submit to her, she drives the third in an excess of passion to murder him. All this is told in flashback, and at the end of his tale the murderer returns to Atlantis and his fate.

Largely unworthy of the mature Feyder, the 1920 *L'Atlantide*

Brigitte Helm as Antinea in Pabst's version of L'ATLANTIDE

has some outstanding features, mainly the desert setting and slow though impressive camerawork. The design, no doubt up to date in 1920, relies heavily on a fussy quasi-Turkish style, and Antinea's bedroom is a riot of over-decorated furniture, cushions and elaborately carved columns. Even the cells in which the legionnaires are confined have sconces on the doors. Elsewhere, the design struggles to be modern with chairs of a hideous discomfort and a library littered with the latest issues of popular periodicals, but fails just as completely. The hall of mummified lovers is partially successful, yet even this, with its marble floors and neatly ranked "galvanised" bodies with brass name plates on each has the look of a war memorial.

Feyder's *L'Atlantide* echoed its time and its filmic attitudes;

fantasy was merely a matter of decoration, an excuse for weird *décor*. Pabst's *L'Atlantide* (1932), springing from a cinema no longer content with elaborate decoration for its own sake, has the erotic bite of the best German films, and a visual *élan* that makes it a modern classic. Predictably, Pabst's Antinea is no simpering sexpot but a cold and imperious queen who delights like Brunhilda in competing with her lovers and destroying those who cannot match her. Declining to become involved in the tedious details of the legionnaires' discovery of Atlantis, Pabst explores at length the story of Antinea's birth, the daughter of an Arab sheikh and a Parisian can-can dancer. As Antinea, Brigitte Helm is a worthy successor to the robot Maria of *Metropolis*, her axe-hard profile used by Pabst to good effect in a design that echoes it in a succession of huge images of her face filling the halls of lost Atlantis. Shot like Feyder's version partly in the Hoggar desert and other Moroccan locations, Pabst's film is in every way a superior work, one of the finest romances from the golden age of the German cinema.

The undistinguished versions which followed Pabst's film have not equalled it, least of all *Siren of Atlantis* (1948), in which Maria Montez impersonated Antinea with the waspish *hauteur* of a disagreeable shop-girl. Edgar Ulmer's version *Antinea, L'Amante della Città Sepolta* (1961), made in Italy and released variously as *The Lost Kingdom* and *Journey under the Desert*, has occasional snatches of the Ulmer mystique, specifically in the conflicts that their kidnapping sets up among the three oil prospectors whose helicopter is forced down in the region of Atlantis, but in general it is a tedious travesty. Perhaps its greatest claim to remembrance is the way in which the writers have altered the plot, as did Pabst, to reflect contemporary attitudes. Instead of Benoit's (and Feyder's) diminuendo ending, Ulmer gives us a machine gun duel between the escaping men and Antinea's guards carried on under the looming menace of an atomic testing tower. If Atlantis cannot go to the world, then the world will come to Atlantis.

Of all the lost kingdom fantasies brought to film, Frank Capra's version of James Hilton's novel *Lost Horizon* (1937) is the greatest, reflecting both Capra's almost mystical belief in the power of in-dividual man and the misty altruism of Hilton's between-the-war romance. Set in Tibet, Hilton's book extolled peace through reflec-tion, and his Shangri La was a living symbol of what the world might be without war and misunderstanding. True to this vision, the film's design is quietly balanced and restrained; white walls, pools that mirror overhanging trees, graceful walks and gardens combine the best of Thirties architecture with an Oriental serenity.

Ronald Colman is one of a group of refugees from revolutionary China who are carried to the secret Himalayan city of Shangri La. There the High Lama (Sam Jaffe) explains that anybody entering Shangri La can never leave it alive, but that should they stay they will live forever. Colman falls in love with the city and a girl (Jane Wyatt), but is finally persuaded to return to civilisation. However all his companions die of the effects of their stay in

The Oriental serenity of Shangri La in LOST HORIZON

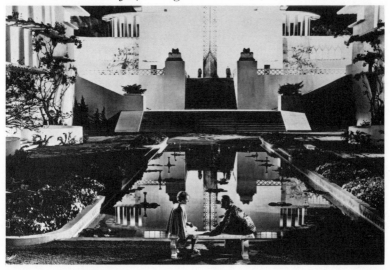

Shangri La, and Colman, after briefly taking up his old life, decides to return; in a final shot we see him spidering up the mountainside in a blinding storm, struggling to regain his paradise. Despite its similarities to Atlantis, Shangri La is vastly different in mood. Without the violence and decay of Atlantis, it offers a cooler, philosophical fantasy world, detached and unreal as was the literature that produced it.

As the lost kingdom films all derived in some form from H. Rider Haggard's *She*, another part of the *genre,* the lost world films, sprang from a similar single source, Sir Arthur Conan Doyle's 1912 romance *The Lost World.* Written long after the *succès d'estime* of the Sherlock Holmes stories—in 1912, Doyle was fifty-three—it harked back unashamedly to a simpler era of personal adventure and gentlemanly exploration. Basing his character on old associates and projections of himself, Doyle created the noisy, brilliant, black bearded Professor George Challenger, an iconoclastic scientist who leads an expedition into the wilds of South America in search of a lost plateau where creatures from prehistoric times still survive.

The first film version of *The Lost World,* directed by Harry D. Hoyt for First National in 1925, starred Wallace Beery as Challenger, but even the blustering Beery could make little headway against a script that, except for brief framing passages, consisted mainly of effects sequences contrived on a model stage, using forty-nine miniature dinosaurs created by Willis O'Brien and animated by his assistant Marcel Delgado. O'Brien, who had been working with the animation of dinosaur models since the early part of the century, had already made a number of short sf films with prehistoric settings, and his success with *The Lost World* was to lead to *King Kong* and its sequels, establishing the lost world *genre* as a permanent part of the sf film field. His system of covering movable wooden frameworks with flexible rubber material and then using animation techniques to counterfeit movement is still the basic method, and the "Dynamation" techniques developed by his pupil Ray Harryhausen merely perfections of it.

Generally the animation of *The Lost World* is crude and jerky, though scenes of monsters gliding through dark jungles, their shapes half-obscured, are eerily effective. The escape from the plateau is also brisk, in contrast to the unreality of the model work that precedes it, but models again prove remarkably impressive at the climax, when the brontosaurus and pterodactyl which Challenger has brought back to London escape to ravage the city. The pterodactyl wheeling in the lecture hall above the startled audience and the brontosaurus bringing down Tower Bridge in ruins have the same impact as later productions with vastly greater resources.

The success of *The Lost World* precipitated a series of similar films, some of them making use of O'Brien's genius. The greatest of them is certainly *King Kong* (1933), a crazy fantasy that has still not lost its Thirties charm. Conceived by producer Merian Cooper, it allowed O'Brien's effects full rein, a challenge he took up with alacrity. His animation of the giant ape that explorers find on a mysterious African island is still a model for this type of work, and re-makes, including O'Brien's own, have not surpassed it. Kong battling with a giant snake in a misty cavern, then fending off a marauding pterodactyl; the screaming half-naked girl (Fay Wray) who is his captive and sexual toy; Kong crushing native huts as if they were egg-crates, batting off spears and grinding a baby into the dirt; the monster triumphant on top of the Empire State Building, snarling his defiance at the world until aircraft blast him to the ground; these are sequences that remain indelibly in the mind.

O'Brien's projects usually outran his facilities, and many of them never saw production. His most ambitious, *Creation*, was to have shown the entire evolution of man and animal life, *Gwangi* a group of cowboys who discover prehistoric monsters on a Texas mesa, but though echoes of both occur in many of his films, the projects remained unrealised at his death in 1962. Unfortunately, the films that he did produce in his long career seldom did justice to his genius, re-working the more trivial and comic aspects of *King Kong*.

Son of Kong (1933) offered little that was new, being content to repeat the original on a slightly less ambitious scale with an East Indian location. Robert Armstrong, the hero of *King Kong*, is

A voluptuous Raquel Welch: ONE MILLION YEARS B.C.

searching for a comparable attraction when he discovers "Little Kong," a twenty foot high version of Kong with rolling eyes, a hang-dog expression and the instincts of an amiable puppy. After some predictably efficient natural disasters, including an excellent flood, O'Brien has his lovable monster hold Armstrong above the waves, saving his master's life at the expense of his own. Occasionally impressive, more often careless and silly, *Son of Kong* is unworthy of O'Brien. But *Mighty Joe Young* (1949), also known as *Mr. Joseph Young of Africa,* is more effective, and gained O'Brien his only Oscar, a belated recognition of his contribution to the cinema.

Some of O'Brien's *Gwangi* material finally saw the light of day in *Mighty Joe Young,* though to do this it was necessary to contrive an unlikely plot in which the ubiquitous Robert Armstrong organised a cowboy expedition to Africa to capture animals for his new nightclub, The Golden Safari. The cowboys discover "Joe Young," the twelve-foot gorilla pet of Terry Moore, and after failing to lassoo it persuade her to return with Joe to America. Exhibited as a freak in the Golden Safari—dressed as an organ grinder's monkey he capers for giant-sized paper coins flung by the audience, or engages in a tug of war with twelve wrestlers, including the hideous Swedish Angel and a down-and-out Primo Carnera—he finally revolts and wrecks the club in an incredible orgy of violence, swinging from a huge artificial tree to spill the orchestra to the ground and tear the building down around his ears. Despite the remarkable finale, with Joe rescuing children from a burning orphanage, only these nightclub scenes, with the tetchy creature held in check only by Terry Moore's halting rendition of "Beautiful Dreamer" (his favourite song) on the piano, are worthy of the man who made *King Kong*.

O'Brien's influence was strong on the field of fantasy cinema, but without his models producers found it difficult to mount films with prehistoric settings. An inadequate alternative to model animation was the use of lizards and spiders that, photographed in out-of-scale sets and with travelling mattes, would give reasonable verisimilitude. The first ambitious use of this system was in *One Million B.C.* (1940), portions of which were directed by the ageing D. W. Griffith. Photographed on the same California locations as David Butler's *Flying Elephants*, and with Victor Mature and Carole Landis as prehistoric lovers, the film does convey some sense of the past, though the ineptly organised battles between lizards are less impressive than Mature's shambling ardour.

An indication of how powerful this subject would have been in O'Brien's hands came in 1966, when Hammer re-made *One Million B.C.* as *One Million Years B.C.* with effects by Ray Harryhausen, O'Brien's pupil, and the identical script of the 1940 version. Although some lizards were used, Harryhausen created a remarkable giant turtle that, along with more conventional monsters, was cleverly utilised by director Don Chaffey. Bleak hills of black volcanic ash, an underground grotto inhabited by hairy "missing links" and the voluptuous Raquel Welch provided an adequate evening's entertainment, but the subject was by then fossilised, a throwback to another decade. The same was true of Irwin Allen's American re-make of *The Lost World* in 1960. After some magnificent footage of towering jungle bluffs in the Amazon basin, the story degenerated sharply, and even such bizarre features as Jill St. John in shocking pink knee boots and an unexpected subterranean climax did not compensate for the lack of content.

Producers remaking classic fantasy subjects have seldom bothered to weave new patterns around the traditional set-pieces. In his production of *She*, Merian Cooper at least altered setting and character, but the Sixties *One Million B.C.* was identical to that of 1940. An exception to this rule, however, was *Teenage Caveman* (1958), a clever Z picture given some ingenious twists by Roger Corman. The film has its faults, like the performance of Robert Vaughn, well before his *UNCLE* days, as the hero, but R. Wright Campbell's script is original enough to cover most of them.

The setting is a stock prehistoric encampment with fur-clad men and women existing on small game. Vaughn is a young hunter, his father the Symbol Maker, a sort of tribal shaman. Wondering what is on the other side of the river, Vaughn is dissuaded from finding out by a limping, bearded Frank de Kova, who warns him of the legendary Monster That Kills With A Touch. Refusing to be put off, he investigates, to discover that the Monster is an old man dressed in a fright suit to scare off marauders. All of the tribe, he reveals, are survivors like him from atomic war; this is not prehistory but our own immediate future.

Cleverly contrived, Corman's world is odd enough to be subtly wrong despite its similarities to prehistoric film worlds we know. Obsessed by ritual, the tribal elders mouth a variety of meaningless laws, their physical expression three men who endlessly labour over a ritual fire, wheel and pile of clay, the "three gifts of man." Long tracks through the forest disguise the familiar greenery and

Vaughn's ineptitude, while the even less competent acting of Darrah Marshall as Vaughn's girl friend is turned to advantage in a nude swim where the girl is so *gauche* and embarrassed that one momentarily believes this least real of all movie rituals. Crisp, economical, *Teenage Caveman* is a good example of Corman's genius.

Lost worlds are a major part of fantasy fiction. They embody the need for a detached, unreal *milieu* in its most extreme form. Significantly, the most enduring fantasists—Conan Doyle, Verne, R. E. Howard, J. R. R. Tolkien, Edgar Rice Burroughs—have all created lost kingdoms in which they could act out their dreams free of temporal considerations. Damon Knight has pointed out also that these men are usually more detached from reality than others, less part of the mainstream of life. Howard was morbidly attached to his mother and killed himself when she died, Conan Doyle on a less overheated level identified so much with the character of Professor Challenger that towards the end of his life, he imitated his talk and appearance. Perhaps this is why lost worlds do not transfer well to the screen; only in the mind can they achieve their complete reality.

8. British Science Fiction Films

Bᴿɪᴛɪsʜ sᴄɪᴇɴᴄᴇ ꜰɪᴄᴛɪᴏɴ has always existed apart from the American sf field, content to develop independently with only the most casual reference to the livelier material produced across the Atlantic. While the work of Arthur C. Clarke, John Beynon Harris (John Wyndham) and other top British writers has always enjoyed some popularity in America, it is unusual to find any British author influencing American compatriots, and the most usual reaction is a feeling of detached mutual admiration.

In sf film, this isolationist attitude is even more apparent. British science fiction films are rare, and those that qualify for the title—

e.g. *The Man in the White Suit* and *The Sound Barrier*—are sf by accident, their real source lying in the serious novel rather than in popular fiction, as does that of almost all the science fiction film produced in the British Isles. Lacking the comic books and pulp magazines from which American sf film drew its inspiration, the English sf cinema has never developed the popular mythology that sustains the American field, and as long as American studios continued to supply the American product to English audiences, no incentive existed to attempt any indigenous form of British sf film.

The sole exceptions have been films produced from books and other material of proven commercial worth. Nigel Kneale's B.B.C. television plays and serials are an interesting example of this. Despite mass screening on television during the Fifties, all three Quatermass serials and *The Creature* were filmed, and proved equally popular in the cinema. John Wyndham's novels *The Midwich Cuckoos* and *The Day of the Triffids,* Charles Eric Maine's radio play *Spaceways,* the TV series *Doctor Who*—British studios capitalised on the popularity of all these properties by filming them, in contrast to American studios which have seldom used any departure point except the comic strip. In America, the field exists in a vacuum, but has the benefit of a hermetically sealed and self-contained mythology little influenced by other stimuli; British sf film, on the other hand, is closely involved with other fields, a relationship that often leads to blandness and dreariness of setting, but also occasionally encourages audacious and thought-provoking films.

High Treason (1929) was one of the earliest British essays in sf, and predictably came from a play (by Pemberton Billing) that had already been performed in London. Despite its setting, Europe in 1940, *High Treason* belonged more to the years following the Great War, when concepts of world organisation and abiding peace based on mutual respect were central to liberal thinking. Combining this already outdated idea with a variation on *Metropolis,* Maurice Elvey produced a drama of doubtful moral worth in which the President of the United Nations averts a world war by murdering the leader of one bloc, after which he offers himself up for execution to the High Court. Halting attempts at *Metropolis*-like sets, featuring the ubiquitous Channel Tunnel, do little to enliven the story, and primitive sound recording techniques make the film, as it was in its time, a chore to follow. After one of the first screenings a bewildered critic commented, "Does Mr. Goddard still think that a stutter adds to the humour of a character, or is this the effect of the sound reproduction?"

Apart from isolated works like *Things To Come*, the Thirties produced few British sf films, mainly because of the dominance of American product and the British preference for fantasy rather than the tougher modes of sf. Korda's *The Man Who Could Work Miracles* (1937), directed by Lothar Mendes, adapted H. G. Wells's slight fantasy to the screen with Roland Young in a convincing performance as the little man who is made omnipotent by some speculative gods anxious to settle a bet, but its sf elements are limited. Nearer to modern ideas, *Miracles Do Happen* (1940) postulated the invention of synthetic milk, and *Time Flies* (1944) sent Tommy Handley and party back to Elizabethan England in a "Time Ball" invented by fuzzy scientist Felix Aylmer; the result was a feeble comedy featuring the usual helping-Shakespeare-write and laying-down-cloak-for-Queen-Elizabeth jokes with which we are now familiar, not to mention the unaccountable use of jazz violinist Stephane Grappelly as a minstrel. The settings, however, are extravagant, the special effects occasionally effective, and Aylmer's other inventions, including a combination film projector/camera, have the ring of authenticity.

The war years produced little of interest in the field, aside from a version of Barré Lyndon's play *The Man in Half Moon Street* (1945) which, though departing little from the Boris Karloff medical fantasies, still offered some chilling effects in its story of a doctor who remains immortal as long as he replaces a vital gland every few years by one taken from a murdered victim. A 1949 re-make, *The Man Who Could Cheat Death*, with glacially evil Anton Diffring as the doctor, is still one of the most stylish and grisly of all modern horror films. Other wartime productions were, however, rare, and it was not until the late Forties that the fantastic again appeared in British cinema.

1949 was a vintage year. It produced Henry Cornelius's bitterly funny *Passport to Pimlico,* in which a tiny London suburb finds that it is legally part of the old Burgundian empire and gleefully secedes from a Britain of ration books and postwar austerity, and *The Rocking Horse Winner,* by Anthony Pelissier, suggesting some of the horror of a "wild talent" in the story of a little boy who, after working himself into a trance on his rocking horse, can predict racing results. The ability to pick horse-race results is probably British sf's only genuine contribution to the list of sf film elements; it appears in a number of English films, and was borrowed by Hollywood in 1947 for *My Brother Talks to Horses* (Fred Zinnemann). In fact, the excessively popular film series based on Francis, the Talking Mule produced by Universal in the Fifties, is probably an example of this intrinsically British sf element mutated by Hollywood.

Passport to Pimlico and *The Rocking Horse Winner* were only partly sf, but 1949 did produce a British sf film which is still one of the field's rare comedies and perhaps its only example of intentional farce. Bernard Knowles's *The Perfect Woman* is a sinister little comedy built around the invention of "a robot indistinguishable from a normal woman." As in *Metropolis* the scientist gives his creation the appearance of an actual woman, in this case the readily available Patricia Roc. Emboldened by his success, he hires a rather thick man-about-town (Nigel Patrick) to take out the robot as a final test, but the plot degenerates sharply into farce when he meets the real girl and falls for her.

Much of the film is conventional, mistaken identity comedy, but towards the climax it takes on a fetishist verve not easily forgotten. Struggling to dress the recalcitrant robot, Stanley Holloway is only able to ease it into a set of black lace corsets. He calls in Patrick and between them they attempt to complete the task, but their efforts with the corpse-like robot only involve them in a variety of obscene poses which, had the principals been nude, would have graced any set of French postcards, a fact noted by the baffled but delighted waiter who arrives in the middle. None of this, however, equals the mania of the last scenes, where the robot, incapacitated by some internal malfunction, reels off down the hotel corridor in a stiff-legged imitation of Frankenstein's monster, spouting sparks and smoke, and brings down the whole collonaded hall on its head.

The flippancy exhibited by *The Perfect Woman* is uncommon in sf, British directors like those in America preferring to approach scientific subjects with a mixture of straight-faced solemnity and plodding worthiness. The spirit that James Whale brought to his horror films in the early Thirties, a cynical, slightly camp black humour that mocked both material and audience, has never caught on in science fiction, perhaps because its proper execution requires a director and scriptwriter with the unique qualities Universal found in Whale and Philip Wylie during the Thirties. However, one film did recall some of this bitterness and wit, a clever satire made by Ealing in 1951 and starring Alec Guinness—*The Man in the White Suit.*

As science fiction, *The Man in the White Suit* has more claim to eminence than most other films concerning technological marvels. The invention by a bookish Cambridge scientist of a fibre that neither wears out nor gets dirty is a plot no better or worse than any other, but the excellent script, mainly by director Alexander Mackendrick, marshals a wide variety of situations to attack the less logical features of British life. Guinness, after he has emerged from his laboratory, with its tortuous maze of bubbling glass retorts and tubes, becomes an apt symbol of British individuality and clear-headedness, best summed up in the scene where, assailed by pursuers in a cramped rear corridor of a block of flats, he flourishes a dustbin lid and chair-leg like the sword and shield of an ancient warrior.

The central conflict between labour and management that motivates the comedy is explored by Mackendrick with his usual flair (like Val Guest, interestingly, Mackendrick has an American background), and although some of the plotting is obvious—naturally,

Guinness falls for the sympathetic daughter of his boss (Joan Greenwood)—there is considerable imagination in some of the casting, such as Ernest Thesiger as the commercial baron, a withered octogenarian in muffling clothes reminiscent of the ancient pyromaniac in Whale's *The Old Dark House*. In the film's context it is even possible to accept the creaky symbolism of the scene where Guinness knocks down a bronze bas-relief showing the union of labour and management, but the white suit itself is always the "hero" of the film, a fact recognised by Mackendrick in planning the climax; Guinness surrounded by his enemies after a night-time chase, the almost supernatural way in which the suit suddenly begins to rot, and is torn to shreds by the mob; and the final moment when, walking away from what seems like a shattered career, the chemical genius stops, says quietly to himself, "Of course!" and hurries off to start over again. *The Man in the White Suit* is, on one level, nothing more than a stylish Ealing comedy, but its universality of subject and expression qualify it as the best type of science fiction.

David Lean's *The Sound Barrier* (1952) may seem an even more unlikely candidate for the title of sf, but in its picture of an old society succumbing to a new scientific age it is one of the most persuasive technocratic tracts ever put on film. Terence Rattigan's script indefatigably contrasts old and new; a jet 'plane howling across England bowing the eternal wheat; the young couple jetting from England to Egypt in a few hours, scribing a white line across the sky above weather-worn faces of Greek statues, suspended between a worn-out earth and a virgin midday moon.

The story is elegant but trivial; aircraft tycoon J. R. Richfield (Ralph Richardson), obsessed by the problem of breaking the sound barrier, drives his family and staff furiously to discover the secret. His son dies trying to master the art of flying for which he is totally unfitted, and his son-in-law (Nigel Patrick) is killed in a jet test flight. Against his daughter's wishes Richfield continues with his experiments, and finally another pilot succeeds. But this is just a step; in a final shot we see Richfield's baby grandson sitting on a map of the moon while above, through the slit in an observatory, the stars beckon.

The Sound Barrier was one of the first films to offer the suggestion that a new technological society had been born, a group of people to whom emotional and social allegiances were of little importance. Riveted by the howl of a jet turbine seeping into the calm country air, Patrick says quietly, "I think it's the most exciting sound I've ever heard," and when he and Richfield enter the jet test-bed both remain inside with the engine while Richfield's son and daughter stay outside, wincing at the noise. In another shot, Richfield, examining the first model of the new jet, sails it gravely past the face of a Victorian bronze head, a technological flourish under the nose of art. Although the agony of Richfield listening to the last tapes of Patrick's death in an empty factory and Joseph Tomelty's quietly humanistic playing as the ageing chief engineer argue that progress has its price, we are wholly on the side of Richfield, Patrick and the other New Men. The seeds of John Frankenheimer's cold scientific fantasies are in this sensitive early work, but of all those who have attempted to re-state the case, few have rivalled Lean's rich statement.

While Rattigan and Lean were probing the subleties of the new technocracy, cruder aspects of the same pattern were showing themselves in the United States. During late 1950 and early 1951 science fiction, mainly due to the success of George Pal's *Destination Moon,* suddenly became big business. Magazines proliferated, paperbacks flooded the market, sf films were a gilt-edged financial proposition. The sf boom was on, and although it was never as big in Britain or elsewhere as in America, the repercussions were apparent all over the world. The larger American magazines began British reprint editions, and a number of English publications sprang up or expanded to cope with the demand. Meanwhile, at the B.B.C., plans were under way to film the first of a number of sf serials, produced by Rudolph Cartier and written by Nigel Kneale, the first of them to be called *The Quatermass Experiment.*

Kneale did three sf serials for the B.B.C., built about the character of Dr. Bernard Quatermass (see *A Note On SF For Television*).

All of them were later filmed, and a film version was also made of *The Creature,* Kneale's play about the so-called "Abominable Snowman." All the films are of a high standard, but *The Quatermass Experiment* (also called *The Creeping Unknown,* 1955) and *Quatermass and the Pit* (also known as *Five Million Years to Earth,* 1967) are especially fine. In its time, *The Quatermass Experiment* was a pioneering sf film, Val Guest's direction showing a combination of American expertise and British sensibility reflecting his American publicist background. As Quatermass, an ageing Brian Donlevy was stiff but convincing, his acting making it easier to accept the doubtful sets; a space ship returning to Earth is stuck in the ground like a dart; the ship interior seen in films looks like an empty bus. Much of the film is saved, however, by Richard Wordsworth's playing of the expedition's sole survivor. Agonised by the disease he has contracted, he drags himself across the junk-littered vacant lots and canals of London's slums in a moving example of tragic mime, one of the finest such performances since Karloff's triumphs of the Thirties.

Donlevy repeated his role in *Quatermass II* (1957), a faithful but ponderous adaptation of Kneale's TV sequel. There are effective sequences, director Guest and cameraman Gerald Gibbs shooting with light lancing up through the shadows in a manner reminiscent of Jacques Tourneur's *Night* (or *Curse*) *of the Demon.* Otherwise the film is indifferent. Even less magic attaches to *The Abominable Snowman* (1957), which had Guest again in charge and a superannuated American star (Forrest Tucker) in a main role. In re-creating a peak in the Himalayas, the set designer had more control over the film than the director, and despite some tense action the story drags. Much might have been done with Kneale's interesting idea that the Snowmen were super-intelligent creatures, wise beyond our understanding, but the hairy monsters supplied by the prop department did not support this view. The echoing honk of the Snowmen over some well-chosen actuality footage of Himalayan snowscapes does, however, continue to exercise a certain eerie influence.

Barbara Shelley in QUATERMASS AND THE PIT

The project of adapting the last of the Quatermass serials, *Quatermass and the Pit* (also known in its film version as *5 Million Years to Earth*), was left in abeyance until 1967, when Hammer, in association with M-G-M, produced it with Roy Ward Baker directing a Nigel Kneale script. One can understand why the film was not made earlier; in content and playing it offers challenges to test most Fifties producers, while its thoughtful subject matter would have been box-office poison at the end of the sf film boom. Today, we can see *Quatermass and the Pit* as Kneale's finest idea, the culmination of everything in the other serials, a powerful statement of the evil and good that can lie in science, and a thriller of impressive skill.

Extending the London underground near a cul-de-sac called Hob's Lane (in the TV serial, it had been Roman excavations), workers uncover a buried spaceship embedded in the red clay. Inside they find the putrescent remains of alien creatures buried there since prehistoric times. Other evidence—distorted skulls of earth-men "changed" to increase their intelligence; ancient drawings of goblins and monsters; the sinister name of the place itself, "Hob's," i.e. "The Devil's" Lane—shows that these aliens hoped to enslave Earth, but failed. But even though the aliens are dead, their ship remains in working order, and when investigation activates it, it conjures up a huge transparent vision of its makers, draws on the mental power of the Londoners, and attempts to take over the city, until James Donald resourcefully quenches it with the time-honoured specific for demonic intervention—cold iron, in the form of a huge crane plunged into the image.

Baker's unravelling of this crisp thriller is tough and involving. Typically, Quatermass bulls into the investigation, first pressing a policeman to explain the weird scratches in a house near the excavation. Terrified, the bobby mutters "Kids Playing, sir, kids playing," and scuttles out. Tristram Cary's music, heavily influenced by his work with the B.B.C. Radiophonic Workshop that did the music for *Dr. Who*, provides a terrifying howl for a diamond drill as it tries ineffectively to penetrate the spaceship hull, and an abrading crackle of splintering glass to symbolise the decay of the chambers in which the alien corpses have been rotting for aeons.

The film has moments of pure terror, perhaps the most effective that in which the drill operator, driven off the spaceship by the mysterious power within is caught up in a whirlwind that fills the excavation with a mass of flying papers. Possessed, he goes whirling out of the station into the night amid a cloud of dust and rubbish, capers down the street like a medieval plague victim, destroys a pie stall, sending its paper plates spinning, then staggers through an old church-yard to collapse among the graves as the ground heaves and ripples under him. Watching this, and later seeing men under the influence of the machine using telekinesis to bombard victims with paving blocks torn from the road, one does not find it hard to accept the ancient legends of the demon and his power.

Quatermass and the Pit is an apt symbol of the rich revival of sf film all over the world in the late Sixties, and contrasts impressively with the feeble imitations of American successes that British producers attempted in the Fifties to cash in on the world-wide sf boom. *Behemoth the Sea Monster* (1958), *First Man into Space* (1958), *The Strange World of Planet X* (1958) were typical of these films. Almost always using a fading American star in a major role and often attempting, with scant success, to suggest that the film was shot in the United States, they reflected poorly both on the field and the men who made them. Only the genius of Eugene Lourié, who co-directed *Behemoth* after distinguished work on such classics as *The Beast from 20,000 Fathoms,* brings anything to this isolated backwater; some of the effects, like a dark lab lit by the phosphorescent glow of an irradiated fish, clearly bear his trademark.

Reflecting a more extreme example of the belief in copying popular successes in other fields, British film-makers adapted two of George Orwell's best books to the screen, *Animal Farm* in 1955 and *1984* in 1956. The former, an animated feature by John Halas and Joy Batchelor, was vitiated by elements of parody in the characterisation, but its visual impact is undeniable. Used to the representational and feminine style of Disney, British audiences found it difficult to accept the ferocious dynamism of John Halas's vision—a ferocity, interestingly enough, that later appeared in some of Disney's work, notably his towering image of the evil fairy in *The Sleeping Beauty* (1958). Orwell's parable of the Russian revolution and its decline was not a good choice for an animated feature, especially considering the in-built resistance to animation on the part of the adult public, but it is one of British film's more honourable failures.

1984, while a failure, is not especially honourable. Again hedging their bets with American stars (Edmond O'Brien and Jan Sterling) the producers offered a boiled-down version of Orwell with an indecent accent on horror and the benefit of alternate endings for various markets. That in which Winston Smith, the rebellious hero, recants and denies his love, was seldom seen, most distributors preferring the bitter-sweet alternative in which Smith, breaking away from his captors, dies with his lover in the blowing leaves, his fingers entwined with hers. Michael Redgrave's inquisitor brings to the film its only hint of Orwell's original nightmarish inexorability; built on the lines suggested by his characterisation, *1984* might well have been a work fit to be spoken of in the same breath as its original.

With the end of the sf boom in the middle Fifties, studios all over the world sharply curtailed their sf output, and the trickle of British imitations dried up. Producers no longer cared to risk their money on nebulous chances of American release, and as a result began to explore the possibilities, as they had earlier, of cashing in on literary successes. John Wyndham's books had long been the most successful British sf, and in 1960 an attempt was made to adapt one of the most cinematic of them, *The Midwich Cuckoos*. Directed by Wolf Rilla and released as *Village of the Damned*, the film is a routine reading of Wyndham, deriving little atmosphere from the story of an English country village all the women of which are impregnated by some alien force and give birth to a group of quiet blonde children with awesome mental powers. George Sanders as the investigator of this phenomenon has the right air of icy detachment—he played one of the Gods in *The Man Who Could Work Miracles*—but the story is told with a slowness and lack of involvement almost worthy of silent cinema. Even the best effects—a tractor grinding around an empty field after its owner has collapsed; the image of a crumbling wall to symbolise Sanders's will collapsing before that of the children—recall silent technique, but unfortunately the entire film lacks a coherent style.

Curiously, a semi-sequel, the forgotten *Children of the Damned* (1963) is an infinitely more effective interpretation of Wyndham's idea. Bypassing the first story, John Briley's script has six "super-children" discovered in six different continents and brought to London. Two UNESCO investigators (Alan Badel and Ian Hendry) attempt to communicate with them and gain their trust, but personal problems intrude. The two men live together in what seems a loose homosexual relationship, and when the less dominant of them becomes involved with a woman, the other, played with malicious authority by Badel, throws himself actively into destroying the children. Hendry sees that they mean no harm, but is unable to prevent Badel from creating a climate of hatred around them. Finally the children are hiding in a ruined city church, surrounded by army units. A screwdriver rolls accidentally across a control board, a careless hand flicks a switch in stopping it, and the streets erupt in a blast of artillery, destroying the church. The allegory is plain, but on the way to its presentation director Anton Leader has given us one of the finest pieces of sf cinema to come out of England, or for that matter of any other country.

Children of the Damned is that rare film which sums up what a country might do given proper incentives and encouragement. Of late, British sf film-makers have involved themselves in small-budget features, like John Krish's skilful *Unearthly Stranger* (1963) and in tangential works like the meticulously re-created *It Happened Here.* Its "new wave" sf, exemplified by Watkins's *The War Game, Privilege* and *The Gladiators,* is clever, original and technically impressive. But the field in Britain has never equalled in imagination the work of its writers, and attempts to emulate their successes have been compromised by commercial considerations or artistic lethargy. Only *2001: A Space Odyssey,* with its echoes of Clarke's *Childhood's End,* is a candidate, and paradoxically this was directed by an American. The great British sf film has yet to be made.

9. Springtime for Caliban

A MERICAN SCIENCE FICTION FILM might have continued in the Sixties exactly as it did in Great Britain, providing part of the spectrum of popular cinema but never competing seriously with the Western or the 'teenage picture. However, in 1950–51 sf film underwent a drastic change, making a strong bid for leadership in the field and becoming for a few years one of the hottest commercial propositions in Hollywood. This boom in sf film, reflected in the wider area of written sf, encouraged a proliferation of magazines, a rash of the more lurid paperbacks and a belated entry by sf into fields like TV where it had never been a serious contender. For a while, sf was big business.

The "boom," however, was an illusory one. The public was not interested in pure sf but in the simpler fare of the movies; audio-visually oriented, it could not cope with the more complex media of magazines or paperbacks, and although this popularity did draw to written sf a new generation of readers, they were readers who would have come automatically to it during the next few years. Analysis reveals that, apart from this galvanic twitch, the sf market has remained fairly constant in relation to population since the Twenties; writers who expected more, however, could not be blamed for fixing on the cinema as a scapegoat, since it had both instigated the boom and gained most from it. Foremost among the objects of their scorn was a producer of sf films who shrewdly judged the market and milked it with consummate skill— George Pal.

Like others involved in sf, Hungarian-born Pal has seldom moved far from the field, and even those productions outside it—*tom thumb* (1958) and *The Wonderful World of the Brothers Grimm* (1963)— reflect a delight in the fantastic. Additionally, his involvement with special effects, for which his films have won six Oscars, is typical of the American field, where the literal depiction of the fantastic demands technical skill rather than cinematic genius. Beginning with his "Puppetoons" commercials and short films of the Thirties and Forties, and extending to such brilliant exercises as *The Power*

(1967), George Pal's combination of technical facility and business acumen has made him a central figure in modern sf film.

Pal's first feature as a producer and the one that began the sf boom of the Fifties was the relatively cheap *Destination Moon*. Trivial in plot, it derived originally from Robert Heinlein's juvenile novel *Rocket Ship Galileo* (1947), a property purchased more obviously for its scientific detail than the unwieldy story of three boys and their scientist uncle discovering a Nazi revival on the moon. Heinlein's background has been retained, the rest scrapped in favour of a routine voyage to the moon yarn. Viewed today, *Destination Moon* is less than impressive; the rocket journey is ploddingly consistent with the scientific standards of 1950, the occasional moments of drama, like the loss of a crewman "overboard" and his rescue using an oxygen tank as a space-boat, do little to save the film from the flat acting of its faceless stars and the generally tepid air.

Despite its artistic aridity, however, *Destination Moon* is an historic production. Cleverly, Pal gauged the nature of the American sf film market and pitched the film directly at it. In production value, it had severe shortcoming; the principals were unmemorable second-leads, the director, ex-actor Irving Pichel, a competent, inexpensive technician, while cinematographer Lionel Lindon had not then progressed through his auspicious TV career to work with John Frankenheimer. The team was undistinguished, but Pal added to it a group of men who, though unable to make much contribution to the film's polish, could influence its success as science fiction. Foremost among these were veteran set designer Ernst Fegté, astronomical artist Chesley Bonestell and rocketeer Hermann Oberth, the last adviser also on Lang's *Frau im Mond*. The animation of skilfully engineered models against Bonestell's meticulously created backdrops and Fegté's fissured and chillingly authentic moon surface gave *Destination Moon* the feeling of realism that Pal recognised was most desired by the American public, and the film struck it rich.

Anxious to capitalise on his success, Pal produced *When Worlds*

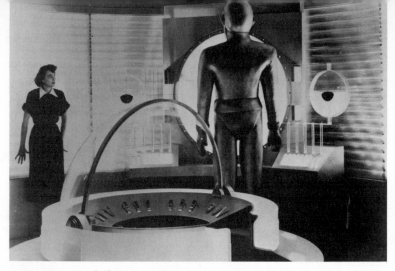

Patricia Neal (left) in THE DAY THE EARTH STOOD STILL

Collide in 1951, though by then the popularity of *Destination Moon* had encouraged a flock of imitators, including such catchpenny productions as *Flight to Mars* (1951) and *Rocket Ship XM* (1950), the latter actually beating Pal's film to release by a few weeks. These films, as cheap in casting and techniques as *Destination Moon* but lacking the vital skill in special effects, faded quickly, but not before the success of the *genre* as a whole had stimulated the imagination of larger studios. *Destination Moon* had been made independently by Pal, but now the studios were interested. Two of the largest, Fox and RKO, planned sf films which, with the full weight of top directing and technical teams, aimed to take over the market so accurately gauged by Pal. Neither succeeded, but the films are classics of their kind.

Today, all that Robert Wise can remember of *The Day the Earth Stood Still* (1951) is an impression of great haste, and of an attempt to warn people of the folly of atomic war. The haste shows, not in technical shoddiness, but in a sense of pace typical of a man whose contribution to the structure of *Citizen Kane* and *The Magnificent Ambersons* extended well beyond mere editing. Furiously fast, Wise tells the story of an alien's brief visit to earth in a series of brilliant action sequences, linking them with rush trips around America and the world to show reactions to the landing, consternation at the alien's revelation that he is there to warn earth against self-destruction, and astonishment when the world's technology grinds to a stop as he drains its power in a telling dramatisation of his strength.

As the alien Klaatu, Michael Rennie is suitably lofty, though human enough to enter into a believable relationship with a young Washington widow (Patricia Neal) and her son. While his lumbering robot Gort is effectively used as a symbol of mindless power, the film declines to copy the original ending of Harry Bates's story *Farewell to the Master* on which it is based; no longer is the robot the master, the humanoid alien a servant. We are left with a sincere attempt to convey some of the lunacy of nuclear war, best summed up when an incognito Rennie, asked by a reporter to comment on reactions to his own landing, speaks out against "fear replacing reason," but is cut short by the reporter impatient for scare comments. The Washington backgrounds are well used, especially in night sequences where stark side-lighting (Leo Tover) gives a hard-edged intensity to the white flying saucer squatting in a park. Klaatu's recipe for peace; a robot police force insusceptible to corruption or scientific tampering—sounds alarmingly Fascist but whatever its political pedigree, *The Day the Earth Stood Still* remains one of the most entertaining excursions into sf yet attempted by Hollywood.

Mystery surrounds the making of the second of Hollywood's ambitious sf films, the unappetisingly named *The Thing*, with credits attributing production to Howard Hawks and direction to Christian Nyby, Hawks's editor on a number of his films. Hawks will admit to preparing the script and supervising production, but *The Thing* is so typical of Hawks in style and ethos that it is hard to believe Nyby occupied more than a minor position in its making. Everything supports this theory—overlapping dialogue, the central idea of the conflict between men of ideas and men of action, the skilful direction of large groups, even the predominantly male cast are characteristic of the mature Hawks. Nyby, who wanted a director credit for union reasons, may have been involved in some aspects of the film, but in every major way it is pure Hawks.

Loosely adapted from John Campbell Jnr.'s *Who Goes There?*, written, like *Farewell to the Master,* in the golden age of magazine sf in the middle Forties, the story has a basic Hawksian flavour. A far northern American base receives word from its North Pole crew that a UFO has crashed in its area. A disobedient yet capable airman (Kenneth Tobey) is sent to investigate the matter, but goes mainly because of a girl at the base whom he wants to see again. She rejected him just before leaving for her tour of duty; his visit seems aimed at finding out how she could possibly do such a thing.

Flying over the Pole, they see a cleared path of snow at the end of which new ice marks where the ship melted the ice and sank. With the approach of a blizzard adding to the tension, the men walk out onto the clear area and are directed to space themselves around the perimeter of the shape in the ice. The moment when they slowly group themselves into a circle, indicating the "flying saucer" below them, is chilling. Ineptly, Tobey sets a thermite bomb to expose the ship, but succeeds only in incinerating it. They save, however, the body of the crewman, and take this back still frozen in a block of ice. Placed under guard in the store-room, the windows of which Tobey ruthlessly smashes to guarantee continued cold, the block is accidentally melted by an electric blanket and the creature brought to life. Efforts to subdue it constitute the rest of the film, with the humanoid alien (James Arness) pursued about the base until Tobey destroys him.

Typically for Hawks the characters quickly separate themselves into professionals and dreamers. The airman, the reporter he takes with him and some of his crew are professionals; the scientists, and especially their leader, are dreamers. Hawks's contempt for the former comes out clearly in the various exchanges at the base,

106

science and scientists generally shown as being incapable of adjusting to the real world. The fact that Tobey is almost always wrong in his decisions does not prevent him from emerging as the most favourable character. Even a wrong tough guy is better than no tough guy at all. Although the head scientist does everything that a logical man should do to communicate with the creature, he is smashed down, and it is Tobey who finally destroys it with an electrical trap, cooking it to ashes so that, like all monsters, it is destroyed by the fire which, in a way, created it.

The atmosphere of terror and tension is conveyed by half-heard sounds and judiciously surrounded silences. One remembers the slow drip of water as the ice block melts, the hushed awe of the scientists as they huddle over a specimen of alien tissue, the fact that it is not seen giving the object a grisly fascination. Crowded rooms and overlapping dialogue support the mood, as does the use of a beeping, flashing geiger counter to warn of the approaching monster. Tension builds unbearably as the beeps become more frequent until the creature bursts into the room, is doused with kerosene, set alight and sent flaming into the snow. Not materially different from *Frankenstein* in plot or ambience, *The Thing* is the furthest beachhead ever established by Germanic horror on the body politic of American technology.

The Day the Earth Stood Still and *The Thing* were the most serious attempts by Hollywood to render sf ideas on film, and although both showed skill and intelligence, neither was a serious competitor with written sf in the area of ideas. Both are, in fact, as squarely opposed to the spirit of science fiction as the monster pictures Damon Knight so roundly condemns. The two fields of sf and cinema do not mesh; sf films usually succeed as cinema in proportion to the degree in which they fail as sf. George Pal, realising that it was pointless to attempt serious sf ideas on film, continued in his policy of combining intricate special effects with colour, music and action, sensing like Laemmle in the Thirties that as long as the patrons could see the fantastic happening before their eyes there would be no criticism of limited plots.

When Worlds Collide (1951) and *War of the Worlds* (1954) are dealt with in Chapter Eleven. Colourful, cleverly worked out, the latter using the art of Chesley Bonestell which had succeeded in *Destination Moon,* both were predictable successes. *War of the Worlds* also marked the beginning of a durable collaboration between Pal and director Byron Haskin, head for many years of the Special Effects department of Warner Brothers. Together they have made a series of sf films which, for the literal depiction of the fantastic, are hard to fault. No stylist, Haskin brings to his films a stolid realism which is ideally suited to his stories of space exploration and alien worlds. In his hands, the already impeccable special effects seem even more real.

After *War of the Worlds,* Pal and Haskin did *The Naked Jungle* (1953), an odd adaptation of *Leiningen vs. the Ants,* a short story by Carl Stephenson which appears frequently in anthologies. Charlton Heston is Christopher Leiningen, a morose and sexually repressed Amazon planter who defies a horde of marching ants, defeating them at last by struggling through the biting, seething column to blow up a dam and flood his plantation. Not properly sf, the film has some of sf's mood, while the ants make an unusual "monster." The script, by veteran writers Philip Yordan and Ranald MacDougall, introduces to good effect a Hawksian sexual conflict between Heston and Eleanor Parker, the mail-order wife he has brought to his mansion to decay slowly with the furniture. Their tentative love affair is interestingly handled but the effects, achieved mainly by anointing Heston with honey and having the ants crawl all over him, are the film's most memorable feature.

The Conquest of Space (1955) returned again to the country of *Destination Moon.* Derived partly from the Willy Ley/Chesley Bonestell book (then a coffee-table favourite), the film gave Pal and Haskin an excuse to show realistic take-offs, space manoeuverings and a landing on Mars that, despite its present-day redundancy, was achieved with some flair. Drama in the shape of a religious maniac at the helm detracts little from the essential narrative, and some of the detail is clever, such as a space burial with the suited

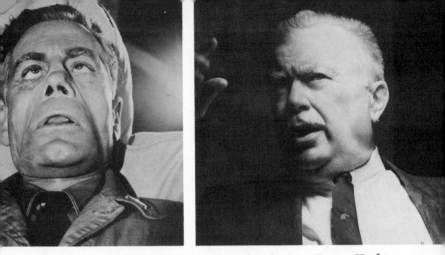

Left, THE CONQUEST OF SPACE; right, director Byron Haskin

corpse sliding slowly on a long fall into the sun. Other moments, like a meal of pills with predictably heavy chaff, and a space station crew watching, unaccountably, a circa 1955 musical, are less convincing.

Little of H. G. Wells's vision remained in *The Time Machine* (1960) produced and directed by George Pal. David Duncan's script suggests nothing of Wells's polemic, and abandons the specific social allegory of the original in favour of some thin moralising about initiative and independence. Wells's suggestion that workers and the aristocracy might one day decay to troglodyte cannibals and effete food animals has disappeared, as has the voyage to a distant future with its giant cockroaches and swollen dying sun.

What remains is a rough version of the book's first section, with the explorer (Rod Taylor) demonstrating his invention to (unlike the book) incredulous friends, and the conflict between Eloi and Morlocks. Differences are rife. In the film, the traveller's friends want him to turn his efforts to making munitions for the Boer War, a view that Wells would have found laughable. Its best features are the special effects of time travel (Gene Warren, Tim Barr, Academy Award 1960) and the Victorian *décor* of the traveller's house, full of chiming clocks; the machine itself, a rococo arm-chair of quartz, brass and plush, with a metal plate attributing its manufacture of "H. George Wells"; the ruined dome where the Eloi live, and the casual arrangement of white crockery and bright fruit inside; sneering sphinxes of the future; the use of "white-out" when matches are struck to drive off Morlocks in their catacombs; rotting books crumbling at a blow from Taylor. The details, however, do not add up to a coherent whole.

Pal and Haskin did not return to sf until 1967, when the team produced the magnificent *The Power* (see Chapter Thirteen). Other studios, following Pal's example, did, however, use his system with some success, one of the most effective efforts being Universal's *This Island Earth* (1955), directed by Joseph Newman. Energetic and colourful, the film is a plausible sf adventure yarn which opens in familiar surroundings and expands to take in interstellar travel and inter-planetary war. Rex Reason, stolidly inappropriate to the part of a progressive young physicist, does well enough with the equally flat Faith Domergue, but special effects and colourful photography of ethereal settings engage our attention and divert it from the actors.

When his private jet flames out on a routine flight, physicist Reason is saved by a green light that bathes the ship and lands it for him. Later, at his lab, he is surprised when a mysterious electronics catalogue offers him parts patently the product of a superior technology. Working from catalogue plans and parts supplied apparently from the blue, he builds an "Interociter," disappointingly nothing but a colour TV set with inverted pyramid screen. The face that appears congratulates him on having passed his test, destroys the machine and tells him to expect a 'plane to take him to his new job. Later, as one member of a brains trust working a Georgia mansion, he finds that his "examiners" are aliens, their task to pick earth's best minds for a means of saving their planet Metaluna from destruction in an interplanetary war.

Jeff Morrow, Rex Reason and Faith Domergue
in THIS ISLAND EARTH

This Island Earth, despite the political allegories attributed to it by Raymond Durgnat,[11] is primarily a crisp sf novelette, cleverly presented with the accent right where shrewd producer William Alland knew it must be, on special effects. But the film shows some of the imagination Alland brought to his films with Jack Arnold. The shattered surface of Metaluna, the space landing and take-off, the enemy boring in with captive meteors to drop on the planet; these are given lavish attention, in contrast to the flaccid direction of actors. Appeals to a gadget-minded audience abound; the Interociter sequence, a montage of plan-littered floors, intricate circuitry and intent faces; the alien trick of burning through a thick lead shield to show that even behind such a cover conversations can be heard. (The humans learn their lesson; from then on a cat, sensitive to alien rays, perches on top of the disfigured shield as they plot to escape, a clever technological joke.)

Although *This Island Earth* had been lavishly and smoothly made, it paled in comparison with the effort mounted by M-G-M the following year. Elaborate beyond the dreams of sf fans, *Forbidden Planet* (1956) was and still is the most remarkable of sf films, the ultimate recreation of the future, a studio-bound extravaganza where every shot is taken under artificial light and on a sound stage. The system begun by George Pal had reached its logical conclusion; everything was false, everything controlled. Reality was not

*Robot Robby, Leslie Nielsen, Walter Pidgeon
and Anne Francis in FORBIDDEN PLANET*

permitted to intrude on this totally manufactured, totally believable world.

Leslie Nielsen is Commander J. J. Adams of United Planets Cruiser C57D, more than a year out on a mission to the great main sequence star Altair. As his palatial flying saucer skims through space, the trip is enlivened by egalitarian banter with intellectual ship's doctor (Warren Stevens), studious engineer (Richard Anderson) and comic cook (Earl Holliman). Arriving on Altair IV to investigate the fate of a colony planted there years before, they find one survivor, a saturnine philologist named Morbius (Walter Pidgeon) and his slightly thick daughter Alta (Anne Francis). Immediately the parallels with *The Tempest* become clear; Morbius is Prospero, his daughter a Miranda who has never seen men. There is an Ariel, in this case a cheeky robot named Robby who can do everything but see a joke. And also Caliban, in the shape of an invisible monster that, Morbius alleges, killed all but him and his wife during the first year of settlement.

Pressing, Adams finds that Morbius is sitting on the remains of a buried civilisation, abandoned millions of years ago by its alien builders, the Krel, but maintained by the same awesome technology which built Robby. Morbius takes them on a tour down a subterranean tram tunnel ("Prepare yourselves, gentlemen, for a new scale of physical scientific values") into a buzzing, howling, throbbing world like the blown-up belly of a computer. "Eight thousand cubic miles of Klystron Relays" keep it going, and the Krel's atomic furnaces are self-maintaining. What happened to the Krel? It emerges that in Allen Adler's ingenious original story they defeated the tyranny of matter by perfecting a means of transferring energy in any form to any part of the planet by mental power alone, forgetting in an alarming lapse of foresight that this would release unlimited forces into the hands of their subconscious and awaken "The Monster from the Id." The Krel presumably tore each other to pieces in a single night, and their city remained undiscovered until Morbius.

Unaccountably the monster from the Id appeared again, first to kill the colonists and smash their ship, the "Bellerephon," next to attack Adams's crew and tear one member to pieces. The ship's doctor, sacrificing himself to a brain-boosting machine to discover the truth, finds that Morbius has now gained access to the same power source that destroyed the Krel. As Morbius shouts when the creature is searing its way into the lab in which the three of them are hiding, "My evil self is at that door and I have no power to stop it." Finally, however, he throws himself at it, is mortally wounded and, dying, ensures that a switch is thrown which will destroy the planet within a few hours. (What such a switch is doing so close at hand is never adequately explained.) From space, the crew, Alta and Robby watch the brief nova, then return to Earth without a backward glance.

Switched on to magazine sf, *Forbidden Planet* uses such elements as Asimov's "Robotic Laws" which forbid robots to harm human beings, terms like "blaster" and other paraphernalia of the literary field, but Robby's dialogue has the same gadget-mad humour as *This Island Earth*. Stolidly he remarks that, if required, he can speak English, as well as "187 languages plus dialects and sub-tongues." Lumbering towards the ship with a huge load of shielding, he says offhandedly, "This is my morning's batch of Isotope 217. The whole thing hardly comes to ten tons," while, when Francis asks him for star sapphires, he croaks, "Star sapphires take a week to crystallise. Will diamonds or emeralds do?" "So long as they're big ones," Francis says. "Five, ten, fifteen carats are on hand," Robby replies smugly.

The look and sound of *Forbidden Planet* contribute much to its mood. Little is made of the landscape of Altair IV, with its green sky, cloud striped oversize moon and red earth, but the space effects are remarkably expert, especially an eclipse where an enormous sun is blocked by a planet, leaving only the saucer silhouetted by its corona. Model work is skilfully used in the vertiginous shots of vast Krel shafts occupied by zapping machines, and George Folsey's bright and cheerful lighting shows the talent that made him one of M-G-M's top cameramen in the Thirties and Forties.

The soundtrack, "Electronic Tonalities" by Louis and Bebe Barron, collaborators at one time with avant garde composer John Cage, is dubiously reminiscent of Karlheinz Stockhausen's work in this field, specifically his "Kontakte." Nevertheless Robby's coffee-pot plopping theme and the whooping shriek of the invisible monster as it attacks are superbly used. The isle is indeed full of voices.

Smooth and cynical, *Forbidden Planet* makes nonsense of the idea that only people who know science fiction can create good sf film. Director Fred McLeod Wilcox is a routine craftsman whose most successful film was *Lassie, Come Home*. Folsey, designer Arthur Lonergan and the other technicians are film-makers first, sf fans last, if at all. What attraction the film has stems from their consummate use of the film medium; Ferris Webster cutting between Alta's nightmare and her father suffering in the lab as he drives his monster to attack Adams and his ship; Cyril Hume's crisp if unlikely dialogue for the crew members and their captain; special effects by Disney's Joshua Meador who had created those for the "Rite of Spring" sequence of *Fantasia*. The scientific accuracy or otherwise of the film seems immaterial beside their ingenuity.

10. Lucifer: The Films of Jack Arnold

A SOLEMN VOICE intones the words of Genesis as a camera prowls through writhing mists and half-glimpsed landscapes; the sea rolls endlessly to the horizon, and as it washes on a dark and empty beach, formless footprints are seen leading from the water up into the darkness. Creation—but of the darkest and most bizarre kind, a mirror image of the exaltation that motivates biblical stories of the world's beginning. This, one imagines, is how Lucifer might have conceived the world; a place in which creatures, born from the womb of darkness, would live out lives of violence and terror, the forces of what we know as good harassing them for being no more than what they are. And just such an impulse does pervade the film from which this sequence comes, *Creature from the Black Lagoon,* as it does all those made by the great genius of American fantasy film, Jack Arnold.

From 1953 to 1958, reaching across the boom years, Arnold directed for Universal a series of films which, for sheer virtuosity of style and clarity of vision, have few equals in the cinema. His dramatic use of the Gill Man, initially no more than a routine Universal "creature" designed by make-up genius Bud Westmore, has raised it to the pantheon of mythopoetic figures along with Dracula and the Frankenstein monster, and today his strikingly original conception of this beast/man has made it a central one in Twentieth century mythology. Adopting the pale grey style of sf film, he raised it briefly to the level of high art, by-passing the cumbersome attachments of twenty years' misuse to tap again, as Whale and Kenton had done, the elemental power of the human subconscious. No imprint lingers so indelibly on the face of modern fantasy film as that of this obscure yet brilliant artist.

Working most often with producer William Alland (Orson Welles's *protégé* with the Mercury Theatre, and an actor most remembered as the inquiring newsreel reporter in *Citizen Kane*), Arnold dominated the sf field during his brief career. His occasional excursions into other forms—a taut thriller called *The Tattered Dress* (1957), the thought-provoking Audie Murphy Western *No Name on the Bullet* (1959), and perhaps most ingenious of all a mad college drama called *High School Confidential* (1958)—show a talent that could operate independent of any outside influence and mark every project, no matter how tawdry, with a brilliant personal vision. Quiescent since the early Sixties, Jack Arnold exists as an *éminence grise* on the horizon of fantasy film, inscrutable, mysterious, almost impossible both to analyse and to ignore.

It is important to discard conventional concepts of cinematic style before considering Arnold's work, or for that matter the work of most other modern sf film-makers. None of them offer the looming low-angle images of Welles, the bravura cutting of Kubrick, the complex philosophy of Siegel. Formal photographic brilliance, montage and arresting acting performances have no place in a form that is mostly mime and masque. Many of the most important and beautiful scenes in Arnold's films might well have been directed for the stage. Entrances are bluntly direct, from right or left of frame, action carried on, as it is in the more recent films of Howard Hawks, without any attempt to underline it with cutting or photography. Whereas most directors look on the frame as a window, for Arnold it is a proscenium. Recognising it as a formal boundary to the image he employs it skilfully as a means of hiding action, just as a stage director might use the wings. Tension is not imposed by style but engendered by friction between characters, or counterpoint between people and landscape. Shadows are avoided, action presented in pale patterns of grey and white. Like Alfred Hitchcock, Arnold has realised that the film medium is strong enough to stand alone without tricks derived from graphic art.

An early indication of Arnold's flair came in 1953, with *It Came from Outer Space*. Based on an original treatment by Ray Bradbury,

Technical artistry: IT CAME FROM OUTER SPACE

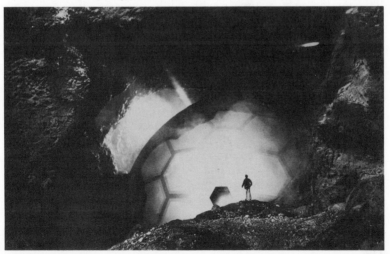

the script that Bradbury wrote was discarded, and the slim plot re-done, probably for the better, by Harry Essex. The film is a basic statement of Arnold's style and predilections. The setting, the Arizona desert, was one that he was to use often in the future, and that sf film-makers were soon to make peculiarly their own. His star, Richard Carlson, became the most popular actor in sf film, embodying the clean-cut intelligence that audiences demanded in their scientific heroes. The film was also in 3-D, sf being a con-venient form for this least viable of all filmic experiments. But the real importance of *It Came from Outer Space* lies in its technical artistry, and in the mood of quiet disturbance which Arnold conveys with such restraint and power.

Initial long shots of a small Arizona desert town at dusk set the film's elegiac mood, as does a commentary using one of the two lines retained from Bradbury's original treatment—"The town . . . resting after its daily battle with the sun." That night amateur astronomer John Putnam (Richard Carlson) sees a space ship land and bury itself in the desert. A week later he is still trying to con-vince the authorities of this when two electricity linesmen disappear, then mysteriously re-appear with oddly different characters. One by one other people are changed, including his girl (Barbara Rush). Putnam is finally able to rouse the townspeople, but he is then told by the alien visitors that they are merely repairing their ship, and will soon leave, restoring all their victims to normality. Prudently, he seals the mine in which they are hiding, giving them time to escape.

Despite some laboured compositions demanded by the need to exhibit the 3-D effect, the film's setting and playing are brilliantly managed. The desert is a character, exercising a mysterious influ-ence over those who live near it, a fact underlined by the remaining Bradbury sentence, given to one of the linesmen. "You see lakes and rivers that aren't really there, and sometimes you think the wind gets into the wires and sings to itself. . . . " Slow helicopter shots of cars moving quietly along dark desert roads; a carefully suspenseful sequence of tracking blood-stains from the road to find no corpse

118

but a dead animal; moments of pure fright as hands leap into the frame to grasp shoulders; all involve us in the desert and the world of the people who live there.

Deprived by his limited budget of elaborate special effects, Arnold cleverly uses disturbances in behaviour to convey mood. All those people who have been "taken over" behave in a way slightly but eerily out of key; the two truck drivers, glimpsed in town by Putnam and cornered in an alley, emerge from the shadows *holding hands,* while one of the men, his attention drawn to the blazing sun, looks up and stares unblinkingly into it. When Putnam faces his girl on a windy hillside at dawn, she stands untroubled by the chill desert wind, while he must pull up his collar and flinch against its bite. Economically we are told that there is something outside our experience, a "different-drummered" world beyond our own. *It Came from Outer Space* is Arnold's first brilliant exercise with the elements of fantasy film and by setting it in the desert, a location assuming at times the status of a character itself, we are given fair warning that from now on Arnold is to discard studio conventions and unleash his creatures on the real world.

Fantasy and reality interpenetrate in *Creature from the Black Lagoon* (1954) a film that fulfils every promise Arnold made in *It Came from Outer Space.* Again our environment acts as the stage for a confrontation between good and evil, again Arnold's cool style involves us totally in an allegoric conflict wherein Man, puny and confused, struggles to subdue a creature deriving its strength from wells descending perhaps to hell. For a brief moment Lucifer is risen, and man is powerless to oppose him.

After a quotation from Genesis, and a sequence suggesting the Creation, we see a line of footprints leading from the sea out into the darkness, then flash forward millions of years to a modern anthropological expedition excavating along the Amazon. A careless blow exposes the dessicated claw of a monster jutting from a bank, and while the scientist is away investigating its importance, a similar creature attacks his camp, killing his men with a vicious clutching slash at their faces. Surmising that fragments of the skeleton may

119

have been washed into the Black Lagoon downstream the expedition moves there, to be menaced and almost destroyed by the creature that inhabits it.

The lagoon's still black water and the silent studio jungle which surrounds it are an eerie *mise en scène,* but it is in its underwater sequences that the film succeeds best. James C. Havens's brilliant underwater photography and the miraculous mime of Ben Chapman as the Gill Man convert the depths of the lagoon into a world of mystery as subtly beautiful as that Cocteau conceived for his

Richard Carlson and Julie Adams menaced by the
CREATURE FROM THE BLACK LAGOON

fantastic creations. Black and murky from above, the lagoon beneath the surface is a transparent new world. Sunlight slants through the water as the men drift and spin in their search, but below among murk and drifting weeds, the monster lurks, leprous and pale. Sunken logs bar the way, weeds float and curl in a sinister evocation of a primeval world, while the Gill Man watches with a sardonic and sinister intelligence from the dark pits of the bottom.

A key scene of the film is when the heroine (Julie Adams) enters the water for a swim, unaware that the creature is swimming just below her, admiring. Shots looking up towards the surface show the girl penetrating a Cocteau-like mirror, her white suit with its accentuated breasts, her choreographed leg movements all overtly sexual. Gliding beneath her, twisting lasciviously in a stylised representation of sexual intercourse, the creature, his movements brutally masculine and powerful, contemplates his ritual bride, though his passion does not reach its peak until the girl performs some underwater ballet movements, explicitly erotic poses that excite the Gill Man to reach out and clutch at her murmuring legs.

This conflict continues throughout the film, the Gill Man being presented as a force of elemental power, not maliciously evil but "other-directed," a fragment of a world where our ideas of morality have no relevance. When they do subdue the creature it is with a drug spouted in a white cloud through the water, the black and beautiful fallen angel vanquished by the white power of science. This imagery of religious eroticism continues in the climax; the girl dragged away by the creature into his mist-shrouded cave, and discovered draped over an altar-like rock, symbolically sacrificed. Shot several times, the creature staggers to the water and, drawn back to the depths, slides gracefully over the lip of an underwater ravine, down into the pit. Lucifer has been conjured up, tested and found invincible. Now he can be sent back to hell until Man next feels himself able to test his power.

Predictably, all Arnold's films embody in one form or another the two basic preoccupations of sf film, the threat of knowledge and the loss of individuality, though his main interest is in the first, and the danger of technology when it is separated from human feelings. The Gill Man, like the afreet of Arabic legend, cannot be controlled after he has been conjured up and, as in most mythologies, only pure human responses like love can protect humanity from its power. In the Creature films, this belief is expressed in highly charged emotional and poetic terms, and a style strongly related to the horror film and morality play from which the entire field draws its strength. With *Tarantula* (1955), Arnold briefly abandoned this aspect of sf cinema to concentrate on a story more biting, modern and scientific. The result is one of his most accomplished films.

Performances give *Tarantula* more punch than the average sf film. Leo G. Carroll as a biochemist experimenting with artificial nutrients brings to his role the low-key efficiency that has distinguished most of his work, while John Agar and Mara Corday are smooth enough to make believable a complicated first meeting scene with a touch of Hawksian comedy. Corday, sexily pneumatic in white, is an acceptable successor to Julie Adams, while Nestor Paiva follows his part as the boat's captain in *Creature from the Black Lagoon* with an amusingly overplayed portrait of the baffled sheriff of the town near which Carroll has his laboratory.

Deriving in plot from the "giant insect" cycle that had begun with *Them!* the previous year, *Tarantula* has a not dissimilar beginning. Instead of the little girl fleeing from some unseen "them," Arnold has a horribly distorted man, his head and hands twisted into beastiality, lurch out of the desert to collapse under the credits. As in *The Monolith Monsters*, Universal's desert town standing set is used as a focus of action and a bridge to the rather more threatening world that lurks just beyond the lamplight. After that, it is all Arnold country, and we sense again the affinity he feels for the desert and its ascetic emptiness, a feeling expressed by Agar as he explains to Corday that it was once the floor of an ocean. "Every beast that crawled or swam or flew began here," he says. "You can still find sea shells out there." Fitting, then, that in a bleak bungalow in the middle of this primeval land, Carroll should be growing giant creatures in a misplaced effort to solve the problem of feeding the world, and that two of his co-workers should die after experimenting on themselves. The second of them maliciously injects Carroll, making him too a swollen victim of the unsuccessful nutrient.

The story might have been adequately told using just Carroll's plight, but the introduction of an experimental spider injected with the nutrient allows Arnold to externalise the conflicts implicit in the situation. The spider, swiftly growing to the size of an office block, ravages the countryside, crunching cars in its jaws, striding through the night until the avenging fire of heaven catches up with it in the form of air force jets. In a remarkable final sequence among the most impressive in the field, the spider burns like a creature of straw as the jets wheel around it, pouring down napalm. No monster ever had a more spectacular burial.

After the success of *Creature from the Black Lagoon*, Arnold was pressed to do a sequel, an opportunity that he used to explore further the myth so cleverly tapped by the original. Except for brief sequences at the lagoon where the creature is drugged by white chemical pellets dropped into the water, most of *Revenge of the Creature* occurs in Florida, a *milieu* totally different from the ghostly lagoon. The black creature is now pitted brutally against white concrete, tile and glass under a brilliant tropical sun, and surrounded by the laughing faces of his enemies. Yet triumphantly he defeats them all, carries off his symbolic bride and, at the peak of his victory, discards her to fall back into the pit.

This is Arnold's most assured work outside his masterpiece, *The Incredible Shrinking Man*, cynically playing on the audience's sensibilities with a series of ingenious tricks. The Gill Man (played this time by Ricou Browning) prowls through landscapes far more densely inhabited than those of the earlier films, and his sudden appearances in crowded areas play subtly on city-dwellers emotions. The film's most successful scene is that in which the Creature, brought in a comatose state to a Miami Marineland, is "walked" up and down a shallow pool in an attempt to revive him.

At first fascinated, the watching cameramen and scientists soon become bored, but down in the water, the creature's eyes creep cunningly open. Suddenly he surges up, smashes the terrified keeper, then scrabbles up out of the pool to claw his way through the screaming reporters until beaten back into the pool with a boathook. Afterwards, chained by one leg in a pool with sharks, turtles and fish (a slip here—surely the Gill Man is a freshwater animal), he petulantly tests his bonds, knowing that he can break out at any time but awaiting only an opportunity.

His escape and the kidnap of the heroine (Lori Nelson) are brilliantly staged. Protected by a huge Alsatian—dogs, it seems, have a special place in Arnold's bestiary; almost all his films have one, and much is made of their power to sense danger—the heroine moves confidently through dark gardens, unaware of the creature lurking in the shadows. Paradoxically the rape is carried out not in deserted surroundings but at a waterside night club where she and her lover are dining. Bursting among the dancers at the height of a blaring rock number, the creature grabs the girl and plunges into the water. The search party glimpses her on a clanging bell buoy, but when they arrive she is gone. Finally, she is found by two searchers sprawled unconscious in the manicured park by a river; the creature, needing to breathe, must abandon her every few hundred feet to re-enter the water. When he next does this, the hunters catch him in the brutal glare of a searchlight, her lover drags the girl back and, batting ineffectually at the bullets whining around him, the creature descends back into the dark water.

Revenge of the Creature uses the elements of the first film again but invests them with greater intensity and eroticism. The final kidnap is far more violent than the original, the ending unambiguously sadistic. The creature no longer drifts casually among the weeds, but ploughs violently across white sandy sea-beds, thrashing at the smooth banks of sand as if to destroy this alien environment. Even the obligatory underwater scene is subtly different; again the girl swims against the mirror surface of the water, again the creature admires her, but this time she is not alone. At the

John Agar (at right) in REVENGE OF THE CREATURE

mid-point of the scene, her lover takes her in his arms and they kiss passionately. Voyeuristically the creature looks on, then excitedly reaches out to grab her ankle and draw her down. Playing on our instinctive fears of "something" below us, Arnold shows his complete control of this most difficult of all *genres,* the theatre of fright.

Few established science fiction writers have written for sf film, and those that have, such as David Duncan and Jerome Bixby, seldom had distinguished writing careers. An exception is Richard Matheson who, after producing a number of successful novels and short stories, turned to the film field with the same skill and imagination he had shown in the magazines. It is from his novel *The*

125

Shrinking Man that Matheson adapted the script for Jack Arnold's next film, *The Incredible Shrinking Man,* a fantasy that for intelligence and sophistication has few equals. Written with Matheson's usual insight and directed with persuasive power, this film is the finest Arnold made and arguably the peak of sf film in its long history.

Again the film begins in the real world, pale and bland. Scott Carey (Grant Williams) and his wife are sunning themselves on their boat, the tiny craft lost on a calm sea. Suddenly a small cloud passes over them; Scott, lying in the sun, is sprinkled with glittery particles that quickly evaporate. But six months later he finds that he has begun to shrink. First just a few inches, so that his clothes no longer fit, then a little more. Soon he is only three feet tall, and a national curiosity. At six inches tall he can only live in a doll's house, and even that becomes impossible when his cat breaks in. Scott

Grant Williams fights a tarantula as THE INCREDIBLE SHRINKING MAN

flees to the cellar, his wife thinks he has been eaten by the cat and the door to the cellar is closed, trapping him in the littered room where, menaced by a giant spider, he struggles to survive.

More formally planned than his other films, containing many images of great visual power and beauty, *The Incredible Shrinking Man* is Jack Arnold's masterpiece, interpreting Matheson's script with ferocious precision. The gradual disintegration of Scott Carey's life and hopes is beautifully conveyed, perhaps most significantly when, after visiting baffled doctors for the last time, Scott's wedding ring slides from his diminished finger. Soon after, his marriage collapses, and only his cat provides any comfort. Yet it is the cat that finally precipitates his plight by driving him into the cellar. Inexorably the process continues, and, as Scott changes, the familiar world assumes new significance, an effect which Arnold and Matheson, by careful "planting," make appear even more convincing. The changing role of the cat, from prop to companion to menace, is especially well managed.

"Easy enough to talk of soul and spirit and essential worth," Scott says at one point, "but not when you're three feet tall." His emotional disintegration, parallel with that of his marriage, leads to a sad liaison with a circus midget, though by casting a normal actress in out-of-proportion sets Arnold throws away what might have been a memorable sequence. When he becomes even smaller than the midget, Scott is driven to his final imprisonment in the cellar, where the dripping boiler showers down a steady stream of stunning water drops and life depends on a crumbling castle of cake for which he must fight with an enormous black spider. After destroying the spider with a sword-like pin and gargantuan scissors, Scott finds himself shrinking still further, until he is so small that he can crawl through a ventilator into the world outside. Looking up at the night sky from a forest of grass, he experiences a moment of elation, and of hope. Nothing is created to live a meaningless life, he realises. Somewhere in the universe, even if he continues shrinking, there is a place for him.

Intriguing though one finds the philosophy of *The Incredible*

Shrinking Man, there is more interest in the remarkable control with which Arnold shows Scott Carey's physical and emotional metamorphosis. Robert Clatworthy's art direction provides believable out-of-proportion sets, but Arnold places Williams in them with complete skill. Scott sprawled on a grating after the cellar has been flooded, just part of the debris left behind; the towering edifice of the steps up which he must struggle, the enormous flaming creature that the boiler becomes, the dusty chunk of cake and the careless pile of sewing things in which he finds weapons and tools; impeccably engineered, these settings became completely convincing. The battle with the spider and with the cat are also remarkable, his final despatch of the former counting among the great moments of film, but in the end it is with Scott, the tortured yet triumphant victim, that we are most in sympathy.

After the skill of *The Incredible Shrinking Man,* it is depressing to contemplate *Monster on the Campus,* Arnold's next production. Despite the talents of Russell Metty on camera, the film has little to recommend it, although certain scenes are grimly horrific. Searching through a wrecked house for the monster that has been menacing the town, scientist Arthur Franz moves into the dark back garden, unaware that, slightly out of focus behind him, the corpse of a girl is transfixed to a tree. We also have our fair share of hands reaching out to grab shoulders, and Arnold has never been cleverer in his use of the frame as a formal barrier; time after time victims back into the camera, begging for a monster to jump on them from out of picture.

But apart from this theatrical bravura, the film is lamentably feeble. David Duncan's script is part of the problem. Franz is a scientist who, after importing a coelecanth for study purposes, cuts his hand on its teeth. Shortly after, the town is menaced by a mysterious monster, but though a dog turns into a prehistoric wolf after lapping up some coelecanth "juice" and a dragonfly that drinks some becomes as big as a cat, nobody thinks to suspect Franz, not even after he has discovered the truth and is ready to sacrifice himself to a police search party. Only at the scientifically unlikely climax, with Franz changing from creature to man before their eyes, do the cops wake up to the truth. An index to the plot's unlikeliness comes from the scene in which Franz, after stabbing the giant dragonfly with a letter opener, inadvertently lets some of its blood drip into his pipe. Lighting up again, he draws, grimaces, but then puffs contentedly until the fluid has its effect.

One assumes that Arnold had little sympathy with *Monster on the Campus*, but the master is very much on form in *The Space Children* (1958), last of his classic works. As pale, grey and melancholy as any of his earlier films, *The Space Children* is Arnold's summation, exploring the conflicts implicit in the confrontation between man and the forces of another, alien world, in this case that of childhood. Ostensibly made for children, the film is so bleakly unsympathetic in its study of adults that it must have widened inestimably the gulf between the generations.

A group of children whose parents work on an isolated missile project is contacted by an alien intelligence. Using the children's minds to channel its mental power, the alien sabotages the project, preventing the missile with its atomic warhead being launched into space. As he uses the desert in *It Came from Outer Space,* Arnold in *The Space Children* employs the sea coast of California as his background, a setting which finally becomes a character in itself. Escaping from the bleak cliff-top trailer camp in which their parents live, the children haunt the beach, wandering into the caves that dot it and finding in one of them a glowing brain that grows as its power becomes greater. Benignly disposing of a brutal father when he tries to beat his child, the brain is an adolescent vision of revenge, a chance to "get back" on the adult world.

Throughout, parents are shown as argumentative, unfeeling and self-interested. In the first scenes, as the family drives along the lonely beach road, the two boys feel the touch of the alien mind and look wonderingly at one another, but their parents sense nothing. Faced with a world of domestic bickering and professional friction, the children retreat into a "gang" mentality, their responses coolly believable in contrast to those of the children in films like

Village of the Damned. With the muffled boom of the surf audible in almost every shot and the grey windy world of the sea shore always around them, the children enter into this dream of conflict and reprisal, convincing us with their eerie acceptance of violence and sudden death. Restrained and thoughtful, *The Space Children* contains the best of Arnold's mature work.

Although Arnold's career did not end with this film—he directed the sf-oriented *The Mouse that Roared* in Britain in 1959 and is still active as an independent director/producer—it does provide an abrupt terminator to his best work. By 1958 the boom was over. The creature cycle had burned itself out and so smoothly professional a director as Arnold could no longer continue to produce horror sf films for a dwindling market. Like Michael Curtiz, Jack Arnold was unconcerned with the symbolism of his films. He was in the movies for money, and because it was what he did best. Any art was incidental. But because of this insouciant attitude his work had a calculated cynicism and a special poetry. As in the commercial cinema at large, the greatest of sf film-makers are those who choose not to be involved. Cool like the great jazzmen, they have expressed their contempt for the world, content to have it forgotten like all ephemeral things. We who hear the echoes are fortunate indeed.

11. The Monsters

I F ONE WERE TO GRAPH the American sf film scene between 1950 and 1960, the curve would be a revealing one. After *Destination Moon* in 1950, a slight rise might be detected as producers cashed in on the success of this new untried medium, and during 1952 and 1953, occasional rises would be apparent as film-makers unearthed new elements from the past or conceived new ones to play the old tricks. But it was not until 1953–4 that the peak really came, induced by two films from Warner Brothers which, almost single-handedly, created the whole monster/creature cycle. One was

Gordon Douglas's *Them!*, the other Eugene Lourié's *The Beast from 20,000 Fathoms*.

Art director for Jean Renoir and René Clair, collaborator with Sacha Guitry and a film artist of considerable standing, Eugene Lourié was an odd choice to direct *The Beast from 20,000 Fathoms*. Derived from a Ray Bradbury short story, it was spectacularly American in ambience and approach, but Lourié managed to instill into it some of his expertise and feeling for mood. Just as Freund and Florey in the early sound period were able to adapt cheap materials to their own ends, so Lourié juggled his models and effects, combining them cleverly with conventional material to convey the essential fantasy of the subject.

The Beast from 20,000 Fathoms was very much a template for those films which followed it, and seeing it today we easily forget that, when it was made, the elements were fresh and novel. An atom test in the Arctic wakes a Rhedosaurus frozen in the ice. After causing a few deaths among the icebergs, it makes its way to ancestral breeding grounds off New York, rampages through the city, making defence difficult because of germs in its blood which infect the attackers, but is cornered in the Manhattan Beach amusement park and killed by a radioactive isotope fired into a wound in its throat.

Ray Bradbury's *The Fog Horn* was a moody fragment; a lighthouse foghorn is echoed in the night by a phantom note, the answering call of a last lonely monster. Little of the story remains in the film, and though the creature does wreck a lighthouse at one point there is, paradoxically, no foghorn in evidence. Reminiscent of *The Thing*, the film is let down by a sketchy script full of the solemn philosophising later to become an sf film commonplace, and by some unintentional humour, like a psychiatrist pontificating on the "Loch Lomond Monster." Cecil Kellaway as amiable paleantologist Thurgood Elson is inoffensive, providing a contrast to the contrived romance between his assistant—beautiful, of course—and the dreary hero.

The film is only really at its best when Lourié and effects man

Ray Harryhausen are allowed full charge, specifically at the climax, with the monster lashing about among ferris wheels and roller coasters, the men in white radiation suits creeping through the ruins and climbing the coaster, only to be stuck there when the cars slide away. As the park begins to burn, the creature rears up to lash at the flaming cage that surrounds him, and is shot at close range by a radioactive lance; as usual, the force that creates also destroys.

Most of Lourié's film had been set at night, as a means of enhancing the limited special effects and to support the mood of subtle horror that is typical of European fantasy. Much of the image was also obscured by judicious setting; the monster is initially glimpsed, for instance, during a blizzard, and Elson sees it for the first—and last—time during a bathysphere descent where process work hides wires and rough edges. Such clever and atmospheric film-making was, however, among the first things to be discarded by Hollywood in its search for good box-office. Warner's next production in the field, rushed out after the quarter million dollar *Beast* had grossed part of its eventual five million dollar profit, was bluntly violent, boldly high-key, overbearingly American in tone and style. In the hands of a lesser director it would have been disastrous, but Gordon Douglas's efficient management made *Them!* into a classic.

Points of similarity between the two films are obvious. Again we have a vague scientist, entomologist Edmund Gwenn, while the love interest this time involves his beautiful daughter and a stolid James Arness, who had entered the field as *The Thing*. Again the atom has created the monster, a nest of giant ants hatched (in the desert, naturally) after an atomic test. Variations on the model, where they exist, spring primarily from the control exercised by director Douglas, the taut script by Ted Sherdeman from a George Worthing Yates original and some highly professional playing by, among others, James Whitmore as an enterprising professional soldier who leads the search for the ants.

Cleverly, Douglas takes from earlier work—*It Came from Outer Space* included—the elements he finds most useful. Opening with a little girl stumbling out of the desert, able to talk only of "Them! Them!" the film has a cool introduction with the searchers in the desert discovering smashed buildings, twisted cars, and each time a trail of sugar leading from the site. When the ants' nest is found, poison gas is pumped in and a party sent down with flame throwers to wipe out any survivors. The resulting scene is especially weird, the suited figures moving slowly along the tunnels knee-deep in white mist, an enormous ant plunging through the wall in the midst of them. Even more remarkable is the sequence in which they seek the two surviving queens that have escaped from the desert to breed. Lead after lead proves hopeless, until a call from a city mental hospital takes them to a ward overlooking a huge storm drain. Patients for days have been raving of monsters, but the doctors pass it off. Now they are not so sure. Pouring down the wide concrete gullet of the drain, the searchers find the ants there together with two children caught in the nest. The final battle, with Whitmore saving the children at the expense of his own life, is terrifying.

In terms of output, the five years that followed the release of *The Beast from 20,000 Fathoms* and *Them!* were the most active of all time for sf cinema. Beginning in the U.S.A. but spreading quickly all over the world, the creature/monster cycle instigated by these two films but keyed initially by George Pal's *Destination Moon* became a major feature of commercial cinema, encouraging every type of producer from the largest through the most creative down to the sharpest get-rich-quick promoter to try his hand at the form. In Britain, Germany, Italy, Japan, Spain and France monsters appeared, giant insects ravaged five continents and the whole sf film field choked to death in a belated undisciplined spring.

Focus of this activity remained the United States, though the interest of independent producers meant that Hollywood studios had no corner on the business. Edgar G. Ulmer shot two sf quickies, *Beyond the Time Barrier* and *The Amazing Transparent Man* (1959) back to back on location at the Texas State Showground, commuting from one production to another across the arena until

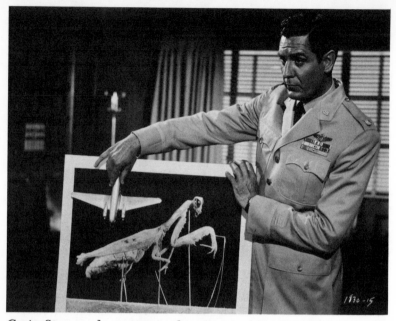

Craig Stevens demonstrates the size of THE DEADLY MANTIS

he ran out of money, whereupon the star brought both films in with his own funds. Ulmer's adventures were fairly typical; the cheapness of the form combined with the juvenile simplicity of the plots made it alarmingly easy to embark on a sf film, though problems of sets and effects generally arose halfway through. The two Ulmer films solved this ingeniously by using ace designer Ernst Fegté, an old associate of the director's, who created a system of triangular module panels from which sets could be created, then easily broken down later. Other directors were not so lucky.

It is difficult to differentiate between the various creature and insect films that dominated the next half-decade. After *Them!* attempts were made at other giant insects. *The Black Scorpion* (1957) incorporated some of Willis O'Brien's effects from *Gwangi* (see Chapter Seven) including impressive battles between the insect, an express train and a helicopter. *The Deadly Mantis* (1957), though marred by worse than usual model work, did achieve convincing tension under the direction of Nathan Juran, but after the success of *Tarantula* and *The Incredible Shrinking Man*, producers realised that the giant black spider played on human fears far more effectively than any other insect; *The Spider* (1958), *Earth V. The Giant Spider* and a score of inept imitations followed.

Evolving parallel with the insect cycle, dinosaur pictures thrived. *The Beast of Hollow Mountain* (1956) set its monster in a Western background, *Dinosaurus* (1960) in the Pacific where lightning revivifies exhumed prehistoric remains. Probably the most impressive of all, however, was Nathan Juran's *20 Million Miles to Earth* (1957) where a returning Venus spaceship crash-lands in the sea, casting up a watermelon-like "egg" from which hatches a tiny Tyrannosaurus Rex, one of Ray Harryhausen's liveliest creations. The baby soon grows to impressive proportions, ravaging cities until destroyed. Set in Italy, the film makes much of the seaside background and warm Mediterranean landscapes (presumably shot in Mexico), though the best sequence is that which opens the film, a rescue party struggling through the wreck of the sinking spaceship to drag out the crew. Artful angling, lots of smoke and some terrifying lurches and sound effects cleverly disguise the fact that the sets are those left over from *The Caine Mutiny*.

The monster *genre* was the first to peter out, its involved special effects making it less and less a practicable proposition as novelty wore off and audiences demanded more sophisticated material, but it continued to survive outside America. Eugene Lourié went to Great Britain to make *Behemoth the Sea Monster* (See Chapter Eight), while *Konga* (1961) and *Gorgo* (1960) were both shot in British studios, the European technicians making minor but effective variations on the established American style. In Sweden, *Reptilicus* (1962) showed a dinosaur laying waste to the countryside, though the film is best remembered for the means by which the monster is discovered, a vicious metal bore bringing up slices of bleeding flesh from the creature lying comatose in a bog.

One of the oddest phenomena of the period was the transference of the form almost intact to Japan, where Ishiro (also Inoshiro) Honda masterminded a series of transparently simple but often technically impressive monster films. Beginning with *Godzilla* (1955) an Asian dinosaur, and *Rodan* (1957) in which a giant pterodactyl hatched out to ravage the world, it continued with *The Mysterians* (1957)—alien invasion; futuristic battles on earth, in space and in the invaders' roomy flying saucer— and *Mothra* (1959), the smoothest of all in which a giant caterpillar destroys Tokyo in retribution for the kidnap of two tiny "magic ladies" whom a Tokyo entrepreneur has put into a vaudeville act. The success of the series spawned a rash of sequels, with new monsters produced to order: Majin, Gamera, Barugon and Ghidorah battled the

Waning cycle: John Sherwood's THE CREATURE WALKS AMONG US

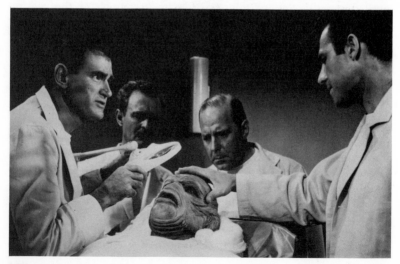

world and each other in a dozen features. Even the venerable King Kong was called out of retirement to participate in the elimination contest. Like sf sequels everywhere, the Japanese monster films have all the signs of catchpenny productions—faded American stars in featured roles, abysmal dubbing, uneven special effects—yet fail, like the others, to compete with Hollywood in what is essentially an American field.

As the cycle began to wane in the middle Fifties, producers looked around for new ideas to spice up the old plots, and created some remarkable monsters. Roger Corman, then producing with directors like David Kramarsky, Wyott Ordung and Bernard Kowalski, created a genre of Z pictures in which large monsters, requiring elaborate special effects, were replaced by more manageable varieties easily fabricated with men in special suits. Traceable back to Arnold's *Creature from the Black Lagoon*, these films—*It Conquered the World* (1956), *Night of the Blood Beast* (1958), *Beast from Haunted Cave* (1959) etc.—soon gave way to grue like *Attack of the Crab Monsters* (1957), *Attack of the Giant Leeches* (1958) and others noted more for violence and horror-film effects than any subtlety of execution. None, however, was as memorably nonsensical as *The Slime People* (1960), an independent work produced, directed and written by its star Robert Hutton, and shot for the most part in a wholesale meat market in suburban Los Angeles, with "slime men" rising from deep freeze cabinets to menace the heroine.

There were a few monsters showing that some film-makers retained an interest and pride in the field. *It Came from beneath the Sea* (1955) offered a giant squid which attacked submarines, including one captained by *The Thing* alumnus Kenneth Tobey. *The Giant Claw* (1957) was an enormous bird, looking most unlikely in close-up but terrifying innocent peasants in Northern Canada in some eerie scenes of night-time horror. Even human beings were pressed into service as monsters but *The Amazing Colossal Man* (1957), its sequel *Revenge of the Colossal Man* (1958), *Attack of the Fifty Foot Woman* (1959) and *The Thirty Foot Bride of Candy*

137

Rock (1959) do not offer much for the connoisseur.

Among the rubbish were the odd gleams of gold, audacious technical exercises and atmospheric fantasies that repay the attention of any serious filmgoer. Kurt Neumann's *The Fly* (1958) is a good example. Adapted from George Langelaan's short story of a man who trades arm and head with those of a fly in an unsuccessful matter transference experiment, the film is a bloody grotesque, rich in black comedy and a Cormanesque glee, and culminating in a grisly scene where the victim's wife mashes her husband in an hydraulic press to put him out of his misery. Vincent Price found it difficult to keep a straight face during shooting, but his plummy playing adds much to the film's crazy mood.

Less amusing, but rising to a special weirdness, was *Kronos* (1954), again by Kurt Neumann. The only serious attempt ever made at a truly technological monster, Kronos is a descendant of the juggernaut, a towering machine like an hydraulic press surmounted by a spherical "head." Deposited at dawn on a California beach, it progresses across the country with pistoning inexorability, raiding power stations to drain them of "food," a surfeit of which finally destroys it. The sight of this strange machine, half creature, half construction, pounding across the hills of America is one worthy of modern "underground" cinema.

In all these films it is possible to see the characteristic American ambiguity about technology. Anxious both to control their environment and to placate the fates, Americans must frequently reaffirm their belief in the overwhelming power of nature, as devil worshippers confirm themselves in their Master's service by ritually sinning in his presence. To American audiences the havoc wreaked on their homes by various dinosaurs is as welcome as the lash to a flagellant, while ritual phrases like "There Are Some Things Man Is Not Meant to Know" assume the importance of a litany; affirm, abase, adore—the prescribed reactions of audiences and congregations are too similar to be accidental.

While the creature cycle turned to its inevitable conclusion, that part of the field responsible for the Arnold films and the quiet, cool masterpieces of the early Fifties continued to flourish, drawing sustenance from the junk films, sneaking material into the theatres disguised under grotesque names or jazzed up with the incidental detail of the horror film. Roger Corman was to work such a system in the Sixties with his Poe adaptations, but in the Fifties Corman was a prolific producer and director of the least impressive horror Z film, other directors using the systems he was to find so convenient a decade later.

Among these was Don Siegel, whose *Invasion of the Body Snatchers* (1956) was a fine film masquerading under a ridiculous title. Adapted from a story by sf veteran Jack Finney, it has all the hallmarks of Jack Arnold's best films—clever use of natural locations, classic conflict between good and evil— as well as a violent energy that is peculiarly Siegel's. Taking the relatively unpromising idea of a Californian community menaced by alien "pods" that have the power to replace humans with soulless simulacra, it fleshes it out with convincing detail until we are totally involved in the fate of Santa Mira and of the young couple who are the only ones to resist the invasion.

After credit titles under which clouds build up ominously, the film opens with an unsatisfactory hospital sequence. Kevin Mc-Carthy tries to explain to Whit Bissell that an invasion is taking place. "For me, it started last Thursday," he says, and the film flashes back to where Siegel had originally wanted it to begin, with county doctor McCarthy returning home by train from a city visit. Low angled camera and a windswept station establish a mood of vague disquiet carried on by the introduction of a small boy who runs away down the road along which McCarthy is driving, and who claims that his mother "isn't my mother any more." In the days that follow, McCarthy begins a relationship with quick and intelligent *divorcée* Dana Wynter, but the epidemic of delusions continues. A little boy is brought in by his grandmother to explain that his mother "isn't real," and even Wynter's sister thinks a relative of hers has "changed."

McCarthy's suspicions, aroused by this, are confirmed when his

139

King Donovan's 'blank' in INVASION OF THE BODY SNATCHERS
(Donovan at left, also Kevin McCarthy and Dana Wynter)

friend King Donovan shows him the half-formed "blank" he has discovered of himself. Laid out incongruously on a billiard table, the "body" is examined by McCarthy as the awed couple looks on, a moody scene well broken at its height when a cuckoo clock goes off. Later the body wakes, its eyes opening in the foreground as the horrified wife looks on from rear of frame, and the nightmare begins in earnest. McCarthy finds a smooth-faced dummy of Wynter in the basement of her house and carries her off into the night in approved "beauty and the beast" fashion; in a greenhouse they find pods exploding like rotten cabbages to foam into obscene "blanks" that McCarthy and Donovan destroy with pitchforks in a horribly graphic sequence.

Soon there is nobody "real" left but McCarthy and Wynter, fugitives hiding in their own town. They watch the invasion proceeding; a gas station attendant puts two pods in the boot of their car when he fills the tank; spying through a window, McCarthy sees a man holding a pod ask his wife, "Shall I put this in with the baby?" "Yes," she replies, "Then there'll be no more crying." The doctor soliloquises on how some people allow their humanity to drain slowly away, and don't realise how precious it is until it is directly threatened, a moving re-statement of this basic sf film preoccupation. Determined to save himself and his girl from a loveless future, McCarthy's means of doing so are direct and brutal. Discovered in his office by two aliens, he and Wynter are prepared for taking over. Two pods are brought and one alien asks almost lovingly "Do you want to watch them grow?" While their attention is diverted, McCarthy fills two hypodermics with drugs and, creeping up behind the men, plunges them into their backs.

Outside they watch the aliens take over. In a particularly horrific shot a fleet of trucks pulls up in the town square and people flood towards them to pick up further pods, their numbers and quiet demeanour indicating the invasion's success. Escaping, the couple flee across the Californian countryside pursued by the pod people, desperately tired but not daring to sleep. Exhausted, they hide in a deserted tunnel, McCarthy secreting Wynter in a pit under some abandoned boards while he goes to investigate the sound of singing they hear in the night. However, it is not the sign of real humanity which he hopes for, but a radio playing while blank automatons load more pods in a field. Returning, McCarthy finds Wynter asleep, kisses her, then as her eyes slowly open into a knowing stare, realises she too is a victim. Desperately he flees to the highway, trying to flag down cars, but they will not stop. "You're next," he yells hysterically, but the cars press on, ignoring him, the last representative of human feelings.

"This is probably my best film," Siegel has said, "I think that the world is populated by pods and I wanted to show them."[31] Passionately involved, it has a fiery relevance that makes it durable even today. In style, it is virile and energetic; the consistent use of low wide-angle shots opens up the frame with cloudscapes, landscapes, all-enclosing buildings crowding in on wide dark streets. The town sequences, shot on natural locations, are almost alarmingly real. Siegel constantly sends his people out of quiet moody two-shots into bright areas; the lovers walking down a staircase to part in a pool of sunlight by the door, McCarthy carrying Wynter out of a dark house to where his car sits under a street light. As in Arnold's films, the effect is of people moving through a vaguely threatening landscape, their lives and relationships safe only as long as they stay close to the light.

If *Invasion of the Body Snatchers* was oddly named, *I Married a Monster from Outer Space* (1958) is surely a candidate for the most unappetisingly titled film ever made, yet behind this grisly label lies a work of more than usual brilliance, directed by ex-editor Gene Fowler Jr. with the crisp efficiency that characterised the distinguished work of Arnold and Siegel. Nor is the plot difficult to accept; on his wedding night, a young man driving home from a bucks' party witnesses the landing of a space ship and is "taken over" by one of the aliens, who assumes his shape. Next morning, his fuzzy reactions are explained away as hangover, and the wedding goes on. Not until the honeymoon night does his wife begin to see that something is wrong, the gloomy nature of the story to come heralded by a horrific scene in which the man, standing on the balcony during a thunder storm, is momentarily frightened by a flash of lightning into dropping his guard. In the glare his face dissolves into a hideous alien mask, then is abruptly re-constituted into human form. Dark, smoothly shot in shadowy interiors that recall the Fritz Lang films Fowler edited, this might well be an episode of Joe Stefano's *The Outer Limits*, which was to bring this kind of atmospheric and disturbing sf to TV five years later.

By the end of the decade films like those of Arnold, Siegel and Fowler were achieving more prominence than ever, and, as the field settled down after the frantic activity of the boom years, their quality became more than ever a matter of interest to film-goers.

Triumph over title: I MARRIED A MONSTER FROM OUTER SPACE

This was the beginning of sf's real maturity, as opposed to the false spring of the early Fifties, when Hollywood tried to force a process that had been continuing for decades. Serious directors like Siegel who saw the value of sf as a vehicle for ideas were able to use it without excessive concessions to popular taste, now they could be reasonably sure of having an intelligent audience.

One of the directors to take this opportunity was veteran Allan Dwan, whose *The Most Dangerous Man Alive* (1961) remains a classic of its kind. Squarely in the tradition of Tourneur and a prime example of the annihilating melodrama, Dwan's story of a gangster turned to steel by an atomic explosion was shot with a cold ferocity and icy lack of feeling entirely appropriate to the subject. After his

143

exposure to the atomic blast, the desperate man scrabbling at a bunker window until the glare burns his image into white, gangster Ron Randell tracks down the men responsible, gleefully demonstrating that the experience has made his flesh impervious to injury. Bullets whine off him as he calmly tears his enemies to pieces, though the real horror of his plight does not occur to him until his mistress (Debra Paget) finds that he is now an impotent automaton. In a desperate attempt to re-awaken some feeling in him, she encourages him to undress her as he kneels at her feet, but even this does not work. Robbed of sexual fire, of every passion except hate, the killer paradoxically meets his fate in the blast of flame throwers which melt him to ash. Accepting the elements of sf film, Dwan like Siegel has cleverly utilised them to record a brutal allegory.

Films like those of Siegel and Dwan began the days of sf as a true medium, a tool talented film-makers could use as they did the Western and the melodrama to convey truths about life. Ideas became more important than effects, sf film entered into a period of sophistication that placed it finally on a level with written material, though in ambience, approach and attitude it still differed markedly from the material offered by the magazines and hardcover houses. Deep in the sf film field ran the same tide of religious imagery, cultural humour, psychological horror and symbolic sexuality that had motivated it in the days of *Homonculus*. Little had changed in the vehicle, and the elements inherited from the past still retained their potency. It was in the subjects sf film-makers chose that one could see the real change in the genre.

12. The End of the World, Plus Big Supporting Programme

A T A CLIMACTIC POINT in Jerzy Kawalerowicz's remarkable *Pharaoh* (1966), the Egyptian high priest gambles on the arrival of a solar eclipse to subdue the revolutionary mob clamouring at the temple gate. High above the crowd, he throws up his arms and demands that the sun god withdraw his light from the earth. Slowly the din subsides and a horrible quiet settles over the crowd as they see the sun's disc eaten away by a cancerous spot. Sinking to the earth, men and women who a moment ago had been proudly confident dissolve in terror, screaming, fainting, burrowing into the dirt. A divine wind howls over their writhing, fear-twisted shapes as they quail before the awful blindness of heaven. For them, the real world has ended; they stare into the infinite dark.

Kawalerowicz's film, though not sf, does rely on a variation of the characteristic science fictional detachment. Like most science fiction, it presents a story in terms of conflicting issues rather than characters. In *Pharaoh,* men are Man, the pressures and conflicts extended so as to have a deeper and wider application. Its end of the world, whether an actual cataclysm or not, has the mood of Judgement Day, and an analysis of the sequence reveals some elements not easily explained away as mere theatre. The wind that springs up has no direct physical justification, while the contortion of the woman who twists herself backwards as if sacrificing her unprotected body to the abyss is an apt symbol of Man helpless before his fate. Is it just an eclipse, we wonder, or has God really intervened to save the religious establishment?

The end of the world, or the threat of it, has always found filmmakers in some confusion as to their philosophies. A few, like Kawalerowicz, suggest that on occasion a divine agency might well intervene to rescue or influence mankind; others, more hard-bitten, prefer to see Man come to his end; sometimes with a bang, more often with a whimper. The theme, with its opportunities for the unbridled use of special effects and stock footage of natural disasters, is a popular one in sf cinema, and has seen some ingenious variations. Often more interesting, however, are the attitudes to religion and divinity which the films exhibit.

There is more than a quantitative difference between the assault of a revived prehistoric monster and the threat of an end to the world. Most monsters are, in a sense, man-made; their revival is a direct result of man's tinkering with nature—atomic explosions, exploration of unknown areas—and the damage they do a punishment meted out by the natural order for the crime of pride. Until recently, however, the end of the world was always shown in sf films as coming from outside the Earth, and although the advent of atomic weapons brought a rash of cautionary films on nuclear destruction, the threat of earth's final ruin almost always springs from what is, basically, a divine authority. And if it is averted, it is through the agency of a supernatural power, unconnected with nature. In sf films, the end of the world and the Last Judgement are synonymous.

Early uses of this theme—Germaine Dulac's *Le Mort du Soleil* (1920), Richard Oswald's *The Arc* (1919)—were secular in concept, reflecting the European experimental cinema's interest in design and psychology rather than any specific attitude to the universe, but European directors travelling to the United States soon found themselves purveying religious-influenced variations on the idea. Michael Curtiz's *Noah's Ark* (1929) succeeds better than most at suggesting the awesome power of a cataclysm which is more than natural, and by interweaving a number of stories in an *Intolerance*-like web of historical duplicity Darryl Zanuck's script suggests that the divine presence has been very much in evidence throughout the life of mankind. The flood itself is a shattering piece of special effects, the hard cutting of Curtiz making it seem as if water is pouring from heaven while the villains struggle and drown around the drifting ark. No tent show revivalist ever conjured up a more effective vision of divine retribution.

In the Thirties and Forties, a retributive God appeared occasionally in the American cinema, though more often the supreme power was shown as a kindly old fellow willing to help frustrated heroes

146

by sending them back to earth for a brief reunion with loved ones. Heaven was usually represented as a cloudy never-never land where the cast waded about up to its knees in CO_2 fumes and strummed on cardboard harps, though in *The Green Pastures* (1936) William Keighley confected a brainless variation in which all-Negro choirs of angels sang spirituals and nestled on clouds made, significantly enough, of cotton. In 1945, Raoul Welsh directed what is probably the oddest of all, *The Horn Blows at Midnight,* with Jack Benny as a member of the celestial brass section sent down to sound the last trumpet, failing through a combination of ineptitude and Alexis Smith.

None of these films took God seriously, but others did. *Gabriel over the White House* (1933) went further, using providence as an excuse for some sinister pamphleteering. Walter Huston is a newly inaugurated President of the United States who, while recovering from a car accident, has a heavenly vision: working under divine guidance, he cleans up America in a series of alarmingly familiar moves. The cabinet is sacked, the unemployed organised into an army, gangsters summarily executed. After he has solved the problem of the national debt by putting on a massive show of military strength and literally frightening the country's creditors into silence, he imposes peace on the United States with a simple Fascist dictatorship. Directed by Gregory La Cava with tongue in cheek cynicism, the film nevertheless has an hysterical undercurrent reflecting the plot's combination of religious fanaticism and political expediency.

In William Wellman's *The Next Voice You Hear* (1950), God again reached out to counsel Man, though with less selectivity. This time the message was general, the effect a complete conversion of the world. (Ivan Butler's recently published *Religion in the Cinema* deals at length with this film.) Not all films, however, granted God such an easy victory, especially not *Red Planet Mars* (1952), probably the most grotesque of all American excursions into the possibilities of divine intervention and an odd parable which may yet become an underground classic. A young American scientist and his wife pick up TV transmissions from Mars, learning that the planet is inhabited by a race ahead of us in technology and philosophy. As usual, knowledge nearly destroys the Western world, civilisation crumbling at the news of Martian cheap power and non-capitalist industry. In addition Mars is ruled by a "Supreme Authority" who, it emerges in the course of the film, is none other than God himself. While Earth listens in fascination to the paraphrased commandments and extracts from the Sermon on the Mount that the screen dispenses, an evil ex-Nazi scientist is hurrying from his eyrie in the Andes to take over the communications equipment, most of it based on his inventions. Before he can do so, however, the American couple and the Nazi die in an explosion that the former has engineered to prevent him from convincing the world that the messages were faked. Over their graves, the President of the U.S.A. delivers an oration and God minutes from Mars, "Well done, thou good and faithful servants."

It is impossible to suggest in words the nutty character of this film, but some of its quality can be gauged from scenes like those showing Russian Communism overthrown by a group of aged revolutionaries whose Christianity has been kept alive by listening to the Voice of America on secret radio sets. Repairing to a field, they dig up the sacred regalia hidden there and soon manage to place a priest on the throne of Russia. (Significantly this scene has been deleted from most TV prints of the film.) The Nazi scientist (Herbert Berghof) carries on like the Antichrist in his Andean hideout decorated with devil masks, while Peter Graves and Andrea King as the hero and heroine seem only one step removed from the pages of Cope's *Book of Martyrs*. Of the concept that God would intervene in world affairs to destroy the international Communist conspiracy and confirm in power the administration of General Eisenhower one can say little except that it is symptomatic of both the period and the sf films which it produced.

Greater maturity of thought was apparent in *War of the Worlds* (1953), Byron Haskin's ambitious adaptation of Wells's classic. Little remains, unfortunately, of the original, and by setting the story in California rather than Wells's beloved English Home Counties Haskin removed the book's most impressive quality, the horror of death and destruction in familiar surroundings, of a society one has known and loved coming apart before one's eyes. Squarely in the tradition of the American sf film, where all attempts are bent to creating a literal depiction of the fantastic rather than evoking a mood, all but two of the film's sequences are shot indoors, and model work extensively used. Despite Haskin's energetic visual style, the film has the smooth unreality of a comic strip.

The atheistic Wells would have cringed at the liberties scenarist Barré Lyndon took with his story, especially the imposition of a heavy religious *motif*. The heroine's uncle, a minister, is built up as an important character during the early sequences, contributing an especially funny scene in which he and the town elders discuss putting in picnic tables and souvenir stands around the Martian spaceship to attract tourists. When, therefore, he decides to approach the advancing Martians with an offer of peace and friendship, walking forward reciting the Twenty-third Psalm with his bible held high and the cross on its cover shining crusader-like in the alien glow, we are not surprised to see him incinerated in short order by the Martian death-ray. Despite this initial set-back God finally has His way, and the last scenes find hero and heroine clutching each other in a church while the Martians fall dead in the streets outside, victims, as Sir Cedric Hardwicke reverently puts it in his narration, "of the littlest things God in His wisdom put on the earth."

Haskin achieves some atmospheric sequences in the course of the film, most of them during the flight of Gene Barry and Ann Robinson across country as the Martian war machines advance. Halfway through cooking dinner in an abandoned farmhouse the whole place is brought down around their ears as a spaceship ploughs into it, and Barry is awakened by the girl washing his face from a torn water pipe gushing like a severed artery. When a Martian from the ship explores the house, they drive it off, not before lopping the horribly intelligent head of the TV probe that is sent in to find them. There is also some clever crane-shooting and cutting in the climax, but Haskin's crescendo is limp compared with the diminuendo ending of the original, with the last stilted fighting machine standing amid the ruins of London, the empty streets echoing with alien screams of agony that slowly die away.

The film's humour, unconscious or otherwise, is its best quality, betraying Barré Lyndon's genial contempt for the project. Gene Barry's atomic physicist is staunchly egalitarian; seen first as a whiskered member of a fishing expedition, he plunges into the social round of the town with a visit to a square dance and an orgy of Coca Cola drinking. Throughout the film he uses few words of more than three syllables, and many of much less. No opportunity is lost to re-introduce the religious *motif;* when somebody calculates that it will take six days for the Martians to destroy the world, the heroine observes piously, "The same time it took to make it." The best line, however, is given to Jack Kruschen, one of the first men to see (and be killed by) the Martians. "What shall we say to them?" a companion asks nervously as they advance towards the ship, white flag upraised. Kruschen looks thoughtful. "Welcome to California?" he suggests.

In David Kramarsky's *Beast with a Million Eyes* (1956), produced by Roger Corman, God's intervention is more direct, and the film is in its way a masterpiece of the Z-movie. Set, predictably, in the Arizona desert, it shows an alien intelligence dominating the domestic animals of a region and turning them against man. In some notably weird scenes, a cow goes mad and savages its owner, and a hitherto amiable Alsatian dog pads quietly around the house searching for someone to kill. After a mentally defective farm-hand has run amok with an axe, the people go out into the desert and trap the alien, which has transferred its intelligence into a tiny desert rodent. As the men pray, an eagle swoops providentially from the sky and carries it away. Abysmal acting ruins the film, but its lack of music and simple exteriors style give it a quality of special horror.

Infinitely more sophisticated on the level of effects, Alfred Hitch-

150

cock's *The Birds* (1963) does not improve on the bleak framework of Kramarsky's film. Evan Hunter's script, however, leaves areas open and ends untied, conveying the cryptic quality that is Hitchcock's trademark. Stripped of these red herrings, *The Birds* is a simple fantasy, inferior to the Daphne Du Maurier story from which it is adapted. As in *War of the Worlds,* the setting has been shifted from England to America, and a love story imposed on the slim plot. Effects are again totally in charge, and while Hitchcock has built cleverly to his dramatic climaxes, in the end they show less imagination than those organised by directors of lesser reputation.

In its plot, *The Birds* is a smooth enough thriller. Tippi Hedren, a madcap heiress, falls for lawyer Rod Taylor, and, on impulse, drives to his home town of Bodega Bay for the weekend with a gift of two lovebirds. As the couple draw closer together during the visit, the birds of the area begin to turn against man. Hedren is pecked by a gull, and a children's party is broken up by a group of them. The next day a man is found pecked to death by gulls, and a flock of crows gathers to attack school children. Fleeing to Taylor's house, where he lives with his possessive mother and young sister, the four of them hide while the whole area is taken over by savage flocks of birds, until finally, battered and torn, they attempt an escape. Calmly the birds let them through.

A number of explanations have been offered of this film, but the real truth seems to be that no overall explanation is possible. *The Birds* merely goes further than most sf films in its contempt for motivation. We don't really believe that an atomic explosion could turn up a prehistoric monster, but it is offered as a token explanation and we accept it. Hitchcock and Hunter don't even bother with the token; the situation, with its inbuilt dramatic and poetic quality, is enough. While it is interesting to note that the birds destroy only those people who have no lasting emotional relationships, any comparison between the birds and the Eumenides, furies who wait to pounce on the lost soul, must fail for lack of evidence. More to the point, Hitchcock has suggested that the film is about the Day of Judgement; and certainly there is some comparison

151

between Hitchcock's vision and that of the New Testament. Even the cryptic conclusion fits in with the picture painted in Matthew XXIV 12–13 "And because iniquity shall abound, the love of many shall wax cold, But he that shall endure unto the end, the same shall be saved."

A heartening aspect of *The Birds* is Hitchcock's drawing of mankind's reaction to the disaster. Apart from the hysterical onslaught of the woman in the café who accuses Tippi Hedren of having brought Armageddon on them, human beings are shown as coping resourcefully and courageously with the attacks, a sharp contrast to the violence, greed and gibbering terror with which they greeted the Martians in *The War of the Worlds*. Since the Twenties, sf filmmakers have universally characterised mankind as responding to the threat of destruction with a return to savagery and it is refreshing to find a film in which some optimism is injected into the proceedings.

Rudolph Maté's *When Worlds Collide* (1951) shared this attitude, perhaps because the original novel by Philip Wylie and Edwin Balmer on which it was based had been published in the mid-Thirties, when many of sf film's *clichés* had not been established. DeMille was originally to have produced the film in 1934, but the project was shelved until George Pal dusted it off seventeen years later in the hope that it would prove as successful as his ambitious *Destination Moon*. Once again Pal poured money into a lush colour production, combining special effects with an intelligent script (Sydney Boehm) and remarkable colour photography. *When Worlds Collide* is in some ways an anachronism, presenting a Thirties vision of Armageddon, but the film's skill is incontestable.

In a deceptively simple opening, astronomers all over the world study mysterious movements among the stars. A young pilot (Richard Derr) is hired to fly a set of photographic plates from a South African observatory to one in the United States. Sensing that the plates contain some shattering information, he resourcefully bluffs himself into the confidence of the American astronomer, who reveals that the earth will shortly be destroyed by the impact of a

Preparing for flight: WHEN WORLDS COLLIDE

roving star, Bellus. Mankind's only hope is for a colonising group to land on Bellus's satellite Zyra, a planet fortuitously possessing climactic conditions similar to those of Earth.

The bulk of the film is concerned with preparations for the flight; building a ship with the millions donated by an embittered industrialist who asks only that he be allowed to go; choosing the crew; accumulating animals and supplies for use on Zyra. Boehm and Maté approach the human problems of the event with reasonable honesty, setting up a conflict for the astronomer's daughter (Barbara Rush) between the young pilot and another member of the group, then working out this parallel with the race to build the ship. Human reactions are recorded with some insight; the pilot lights his cigarette with money in a night club, the unsuccessful suitor leaves his rival stranded on the roof of a flooded house when they use a helicopter to rescue a child, but returns to pick him up after some brief soul-searching.

The approach of Bellus is a signal for a horde of special effects, including an eerie orange tone which bathes the entire film. The ship, built horizontally and designed to be launched on a giant roller coaster up the side of a mountain, glows like gold, while the sky is in perpetual sunset. Friction between the chief astronomer and rich industrialist builds up until, in a morally disreputable finale, the former sacrifices both the millionaire's life and his own so that the ship may take with it a larger, younger crew. While not free of the imputation that the human race would disintegrate under such pressure, *When Worlds Collide* offers a picture of world's end that is both logical and dramatically competent.

Exterior menaces, natural and otherwise, continued to pop up in sf cinema; in *The Day the World Exploded* the threat was a new element brought to the surface, by, predictably, atomic bomb experiments. Expanding and exploding on contact with air, it can be quenched by water, and mankind finally empties its dams into all the cracks of the world and puts the element out. Chemically foolish, the film is not saved by some suspenseful material in a dam powerhouse flooded with poison gas. Fred F. Sears showed his skill to greater advantage in *Earth v. the Flying Saucers* (1956), a tight and plausible little fantasy with excellent Ray Harryhausen effects, including some of the most genuinely convincing alien invaders ever engineered for the cinema, bulky silver automatons who project death rays from the handless ends of outstretched arms. A taped recording of an alien message plays an important part in the plot, and the final scenes of Hugh Marlowe and Joan Taylor trapped in a bunker, listening to the alien voice croaking on the running-down recorder, are moodily disturbing.

Superficially similar to *The Day the World Exploded*, John Sherwood's *The Monolith Monsters* (1957), from a Jack Arnold script, offered a far more atmospheric story and setting. Sherwood, an Arnold *protégé*, is clearly under the master's influence in this film, and much of the direction hints at the Creature cycle. Again the setting is the desert, the action occurring in and around a dusty desert town. An alien element carried to earth by a meteorite expands when touched by water, and can only be inhibited by salt.

Humans overcome by the material are turned literally to stone, and finally the expanded stone advances on the world in the form of crystalline monoliths that tilt, topple, shatter and spear upwards again.

Horror elements are plentiful and harsh; a shattered house, its splintered timbers inundated with glistening black rock and, among the ruins, a terrified and silent little girl; a man turned to stone who, when pushed, falls to the floor with a horrifying crash; faces illuminated by an X-ray plate of a child whose lungs and right arm are slowly being turned to stone. The phony backlot town is cleverly used with a dusty windstorm and some convincing night shots, while the brief cutaways to the meteorite crater at the bottom of which the alien rock seethes and bubbles as water floods in reflect Arnold's dark vision. While lacking the poetry of *It Came from Outer Space*, *The Monolith Monsters* is a worthy exercise in the tradition of desert fantasy and horror.

Despite the prevalence of natural onslaughts, it has always suited sf film-makers to dwell on the more immediate horrors of atomic war as a cause for the world's end. Part of the reason is technical; special effects are expensive and a film based on world war can make use of economical stock footage. But the idea of world self-destruction is one for which this melancholy and pessimistic field has always had a special attraction. The diminuendo of atomic annihilation offers opportunities for finales of considerable drama, and sf film has not been slow to make use of their poetry.

13. The Bomb, and After

EARTH DESTROYED by the actions of its inhabitants is an idea born of the atomic age, but its popularity with sf film-makers since 1945 shows that its values fit well into the *genre*. Atomic destruction embodies and concentrates one of basic sf themes, the threat of knowledge, and sf cinema has always preferred to accept only that part of the Atomic dilemma which bears on this idea. Few sf films deal with the peaceful uses of the atom, with simple radiation hazards, with mutation. Despite the cinematic potential of books like Lester del Rey's *Nerves,* no attempt has ever been made to transfer it or others like it to the screen. (An exception is the Russian *Nine Days in One Year.*) Sf film takes from a concept only what it needs, in this case the possibility not only of danger and destruction brought on by the accession of knowledge but the end of the world itself, a pessimistic vision of truly overwhelming proportions.

An early and hilarious indication of what Hollywood would do with the atom was released in 1946. *The Beginning or the End,* flatulently directed by Norman Taurog under the watchful eye of the U.S. Government, purported to show the origin of the Bomb and the decision which led to it being dropped on Hiroshima. With Joseph Calleia as Fermi and other well-known character actors playing the physicists and politicians involved, the film offered little information about either the Bomb or the people who made it. As a symbol of all the brass who organised the Manhattan District project, Brian Donlevy strides about pointing at unseen installations and saying "Put the cyclotron over there," but due to security requirements his part consists largely of montages of construction machinery and men peering intently at plans. Tom Drake is a doubtful young genius who thinks it should be Used For Peace, but nobody takes much notice of him. Of its many ludicrous scenes, perhaps the best is the fake newsreel that opens the film, in which a group of the film's "scientists" buries a time capsule under a sequoia, an event enlivened by the information that a copy of *The Beginning or the End* is inside. The actors look especially glum at the thought.

Film-makers were quick to see the possibilities of this new concept in the sf field. In 1951, Arch Oboler wrote, directed, designed and produced *Five,* an often laboured excursion into an After the Bomb world that, despite extensive errors of style and philosophy, has gained some critical eminence in France. *Five,* however, is still a film of power, and in its picture of a deserted world inhabited by five brawling survivors occasionally achieves remarkable impact.

Though tied to dialogue, a reflection of Oboler's radio background, *Five* shows some visual flair; the Frank Lloyd Wright house perched on a hill-top to which the refugees flee, a frightened trip into the corpse-choked city in search of a woman's husband, the lonely patch of corn that becomes the focus of their aspirations. *Five* is sometimes cinematically undistinguished, but its importance in the development of the cinema's attitude to atomic war is considerable. It revived the pessimistic mood which had pervaded *Paris Qui Dort* and other early fantasies. One was prepared for the worst when sf cinema considered the future of mankind.

Alfred E. Green was obviously influenced by *Five* in making *Invasion U.S.A.* (1952), one of the first pointed and specific stories of atomic war. Dismissed at the time of its release and forgotten today, the film is an interesting mirror of American attitudes of the period. Opening in a New York bar with a group of drinkers discussing the Cold War, it slides easily into a plotless catalogue of a possible Russian invasion beginning with a mass atomic attack. As the group disperses, its members die one by one in the war, either killed by the enemy or wiped out in the disasters they cause, like the destruction of Boulder Dam. As the last member is killed, falling in a screaming descent from the top of a skyscraper, it is revealed that It Was All A Dream, or, in this case, Mass Hypnosis. Chastened, the people vow to prepare for war, some by giving blood, others by retooling industry for munitions manufacture.

Relying heavily on stock footage of war and natural disasters, *Invasion U.S.A.* does nevertheless have a special topicality. One remembers the *ennui* of the bar, the flaccid discussion of conscription and world tension. Later, people line up at a desk to hear war news of distant areas and a disinterested officer tells families that their homes have been wiped out by a bomb, or occupied or burnt to the ground. The hypnosis device is specious, but by expanding the cross-section sample system of *Five*, Green gives the film enough pace to make its plot defects immaterial. As a mirror of its time, *Invasion U.S.A.* is a fascinating fossil.

John Mantley's allegorical novel *The Twenty Seventh Day* is an oddity of modern sf, and has been reprinted so often that, for some people, it must seem the most important science fiction work of its time. Columbia brought it to the screen in 1957 with William Asher directing a script written by Mantley himself, and with an interesting cast including Gene Barry and the talented George Voskovec. Lacking monsters and without an especially dramatic climax, the film made little impact, but it is not without merit in a field where simple directness of execution is rare.

In five separate locations across the earth, an alien gives an ordinary human being a box of capsules. Any capsule is capable of clearing a continent of human but not lower animal life, the charge responding only to the telepathic command of the person receiving the box. Nobody else can explode them. The gesture is the equivalent of giving a condemned man a loaded pistol; the aliens wish to take over earth but according to their moral code (!) cannot do so by direct aggression. Predictably each nation puts pressure on the recipients to let the capsules be used to wipe out their enemies, but the five, with more intelligence than sf characters are usually given credit for, know that this will mean the end of the world and the beginning of alien invasion. With great difficulty they hide out (Barry in a deserted racecourse) or resist temptation until Voskovec finds out the aliens' secret; it is all a test of Earth's maturity, which naturally it passes.

The plot has echoes of that old war-horse *The Most Dangerous Game*, filmed as *The Hounds of Zaroff* in 1932 and in various guises over the past twenty years. As in Richard Connell's story, people are chosen almost at random and told that their lives are to be forfeit if they do not find hidden qualities in themselves. In both cases they succeed, but it is curious that it should be a science fiction film that provides the most positive affirmation of this optimistic view. Unfortunately the unlikely elements of Mantley's story are carried on in his script, the hardest to accept being the finale in which the capsules kill selectively all the world's villains. "I know you'll find this hard to believe," an announcer accurately remarks, "But the capsules seem to have killed every enemy of human freedom." One

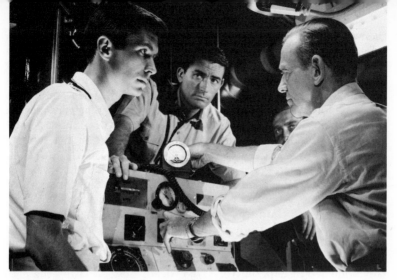

Atomic destruction: Anthony Perkins, Gregory Peck and Fred Astaire in ON THE BEACH

assumes it is only a coincidence that the President of the U.S.A. is not mentioned after this event.

None of these films grappled successfully with the basic reality of atomic war, being content to discuss the prospect in the detached terms of fantasy. Stanley Kramer's *On the Beach* (1959) declined any such assistance. Direct, prophetic, it stood or fell by the worth of its convictions. Like all Kramer's films, *On the Beach* is variable in style, its script sometimes over-written and marred by a tendency to reduce important issues to choices between black and white, but as an exercise in science fiction its worth is undoubted. There is no better film on the mood and feel of atomic destruction, no fable so relevant to our own time. Technically brilliant, this film is one of science fiction's legitimate masterpieces.

In 1964 the people of Australia listen in horror to the news of atomic war in the great continents of the world. Finally there is silence; radioactivity has wiped out the rest of humanity, and a tide of it creeps towards Australia, the last refuge of man. An American submarine arrives in Melbourne, captained by Dwight Towers (Gregory Peck) and reports that the world is dead, as Australia soon will be. After a brief stay, the submarine returns to America, following a phantom radio transmission that may mean a pocket of survivors. They explore the dead cities of America's West Coast, and discover the source of the signal, the random tapping of a morse key by a bottle caught in a window blind; the final, horrifying irrelevance.

Back in Australia people prepare for the end. Old friends draw closer together, new ones—Towers and his cynical lover Moira Davidson (Ava Gardner)—are haunted by the hopelessness of their lives. On the beach it is easy to watch the yachts and imagine that it is all a bad dream, but in town there is the reality of radiation sickness, the cold look of the doctors as they hand out packets of Government Prescription No. 24768—death pills to hasten the end. Finally Towers and his crew decide that it will be easier to die in the places they know best, and the sub sets off on its last voyage. From a headland Moira watches it go, alone on the last beach. Soon they are all dead. Papers blow in the empty streets, a brutal statue of "War The Destroying Warrior" spreads a bronze cloak over the city, and the wind flaps a revivalist's banner with its prophetic legend, "There Is Still Time."

Kramer's presentation of this apocalyptic sermon is immensely assured, aided by Giuseppe Rotunno's lambent photography. The Australian location with its hard sunlight and easy life is a chilling contrast to the reality of the situation. "Dogs go into a corner to die alone, ashamed," someone says. "But what do we do?" The film's focus on people involves us totally in the situation; Towers desperately breaking away from his ship, but drawn always back to the rigid naval life he has been used to; Moira enjoying with him the country pubs and squattocratic social life, yet conscious always of approaching doom, the young couple trying not to think of the moment when they must take the pill, and give one to their new-born child.

Even in its generally released 135-minute version, *On the Beach* is incomplete. Kramer's final cut was close to three hours but the financing company reduced it sharply, curtailing much of its message. The character of Swain, played by Australian actor John Meillon, has been trimmed to a detail, and only in his gesture of deserting ship in San Francisco to die where his parents died does he have an opportunity to display his talent. One scene remains, where he blandly sits in a boat fishing, then conducts a last conversation with the inquisitive periscope of the sub that pokes out of the water beside him, but many others were deleted, as were sequences of people preparing to die and the final shots of empty streets, of which only a handful remain. One will never know whether the longer version would have been more effective, but at 2¼ hours *On the Beach* is still a brilliant film and a moving document.

Lacking the sweep of *On the Beach*, Ranald MacDougall's *The World, the Flesh and the Devil* (1959) nevertheless succeeds in putting forward some intriguing speculation about a similar situation. As in *Five*, an atomic war has left only a few people alive in New York; a Negro miner (Harry Belafonte), a white girl (Inger Stevens), and the obligatory rotten apple, adventurer Mel Ferrer. Even after Ferrer's arrival, Stevens is willing to remain with Belafonte, but the white man can't face this and the two fight with rifles in the city's canyons until both realise the futility of it. In a final shot, the three walk off arm in arm and two cherished ideals of western society—monogamy and racial purity— disappear with the end title, heavily expressed as "The Beginning."

Despite the claim that this film is based on M. P. Shiel's 1901 *The Purple Cloud*, little of the story remains in MacDougall's blunt allegory on racial tensions, although visually there are sequences of great distinction. Belafonte's initial entry into the empty metropolis is morbidly beautiful, and it is hard to forget the wandering man poking along a deserted street pulling behind him a child's wagon loaded with provisions or his discovery by Inger Stevens asleep in an antique bed in a decorator's shop window. The final hunt too is magnificently staged, with the rivals perched high on the cornices of skyscrapers searching the streets for one another. When Ferrer pauses by the United Nations building, reads the biblical injunction about beating swords into ploughshares and throws down his gun, any unease about the scene's moral worth is obliterated by its splendid theatricality.

The boom in sf films during the early Sixties produced its share of unremarkable apprentice works from directors who later achieved some status in the field, including Roger Corman's *The Last Woman on Earth* (1960), a largely forgettable opus with Anthony Carbone as a gangster and Betsy Jones-Moreland as his wife who survive the atomic blast by being underwater, skin-diving, when it occurs. As enjoyable in its way as Corman's earlier exercise *The Day the World Ended* (1955), in which cardboard mutants pursue a group of survivors round a hidden valley, *The Last Woman on Earth* offers little that is new or thought-provoking either in style or content, although a later film, also made under American-International auspices, succeeds where earlier films failed in giving a bleakly credible picture of atomic war and its aftermath.

Based without credit on Ward Moore's short stories *Lot* and *Lot's Daughter*, *Panic in Year Zero* (1962) is a merciless appraisal of one man's reaction to a sneak atomic attack on America. Harry Baldwin (Ray Milland) has prepared himself well for the contingency, and reacts with the assurance of somebody who has known all along it would happen. Escaping into the hills with his family, dumpy wife, sexy daughter and brainless son, he sets about the business of surviving in a world where, he knows, the old ideals of humanity will be first casualties. The men who rape his daughter are mercilessly shot, his necessity to deny food and shelter to those less prepared for the war assumed without sentiment. *Panic in Year Zero* might almost be a manual for the bomb-shelter generation, a styleless and documentary exercise in the transfer of information on how to get along after the attack.

Inhuman and terse, *Panic in Year Zero* is basically a side-track, coming under the heading of sf through its subject matter but reflecting none of the comic-strip orientation or visual imagination of the field as a whole. It is interesting to see how the Russian Mikhail Romm, in his *Nine Days in One Year* (1961) explores yet another side-track without departing totally from the traditions, visual and intellectual, of the field. It is doubtful that Romm is familiar with the American product of the middle Fifties, but his film frequently echoes the work of Frankenheimer in its visual style. The ambience, however, is broadly Russian, and the film, a rich, compelling if slightly sentimental drama, belongs to that humanist tradition of which the Soviet film-makers are past masters.

Exposed to a large dose of radiation during an experiment, physicist Dmitri Gusev (Alexei Batalov) must face the prospect of a lingering death. His wife (Tamara Lavrova) and best friend (Innokenty Smuktonovsky) draw closer together to help him, but the

Russian approach: Alexei Batalov in NINE DAYS IN ONE YEAR

situation is one Gusev must solve himself. Should he continue with his work and risk the second dose of radiation that will almost certainly kill him, or should he settle down with his wife and the safe job offered by his friend Ilya? A visit to his old home village and endless discussions with Ilya and his wife do not really bear on the central problem, which is a personal one. Finally Gusev continues with his experiments, suffers the inevitable second accident, and is told he cannot hope to survive. The only possible chance is an operation hitherto performed only on dogs, and unsuccessful with them most of the time. As he submits to it, we are left waiting to hear whether he will live or die.

As drama, *Nine Days in One Year* is moving and restrained, full of people whom one instinctively likes because of their warts-and-all characterisation: Smuktunovsky, bright, cynical but likeable as the scientist opting for the freedom of journalism; Lavrova plump and pleasant as Gusev's wife, emotional but always thinking hard; Batalov in a diamond sharp performance as the often tedious, always convincing Gusev, wanting to be human but not really believing that a happy marriage is more important than his experiments. The story is set in a research station superbly designed by G. Koltchanov, no asceptic temple of science but a crowded, workmanlike bunker with narrow concrete tunnels connecting laboratories jammed with formidable machines. English subtitling occasionally makes nonsense of Romm's dialogue—the triumphant scientists burst out after a successful experiment with the cry, "Hurrah! Neutrons!"—but the script in general explores perceptively the complexities of a world where technology and humanism have not yet found a meeting point.

Nine Days in One Year is typical of the sf films of the Sixties in that it frees itself of most familiar visual traditions of sf film without abandoning its attitudes. Science is still shown as something alien, slightly threatening to basic human values and certainly not a force with which ordinary people can come to terms. It became common to set parables on atomic war in situations that would elevate them above the tradition of sf film, as if in this way the film-makers could separate themselves from the disreputable connotations of "science fiction," but even *On the Beach,* the most serious of all these films, did not wholly escape from the old traditions. The empty streets of the climax may be good cinema, but anybody who has seen sf films will recognise the sequence as a commonplace of the field.

In *The Day the Earth Caught Fire* (1962), Val Guest and Wolf Mankowitz created a script in which, showing the effects of nuclear delinquency reflected in the activities of a large British newspaper, they hoped to appeal directly to the public and escape sf's catchpenny connotations. This time the subject of censure is atomic testing, a hot topic at the time but *passé* today. By coincidence, both the British and the Russians detonate giant bombs at the same time, and the Earth is pushed out of orbit on a long fall into the sun. As the world goes wild with tidal waves, earthquakes and, in London, unseasonal variations of temperature, the staff of the *Daily Express* struggles to uncover the facts and report them. In the final sequence the world has united to explode four more bombs that, hopefully, will push the Earth back into place; in the newspaper office the camera, recalling *Citizen Kane,* pans over two headlines awaiting publication—*Earth Saved* and *Earth Doomed.* We are left wondering which will grace the Armageddon edition.

In common with *On the Beach, The Day the Earth Caught Fire* shows destruction reflected in people rather than in special effects, and as such derives directly from the European tradition of sf. Apart from the low-key sequences tinted a seedy yellow to indicate the oppressive heat, little effort is made to describe the effects of the cataclysm, and the meagre attempts at spectacle, like a sudden fog boiling up the Thames, have limited impact. More apt is the casting of ex-*Daily Express* editor Arthur Christiansen as himself; despite indifferent diction he is convincing as the man who holds the 'paper together during the crisis, a superb symbol of British constancy and vigour. One remembers his burst of anger at incompetence on the part of reporter Edward Judd, his bulldog drive in dragging admissions from a close-lipped civil servant, the meaningful tone of voice as, after hearing of a first step in the crumbling of English society, he briefly sets the team to work, then quietly directs the switch girl, "Get me my home." Yet for all this, *The Day the Earth Caught Fire* cannot escape its beginnings; the hero and heroine still, after initial antipathy, draw together under the common threat; the crowds still go rampaging through the streets intent on rape and plunder; and there is another of those speeches, delivered this time by a well-cast Leo McKern as a more-cynical-than-thou newsman, in which he suggests "There are some things Man is not meant to know." *Plus ça change. . . .*

By the middle Sixties the atomic war theme had almost petered out. After Cuba the west ceased to believe that mutual destruction was a genuine threat, and Vietnam assumed the mantle of mankind's focus of conscience. The period did, however, produce two films that, although superficially dissimilar, represent a common view of human self-destruction. Stanley Kubrick's *Doctor Strangelove Or How I Learned To Stop Worrying and Love the Bomb*

Nightmare comedy of self-destruction . . .

(1963) portrayed the prospect in terms of "nightmare comedy," while Peter Watkins's documentary-oriented *The War Game* (1966) showed it as a potential reality hovering in the limbo of tomorrow's TV news. Both films, despite high ideals, failed to make any coherent point, but their significance in the decay of an sf theme is considerable.

Scott Fitzgerald once defined personality as "an unbroken series of successful gestures," and it is in this way that both films are best seen. Devoid of any real intellectual consistency, they present instead a string of vignettes, set-pieces and visual poems on atomic war and the negation of human hopes and qualities. Kubrick's system is that of comedy, and his exposition, based mainly on the humour of incongruity, is often grimly amusing. It is hard not to laugh at colonels and generals acting against image as if they were spoilt children, at an ineffectual American President seeking his Russian opposite number from love nest to love nest while the prospect of atomic war draws nearer, at a stetsoned pilot riding an

. . . Kubrick's DOCTOR STRANGELOVE

atom bomb down with the "yahoos" of a rodeo performer. Watkins, on the other hand, offers a series of special effects whose reality eclipses most of our intellectual objections. His gritty black-and-white evocation of an atomic attack on Britain is often horrifying; raging fire storms, the glare and concussion of the bomb; torment and slow death from radiation; mass cremations and buckets of wedding rings. Yet in the final analysis each film is largely a series of gestures, not all successful and not all appropriate. Neither film, despite the intentions of its maker, has any more content than an episode of *Buck Rogers*.

The notoriety earned by both films at the time of their release obscured many of their drawbacks. *Doctor Strangelove* disturbed many with its juxtapositions of Vera Lynn songs and scenes of jet bombers refuelling like copulating metal insects, and with Peter Sellers's grotesque characterisation of idiot president Murphy Muffley and sinister Doctor Strangelove, not to mention its irreverent approach to the subject. Watkins, faced with B.B.C. unwillingness to telecast his film, finally saw it released theatrically by the British Film Institute long after its initial impact had dissipated. It is debatable whether the B.B.C. was justified in refusing to show the film, although the move was one which had the sympathy of most B.B.C. personnel, even Watkins's contemporaries on the editing and directing staff at the time of production. The most explicit violence is still, when shown on the television screen, basically unreal, and one doubts that public response would have been the horror and panic which was suggested at that time. In the fuss, however, few people stopped to point out that Watkins's film is deficient both in concept and style.

The War Game was the end of the atomic war cycle. The final hellfire sermon had been delivered, the peak of special effects recreation reached. Significantly, both Kubrick and Watkins moved on not to other areas of committed cinema but into science fiction, Kubrick to the extravagance of *2001: A Space Odyssey*, Watkins to the social sf of *Privilege* and *The Gladiators*. Apart from pale carbons like *Fail Safe* (1965), the field of atomic war films faded away,

Peter Watkins directing THE WAR GAME

to be replaced by productions reflecting the predilections of a decade more concerned with the war between mental independence
and physical necessity than with ideological questions. Racial suicide was a dead letter, although the films that it produced are re-
minders of a period during which the western world struggled
without success to act out its ideals on the public stage.

Pal and Haskin's ROBINSON CRUSOE ON MARS

14. Renaissance in 2001

THE TIME OF INVOLVEMENT with the problems of the world passed for science fiction film with almost indecent haste. This type of material was never really the point, a fact which soon dawned on producers as they peered into the crystal ball of the box-office returns. For a few years some film-makers inserted a half-hearted mention of racial suicide or the threat of The Bomb, but their hearts were not in it. Science fiction film, they realised, was primarily a field of fantasy, and emboldened by this knowledge they pressed on along the road originally taken by *Destination Moon*.

One of the best of the Sixties films came from the same team that had produced *Destination Moon*. In planning *Robinson Crusoe on Mars* (1964), producer George Pal and director Byron Haskin were not backward about covering again the same ground as their first success, especially since now there was an opportunity to improve on their early model. After the Arnold films, the entire world had, in a sense, become a sound stage. Environment could be framed in such a way that it appeared alien, a fact immediately grasped by Haskin who chose as his setting the eroded nightmare of Death Valley. Grimly like the Mars of more pessimistic theorists, the area is invested by Haskin with his own special effects skill. Falsifying little, he dots the landscape with props and situations that give Earth the mood of another world.

Under a pumpkin-coloured Martian sky, astronaut Paul Mantee struggles to survive after the ship which has landed him on Mars is destroyed along with his partner. His only companion is a tiny monkey, though in nightmares his dead friend (Adam West) returns to bestride the tiny cave in which he now lives. Months later, aliens land on Mars, bringing with them humanoid slaves, one of whom Mantee rescues and makes his friend. Now life can go on until he is rescued, though first they must make a harrowing journey to the ice cap to escape the pursuing aliens.

Haskin's use of his setting is superb. The knife-edge ridges of the valley provide a remarkable background to Mantee's fight for life, and the flat valley floor with soaring mountains behind is the location for one of his most convincing scenes. As the astronaut labours to construct an arrow of stones indicating the direction of his journey, a tiny automatic scanner with a binocular gadget on top revolves gravely beside him, technology constantly on the lookout for the creature round the corner. Influenced by Haskin's use of Death Valley, John Sturges used the same location, not to mention a similar story of astronauts stranded on the surface of the Moon after an unsuccessful space flight, in *Marooned* (1969), a film which in the extravagance of equipment and breadth of budget eclipsed Pal's pioneer effort.

Natural locations again assisted *Planet of the Apes* (1967), a confused reading by Franklin Schaffner of Pierre Boulle's symbolic novel *Monkey Planet*. Scriptwriter Rod Serling, veteran of TV's *The Twilight Zone*, did his best with the book (script credit is shared with Michael Wilson), replacing some of its more laboured allegories with tight dramatic situations and action sequences. Nothing, however, can hide the book's overdone parody. The idea of a world where apes have evolved into an intelligent society and where humans are hunted or enslaved belongs properly with Capek and other social satirists, and is therefore outside sf film's orbit. But Schaffner tries valiantly, and occasionally succeeds. The space ship crash-landing in a blue mountain lake is shot with skimming helicopter shots intercut with frenzied close-ups, while the hunt of human beings by gorillas on horseback is crisply done, underlined by Jerry Goldsmith's growling score. Otherwise the acting is feeble, competent people like Kim Hunter reduced by monkey make-up to mugging and nose-wrinkling, and Charlton Heston's antics giving little indication that he is more than the animal the apes take him for. *Planet of the Apes* is an apt indication of how wrong Hollywood can go when it attempts to combine sf film too closely with any part of visionary literature, parody, satire or science fiction itself.

Extending the premise underlying both *Robinson Crusoe on Mars* and *Planet of the Apes*, that sf film draws its best effects from the

172

relationship between characters and setting, Richard Fleischer's *Fantastic Voyage* (1966) placed a group of "miniaturised" explorers inside the human body, speeding by tiny submarine through the blood stream to wipe out a dangerous lesion in the brain of an atomic scientist. Fleischer, who had created in *20,000 Leagues Under the Sea* (1955) one of fantasy's finest underwater adventures, struggled to achieve something with his plot, but it was apparent that the story rested too solidly on the *cliché* situations of filmic space opera. As in so many other films, the crew has its intrepid captain (Stephen Boyd), sweating villain (Donald Pleasence), and pneumatic cutie (Raquel Welch). The hand of noted sf writer and biochemist Isaac Asimov, who contributed to the script, is less in evidence than that of magazine veteran Jerome Bixby, on whose story the film is based, though its most remarkable scenes spring, as do those of many other modern sf films, from the genius of the set designer. Model sets like the white vaulted cathedral of the heart and the veiled jungle that is the scientist's brain touch, however lightly, the core of wonder that draws us back time after time to fantasy.

Among the brightly coloured and expensively mounted sf films of the Sixties, those less extravagant in sets and slightly lacking in opulence tended to be lost, a fate that befell the most penetrating of all the Pal/Haskin collaborations, *The Power* (1967). Based on Frank M. Robinson's novel published in the Fifties, the film is one of the finest of all sf films, a tightly wound thriller that comes close on occasions to combining the optimism of science fiction with the pragmatism of the cinema, a fact all the more surprising for the film's story, an almost routine thriller of a hunt among scientists at a research institute for the malevolent supermind Adam Hart who is determined to kill them all. As researcher George Hamilton finds his past wiped clean item by item, his name erased from college records, his very existence threatened by the cold mind which hunts him as he hunts it, we sense the horror of alienation which directors like Antonioni have pointed to in the abstract as a symptom of our age's malaise.

173

Bound tightly together by Miklos Rozsa's clever music score, with its echoes of Dvorak's chamber music and recurring motif of the zimbalom, *The Power* gains from an inventive script (John Gay) and performances of remarkable integrity by Hamilton, Suzanne Pleshette, and Nehemiah Persoff as an untidy assistant in the hunt, a role that ends bizarrely in a disordered hotel room after an all-night party. Having struggled to stay awake and stave off mental attack by Hart, all three have gone to sleep. A girl, beginning a strip tease to get the party going again, kisses the sleeping Persoff, then in the middle of the caress stops, screams and jumps back, leaving a red splotch of lipstick on the mouth of the man who, during the night, has had his life snuffed out by the telepath.

Throughout the film, death lurks in the most prosaic locations. Hamilton and Persoff fight desperately in a kitchen, struggling among the suds of an overturned dishwasher, using a glowing hot plate as a weapon, the light of an open refrigerator as illumination. Arthur O'Connell finds himself trapped in an office where the doors have suddenly melted into the wall. And in a penny arcade Hamilton is hounded onto a carousel that whirls to collapse with him clinging to the frantically galloping horses. One admits the plot faults of this remarkable film without once denying its substantial status as fantasy and cinema.

Across the contemporary field groups of films occur like patches of lichen, spreading out from a central focus until the edges blur into other colonies. One such patch is that born of Walt Disney's belated realisation that sf film tapped the same spring of gadget mania as the popular science magazines. Combining his special brand of sinister Americana with routine sf gadget plots, Disney created a viable if short-lived field of his own with films like *Moon Pilot* (1961), *The Absent-Minded Professor* (1961), its sequel *Son of Flubber* (1962) and *The Misadventures of Merlin Jones* (1963). Most showed backyard inventors knocking up, in true Edison

Opposite: top left, THE FANTASTIC VOYAGE; top right, George Hamilton clings to the carousel in THE POWER; below, Charlton Heston on the PLANET OF THE APES

fashion, a new gadget that, after a great deal of polite incredulity from the authorities, vindicates its maker by helping the home team win the college football final or the young scientist his 'teenage sweetheart. Disney plugged rural virtue, individual initiative, modest civic disobedience tempered by a belief in basic human rights, and a healthy scepticism about the value of organised education. The films set learning back twenty-five years without, unfortunately, advocating any of the more pleasurable aspects of ignorance.

A second group of films, more vital, ambitious and cinematically important, sprang again from the ideas of one man, director John Frankenheimer, whose work in the American cinema has marked him as its most important talent of the Sixties. Always fascinated by machines—he had originally wanted to be a racing driver and entered film through the sharply technological world of live TV—Frankenheimer's films express a belief in technology as the most important force in modern life, and a willingness to accept the fact rather than, as other directors have done, fight science as a dehumanising inflluence. In *The Train* (1964) and *Grand Prix* (1966) this preoccupation had its most general and commercial expression, though it is apparent at its clearest in *Seconds* (1966), *The Manchurian Candidate* (1962) and *Seven Days in May* (1964).

By any standard, all three films fall neatly into place as science fiction, showing vulnerable Man eyeball to eyeball with science, the weak being defeated by it, the strong using it to order the world or enlarge their lives. In *The Manchurian Candidate* Chinese scientists plant a brainwashed dupe in the United States, programmed to assassinate the President-elect, but the plan is foiled when the man, awakened to his role, rebels. Another protagonist in *Seven Days in May,* committed by tradition and inclination to a course of action that will result in a military overthrow of the United States government, defies the mighty machine of the U.S. Army and is able to defeat it. And even the poor hero of *Seconds,* embracing the scientific plan that will remake him as a younger, fuller man, instinctively rejects its oiled efficiency and goes, albeit

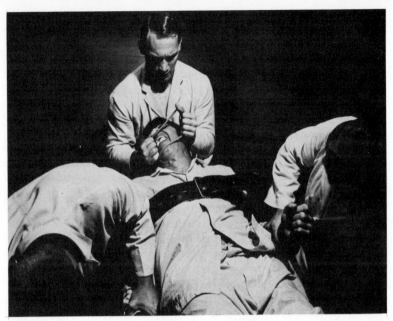

The final outcome: Rock Hudson in SECONDS

unwillingly, to death rather than deny his real self. In no film does science, technology or order appear as a universal panacea, but a belief in the final triumph of "white" science is implicit in all three.

Presenting his thesis, Frankenheimer makes skilled use of technology's outside signs and symbols. One is always aware in his productions of the technological "frame" in which we all exist. In both *Seven Days in May* and *The Manchurian Candidate* television monitors turn a grey unwinking gaze on every action: the Pentagon is littered with them, repeating images along silent corridors, reflecting the suspicious, disturbed nature of life among the technological wizards, and when James Gregory assails the government at a press conference in *The Manchurian Candidate* his image looms on a foreground screen, dramatising his unreal, puppet personality. Martin Balsam in *Seven Days in May* bobs along in a tiny boat, dwarfed by the mountain of an aircraft carrier: Senator Edmond O'Brien is stopped in the desert by a helicopter which, after alighting like an iron dragonfly, frames him in its fretted tail vane as cryptic guards hold him at gunpoint. The machines are all around us. We must gain their trust or die.

While such unlikely luminaries as Disney and Frankenheimer shed considerable light over the sf film scene, earlier talents waned. Roger Corman, key figure of the Fifties, committed himself during the Sixties to the picturesque and the profound, using a science fictional detachment to examine processes like war *(The Secret Invasion)* and crime *(The St. Valentine's Day Massacre)*. His studio, American International, continued however to involve itself in sf as part of the spectrum of fantasy on which its empire is based. Sensing the value of using antique properties as a departure point into more personal worlds of fantasy A. I. filmed Lovecraft *(The House at the End of the World)* and such lesser known works of Poe as *The City beneath the Sea*, a poem which Jacques Tourneur turned into a sub-Atlantis fantasy starring Vincent Price. Few of these films had value as sf. The real sleeper of A. I.'s output, however, was a film which combined sf with another of the studio's specialties, the 'teenage sex musical, in a one-off collage of sensuality, revolution and mad humour.

Barry Shear's *Wild in the Streets* (1968) arrived providentially for its producers at a time when both the public and the critics were disposed to be attentive to the voice of revolution. Civil unrest, assassination, the fall of the Johnson *régime* and world-wide strife had encouraged a cynical disbelief in political solutions. Everybody was ready for a gallows joke about the American power structure, and *Wild in the Streets* was assured of success. The plot is incredible. Max Frost (Christopher Jones), a young pop star, lends his support to a Kennedy-style senator in California, wins the election for him and demands as his price the lowering of the voting age to fourteen. They compromise on eighteen, but once their foot is in the door Frost and his group take over the country. Everybody over thirty-five is put on a funny farm high on L.S.D., the 'teens and 'twenties enter into a paradise of content and fulfilment. But for how long? As the film ends the sub-'teens are muttering, galled by a new and just as irksome control. Another revolution is just around the corner.

Critics who suggested that this plot could be taken seriously were lamentably wide of the mark, but as in most sf film *Wild in the Streets* did contain a genuine social relevance on a symbolic level. Shear and writer Robert Thom, mainstay of the excellent TV series *The Invaders* (1968), contrived to dramatise the new structure of American society, the shift of power that had made young people more competent to cope with the realities of life and extract from it the most exquisite pleasures. The film's young people revel in simple hedonism, opt always for the emotional solution. The pop star who makes love to his mistress (Diane Varsi) while the TV announces his political victory, protests in the only way he knows after his followers are shot down during a demonstration, moving from between the white funereal pillars of a stage set to sing on television a sinister pop song about "The Shape of Things To Come" ("There's a new sun/Risin' up angry in the sky . . . "). The fact that Shear's film is confident about the worth of the 'teenage ethic is not really relevant. When Max says simply about his tiny daughter, "They're better than we are," we sense that this is an expression of a new but valid morality, but it is also obvious that such feelings are less important to him than the urge to fight, dance, make love and go naked in the world. Anti-sf in every way, *Wild in the Streets* remains for all its fantasy an interesting essay on human motivation.

Although Roger Corman occupied himself mainly with Poe in the early Sixties, in 1963 he made a rare excursion into sf in what was probably a trial balloon for more ambitious social dramas like *The Trip*. *The Man with X-Ray Eyes* is a weird, flawed film, but a splendid grotesque. As Dr. Xavier (pronounced Ex-avier), a surgeon who uses drugs to develop X-Ray vision and thus operate better, Ray Milland portrays with some skill the agony of a man physically and mentally tortured. As his gift leads to an agonising necrosis of the eyes, he is forced to do a mental act at a circus, to be a professional gambler, and finally to appear in a slum basement as a "faith healer." Pursued by the police, he escapes into the desert and staggers into a tent show revival meeting where evangelist John Dierkes exhorts his audience, "If thy eye offend thee, pluck it out." Turning his blind eyes, rotted to a silver black, up to the man, Milland tears them out.

Corman's variation on basic sf themes is audacious. As usual the scientist seeking knowledge is betrayed by his discovery. "Only the Gods see everything," a colleague remarks, but Milland rejects this, saying he is "pushing the Gods fairly close." Traditionally such hubris is punishable by death, and Milland's fate is consistently brutal. Corman frequently raises the question of scientific responsibility, with the carnival people suggesting that Milland should help people with his skill. However, when he becomes a "healer" he cannot heal, merely advise; knowledge by itself is useless. Perhaps the Foundation which sacks him and the doctor who wants him charged with malpractice are right. Using colour to odd effect, Corman continually refers us to supernatural sources. Milland stares into space with his super-sensitive eyes and sees a flaring world of crimson and gold, to him the image of some mad God. Perhaps he is right, or perhaps they are only suns blazing in the dark. Either way, we are conscious more than in any other contemporary sf film of the morality play which is a key ancestor of the field.

Corman's film was, despite its novelty of subject, easily identifiable as sf film. The elements were the same as a hundred other films, the shadow of *Homonculus* and *Metropolis* apparent over many of its situations. The same can be said of most other sf films of the period, though on certain notable occasions the film-makers involved in outlining the fantastic found it possible to reject the traditions, and thus moved into areas that belonged properly to other fields. As *Planet of the Apes* took sf film into areas of social satire, so Stanley Kubrick's *2001: A Space Odyssey* (1968) experimented with space-age documentary, creating by the meticulously professional use of special effects an artificial world more real and more impressive than anything previously devised.

Alarmingly simple as to plot, Kubrick's film aims above all else to create the world of 2001. After a long and fragmentary sequence showing the growth of human intelligence, a process accelerated by the appearance among primitive ape men of a black slab of stone that boosts their intelligence, we are flung head first into the Twenty-first century. White space ships whirl against the stars, rendezvous-ing with drifting space stations and decanting passengers into an asceptic world of clinical plastic, colour TV phones and Howard Johnson restaurants, 2001 style. One passenger, William Sylvester, guardedly fends off queries from Russian colleagues about trouble at the American moon base and presses on there, to investigate the discovery of an ancient monolith buried beneath the moon's surface millions of years ago, an artifact identical to that which prodded the ape men into intelligence.

Abruptly we are years further into the future. Two astronauts (Gary Lockwood and Keir Dullea) pilot a vast white ship towards Jupiter, mission undisclosed. On board are further crew members, frozen until required. Fighting boredom, the caretakers jog through a routine of exercise, maintenance, television. Occasionally they play chess with HAL, the soft-voiced computer, a character which assumes sinister significance when it appears to report wrongly on a system malfunction. Soon HAL becomes irrational, killing Lockwood and the frozen crew. Dullea, however, is able to switch the machine off. One of its last acts is to advise him that he has been sent to Jupiter to investigate the possibility that the monoliths emanate from there. A mental contact is made with a race on Jupiter, and after a mind-bending brainstorm, Dullea finds himself confined to a luxurious apartment in which he lives out the rest of his days. Dying, he is transformed into a child, humanoid but not human. In the last shot, the child hangs in space, contemplating Earth turning beneath it. The new millenium begins.

Keir Dullea as an astronaut in 2001: A SPACE ODYSSEY

This story, it might be noted, bears even less serious study than *Red Planet Mars*. Respected sf writer Arthur C. Clarke, who wrote the script and of whose novel *Childhood's End* and short story *The Sentinel* much of the film is reminiscent, seems to have had little to do with it after shooting began in 1966, a fact that is obvious from the muddled development of ideas like the monolith. Originally the monolith during its first appearance had been a vision screen on which an alien demonstrated to the ape men how they might use weapons to kill animals for food. Similarly, when the monolith on the Moon gave off its deafening shriek, it was established that this had been a high-intensity radio emission directed towards Jupiter, a fact that induced Earth to send off its expedition. This fact, not revealed in the release print until the end of the journey, gave dramatic relevance to the otherwise meaningless journey. Additionally, the monolith in the original story did not appear again. When Dullea arrived among the moons of Saturn he found, not the floating monolith of the film, but a gargantuan version of the object that acted as a "star gate." Entering this, he was projected into the fantastic world of the climax.

The film suffers as well from Kubrick's further tampering with the cutting. After first preview screenings, he removed twenty minutes, muddling portions of the Jupiter voyage. In the original, astronaut Lockwood was sent whirling, alive but out of control, into space, was rescued by Dullea but then killed by the machine. Reports on the film-making mention a sequence in which Lockwood is crushed inside his space suit and bleeds horribly to death, but these are no longer seen. When Dullea retrieves the body, it is still struggling, but we are led to believe that he is nevertheless dead. The effect, to say the least, is confusing.

All this said, it must be admitted that *2001: A Space Odyssey* is in many ways an impressive artistic and technical achievement. A vital component of this success is Kubrick's brilliant choice of music. From the opening, with sunrise over a black world heralded by the "Dawn" passage of Richard Strauss's *Also sprach Zarathustra,* the film's soundtrack exercises a spell over the viewer, complemented by memorable images. Shot with the "front projection" system pioneered by sf writer Murray Leinster, background scenes in the form of huge glass transparencies projected to simulate exteriors, the scenes of the Dawn of Man are weirdly real: apes cowering in the dark as beasts howl, a leopard, its eyes glinting violet as it prowls by, then the appearance of the monolith and a triumphant primate orgiastically smashing a skeleton as he discovers the tool.

From the moment when Kubrick shock-cuts from the bone, flung into the air, to a shot of a slim white space ship whirling in orbit around Earth, we can be fairly certain that this film is about the technology which both items represent. As Kubrick develops his thesis, we see that it is technology and the concepts of the tool which is his subject. HAL is a tool, just as the bone was, and like the bone, it was only as good as the man who used it. When HAL malfunctions, the men are forced back on other resources, a fact that Kubrick seems to greet with some pleasure. HAL takes the tool as far as it can go. When it fails, man must find another answer, and Dullea does, moving on as a "star child" to another level of existence for both he and the human race.

Kubrick's use of the "Blue Danube Waltz" over scenes of space ship docking is superbly chosen. Nothing could so perfectly suggest the undramatic acceptance of space travel, an event so commonplace that some lyricism is possible instead of spectacle. Georgy Ligeti's quivering choral works also exercise a subtle effect over scenes of the monolith's appearance, while the drab, depressing sound of Katchatchurian's "Gayeneh" underlines the meaningless drudgery of life aboard the Jupiter ship. It is the opening sequence, however, for which the music is most perfectly chosen. The blasting shout of the orchestra, evoking the joy of the philosopher on contemplating the dawn, conveys the splendour of space and the exaltation of travel in it with overwhelming grandeur.

One of the sources for Kubrick's ideas is obviously the National Film Board of Canada's brilliant documentary *Universe*, in which the special effects department of the N.F.B.C. created planetary scenes of miraculous reality. Kubrick had originally wanted the same team of Colin Low, Sidney Goldsmith and Wally Gentleman to work on the film, and Gentleman did begin preliminary work, though finally the effects were created by Douglas Trumbull, twenty-five-year-old expert in space documentary, with veteran effects men Wally Veevers, Con Pederson and Tom Howard. Many of the effects do, however, depend heavily on the work of Low and his team in Montreal, notably the "mind storm" sequence in which Kubrick's group adapted the basic Canadian idea of counterfeiting enormous scenes by shooting tiny objects with powerful lenses. Starbursts and nebular movements were achieved by focusing on drops of dye moving on glass, or reflections on a tiny portion of revolving metal. Kubrick also rejected the traditional travelling matte process work, for so long a pillar of sf film. Although some mattes are used, most of the scenes that required tiny inset shots of live action over models —the landing of the space ship on the Moon, for instance, with crew members and landing team visible right across the screen—were achieved with 16mm projectors mounted inside the models.

2001: A Space Odyssey is more sf than sf film, stressing the beauty of natural order and technology. Kubrick has conveyed much of Clarke's mysticism, ignoring plot and character in order to evoke

The emergency return: 2001: A SPACE ODYSSEY

the beauty of science and its creations. As Damon Knight has said, "With Clarke, the real protagonist is time," an observation the truth of which is reflected in the film's fragmentary structure. To Clarke, it is no strain to leap a million years in an instant, but in translating this approach to the screen Kubrick has not realised that film is less precise a medium. When he leaps, most of us are well behind him, and as the film goes on we become less and less concerned with overall themes. The show is beautiful, the music superb, but somewhere along the way the point has been forgotten.

With *2001: A Space Odyssey*, science fiction came as close as it could to an alliance with sf film. Whether by instinct or design, Kubrick and Clarke had found a plot device that combined the positive attitude of science fiction with the negative attitude of sf film. They had set the particularising mood of film in the visionary sweep of literature, the mythopoetic basis of sf film in the rigidly real world of Clarke's space fiction. But despite this superficial combination, the tension is still there. One doubts that it can ever be otherwise when too dissimilar fields, for better or worse, are nailed together.

185

15. A Note on SF for Television

A GREAT DEAL OF NONSENSE has been written about sf on television, most of it resembling the stock criticisms of sf cinema. "Inaccurate," "immature," and "illogical" are words frequently used, and it is probably not necessary to reiterate that all three are inappropriate in a field where accuracy, maturity and logic have no place. Potentially, television is an ideal medium for sf—unlike the hard blacks of horror film, sf's glossy greys transfer well to the "cool" television image—but it has seldom been used successfully in this regard.

The basic problem is one of caution on the part of producers. Science fiction is a proven second-line money-maker in the cinema, but its commercial possibilities in TV have always been uncertain. Producers, therefore, always hedge their bets when it comes to sf; no show is put out unless it contains, in addition to its sf elements, a selection gleaned from some other field. Some producers add gratuitous "monsters" from the horror film, others a few situations from family comedy, while a third may push an "educational" angle by including technical surveys or historical "flashbacks." Add to this the fact that sf, by virtue of its plot-oriented approach, lends itself best to the anthology programme, a complex and often unpopular form in TV, and one need not be surprised that science fiction's history in this medium has been a stormy one.

Apart from such primitive efforts as *Captain Video* and *Superman*—TV, like the cinema, used the comics as a departure point—little intelligent sf television was attempted before the early Fifties. The best pioneer efforts were those produced in Britain by the B.B.C. between 1953 and 1960, mainly Nigel Kneale's *The Quatermass Experiment, Quatermass II* and *Quatermass and the Pit*. These three six-part serials provided the first indication that sf could be transferred successfully from cinema to TV. Skilfully combining elements of the horror and sf cinema, Kneale used the medium to create new variations on the old traditions.

Dr. Bernard Quatermass is a scientific genius continually at war with the forces of reaction and order, powers which he succeeds in overthrowing each time only after a superior effort of will. In each serial Britain is faced with a threat of invasion from outer space; in each, despite official scepticism, Quatermass defeats the invaders. There is little difference between the plots, but Kneale is a good enough writer to re-use the themes without excessive repetition. By clever alternation of locales, he succeeds in creating three works which, in mood and feel, differ completely.

As each of the serials was later filmed—*The Quatermass Experiment* (or *The Creeping Unknown*), *Quatermass II* (or *Enemy from Space*), and *Quatermass and the Pit* (or *Fifty Million Years to Earth*)—the significance of their plots has been discussed elsewhere. It is worth however, recognising Kneale's inspired use of the TV medium. In *Quatermass and the Pit*, the setting of a London archaeological excavation is especially brilliant; despite the quality of Roy Ward Baker's film, Kneale's television version is still an eerie classic.

British television, though more adventurous in its programming of sf, has so far achieved little of merit. The two serials *A for Andromeda* and *The Andromeda Breakthrough* conveyed cosmologist-novelist Fred Hoyle's high-powered variation on the Quatermass prototype with limited subtlety. Hoyle's hero may have railed more violently against the establishment which refused to believe that his machine had manufactured a beautiful android on directions received from M31 in Andromeda, but basically his predicament was the same. If the Hoyle serials succeeded, it was in their acting— Mary Morris was an inspired choice for a crusty, brilliant physicist, a young and mute Julie Christie meltingly right for the android girl—and in the incidental gadgetry. The computers chattering out rolls of printed paper and Jodrell Bank's prowling antenna contributed a lot to a Sixties vision of Britain as a scientific power.

Since the *Andromeda* serials, nothing of real interest has been done in Britain. The anthology programme *Out of the Unknown* (1966) differed from others produced in the U.S.A. only in that many British short stories were used as subject matter, while the long-running B.B.C. serial *Doctor Who*, after a promising start, degenerated sharply into repetition and clumsy melodrama. One wishes that this programme could have held to its original high quality, retaining the brilliance of imagination that produced creatures like the Zarbi, ant-like monsters that preyed on humanoid butterflies in an Aubrey Beardsley catacomb of *art nouveau* screens. Unfortunately, the success of the Daleks, dustbin robots with cleverly engineered "mechanical" voices, drew the producers into endless consideration of other corrupt robot societies, and the series collapsed.

Despite this, *Doctor Who* remains a good example of what may be done with limited facilities if a producer has imagination. The Zarbi and the Daleks were flashily interesting, but far more compelling are scenes in an earlier part of the series, where the Doctor and his friends find themselves lost in a future London ruined by atomic war and inhabited by mindless slaves whose electronic helmets dictate their every move. Hunting the small group of uncontrolled humans, three automatons pace to the end of a pier, stand silent for a moment, then at the same moment turn their heads slowly to face the direction of their quarry. The grainy image and natural location, both reminiscent of news footage, convey a special horror.

The fate that befell *Doctor Who* is one to which many sf series have succumbed. There is a strong compulsion to repeat a formula which has succeeded, and most programmes give in to it. Some, like *Lost in Space* (1967), actually invite predictability by setting up a situation so restrictive and complex that internal friction among the characters is enough to produce a story. By combining a space explorer, his family, a handsome lieutenant and a stowaway doctor of monumental rudeness and stupidity, the producers of *Lost in Space* managed to fill most programmes with reports on the romance between eldest daughter and lieutenant, love-hate relationship between doctor and family and other internal problems. As in *The Swiss Family Robinson*, on which the series was based, the problems of keeping alive and staying sane precluded any plot as such.

There were few exceptions to this rule in *Lost in Space*, but a notable one was *Wish upon a Star*, directed by Sutton Roley (1967). With a flexible use of the camera, Roley achieved superb effects despite a restrictive and basically illogical story. The brainless Doctor Smith (Jonathan Harris) discovers a wrecked space ship on the castaways' planet and in it a helmet which, he finds, confers the power to grant any wish the wearer makes. Predictably, Smith secretes himself in the wreck and conjures up a world of luxuries. Roley, cleverly beginning with a close-up and pulling to long shot, shows Smith's beaming face, then slowly reveals him at the head of a table groaning with exotic foods, while behind the throne in which he is lounging hangs the Mona Lisa. Later the mood is broken by the terrifying appearance of the helmet's owner, a faceless creature that erupts from the wreck to demand with explicit roars that Smith returns his property. Directed with flair and insight, this episode is without flaw as visual sf.

The predictability of *Lost in Space* was considered and intentional, but that of other programmes has often resulted from an abrupt change in pattern half-way through a series. *Voyage to the Bottom of the Sea* (1966), based on Irwin Allen's successful film, seized in the middle of a series on the concept of fear as a weapon. For the next thirteen programmes, viewers were confronted with almost weekly variations of this theme; fear gasses, fear vibrations, fear phobias. In one episode, midget Michael Dunn and a group of pirates dressed as clowns take over the submarine by the use of a fear *gun* and produce what must be one of the most bizzare shows in the history of television.

Similarly, *Star Trek* (1968), after beginning well with a cleverly constructed double episode called *Menagerie*, degenerated sharply into stock situations. *Menagerie* is an interesting example of prudent TV production. Originally made as *The Cage*, a one-hour pilot for the series, it starred Jeffrey Hunter as the captain of a space battleship who rescues castaway Susan Oliver from telepathic aliens on a dying world. By the time the series had been accepted, Hunter was no longer available, so the producers incorporated the original hour into a two-hour programme in which William Shatner, the series' eventual star, investigates the circumstances of Hunter's landing, with Hunter, a disfigured and unrecognisable victim of a space accident, beside him on the ship. The first programme was viewed in segments as flashback, some extra action added to tie up loose ends. On the whole an extremely clever piece of reorganisation.

Like so many other series, *Star Trek* became caught in a profitable groove, in its case the idea of worlds in which societies had developed parallel with those of Earth. This preoccupation began with *Tomorrow Is Yesterday,* an early episode in which Shatner's future starship is sent back in time, landing on Earth of the Sixties. Presumably intoxicated by the ease of doing an sf show in stock sets and with formula situations, the producers soon offered a planet like Nazi Germany, another like Chicago in the Thirties. A third story was nothing but a space version of a wartime submarine drama, two space ships hunting each other with sophisticated versions of sonar. Marginally interesting as esoterica, none of these programmes deserve serious consideration as sf.

An exception, however, was an episode called *Charlie X,* directed by Lawrence Dobkin with Robert Walker Jnr. as a telepath which the starship "Enterprise" unwittingly picks up. Adolescent and vindictive, the boy slips from puppy love to childish hatred in a moment, while the crew's reactions convey perfectly the terror of men faced with a power impossible to fight. Walker's acting is superb, an animal contortion of his face horribly suggesting the blast of hate that destroys those who oppose him. With it he melts the pieces of a three-dimensional chess set on which he has lost a game, and later, being angered by the laughter of some crewmen, stops them abruptly. Seen first only as shadows, a girl gropes around the corner of a corridor to reveal her face changed to a smooth mask of flesh. Shape means nothing in his world, and when he turns a girl into a scuttling lizard we imagine when he advances on another with his hand behind his back and the coy offer of "something for her" that is this creature he will flourish in her face. But his hand holds instead a rose. Horror too can have its poetry, evil its own special beauty.

Diverting as all these series may have been, none of them compete with *The Outer Limits*, a programme produced between 1964–65 by scriptwriter Joseph Stefano (*Psycho, The Black Orchid*) and containing the best science fiction ever to be presented on television. Ill-fated and misunderstood, this series was readily accepted by the visually-oriented 'teenage audience when it was run in early time slots on American television, but when increasing sophistication forced programming at a later time, adults found its odd plots and unconventional narrative style impossible to comprehend, and it folded abruptly. But in its brief life *The Outer Limits* gave television some of its finest moments, encouraging directors like Gerd Oswald and writers like Harlan Ellison to experiment with the medium and with the visual possibilities of science fiction.

Like all such series, *The Outer Limits* was variable in quality, although it never descended to the continual re-use of a stock plot. Even though the production company demanded at least one "monster" per programme as a concession to the juvenile audience, the writers managed as a rule to find logical reasons for their inclusion. The best of them were monsters of a subtle though no less horrible kind, and in the programmes directed by Gerd Oswald it was especially clear that the director, not content merely with coming to terms with the restriction, was using it to achieve new and interesting effects.

Probably the finest of the series is *Demon with a Glass Hand*, directed by Byron Haskin and written by Harlan Ellison. Ellison, providentially both sf writer and scenarist, contributed a script of intricate complexity, well thought-out even to the characters' names. Robert Culp is Trent; the aliens who hunt him in some nameless city are Arch, Battle, Brush and Budge. A solemn narration accompanies the first shot of Culp fleeing down a shadowed street. "Through all the legends of mankind—Assyrian, Babylonian, Sumerian, Semitic—runs the saga of the eternal man, the man who has never tasted death, the hero who strides through the centuries. . . ." But then Trent's voice enters, alone and afraid. "I was born ten days ago, a full grown man born ten days ago. I walk on a street of this city. I don't know who I am or where I've been or where I'm going. And They track me down and try to kill me. But the hand, *my* hand, tells me what to do. . . ."

"They" are aliens from the future, nervous, dedicated men in black clothing who wear around their necks medallions that hold them still in time. Tug off such an amulet and the man is whisked agonisingly back into the future. Trent is told about the medallions by his hand, a glowing glass prosthetic that advises him in a cool, unemotional voice. It lacks, however, three of its fingers; without them it cannot tell Trent who he is or why he is in the city. Relentlessly, Trent hunts down the aliens, and regains the missing fingers, only to find that his reason for living is agonising and lonely. Sent back to hide in the past, he carries with him the entire consciousness of mankind engraved on a single piece of wire. With the human race beyond its reach, the alien invaders will retreat, and Man will wait until Trent has lived through the centuries to his own time, to be re-created by him from the matrix he holds. The long wait will not worry Trent, for, as the hand coolly informs him, he is only a robot anyway.

This strange drama is played out in a brilliantly chosen location, a dilapidated office block. Along its echoing marble corridors, Trent pursues his quarry, hunting them down in the shabby offices of private investigators, stamp merchants, tatooists. His hand, pulsing with light and dispensing disinterested advice, is one of science fiction's cleverest inventions, given a sharp edge by Ellison's writing for it. In one sequence it advises Trent to let himself be killed by the aliens. When a woman Trent has met comes to mourn by his body, it directs her eerily to place a wet cloth on its owner's forehead, then crisply reads off figures on pulse and respiration until Trent comes back shakily to life. Here is a "monster" that, like Arnold's *Creature from the Black Lagoon*, combines horror with a dark poetry.

Ellison also wrote *Soldier,* directed by Gerd Oswald with Lloyd Nolan as a scientist struggling to discover the secrets of a man from the future catapulted back in time. Less cleverly written than *Demon with a Glass Hand,* this episode is given point by Oswald's direction, especially his claustrophobic use of the padded pit in which Nolan questions the soldier (Michael Ansara). Ellison's flair emerges, however, in the alien's language, a ritualised snarl that is finally translated as "Name's Twilo Gobridny, Private, M-N-T-N-D-N-D-O"; Name, rank and serial number. Making Nolan a language expert, donnish and good natured, is also a clever touch, as are the details of Ansara's life, built up from gestures—trying to strike a cigarette as if the lighting agent were incorporated into its tip, struggling to communicate with the family cat because in his time they are telepathic couriers.

The Invisibles, a two-hour programme designed as a pilot for a series that was never satisfactorily launched, is one of *The Outer Limits'* most remarkable efforts. If *Soldier* recalls details of horror film's traditions—cats as "familiars"; an alien trapped like a demon, able to communicate arcane knowledge if placated— *The Invisibles* is almost a compendium of them. The scar-faced and sinister George Macready is an agent of an alien race intent on dominating Earth. Luring men to a deserted army camp, he straps them down to a bench and places one of the aliens on their backs. The squealing insect-like creatures penetrate their minds, and they become totally dominated by them. While the plot parallels Robert Heinlein's *The Puppet Masters,* there is little truly science fictional in *The Invisibles.* The search for Macready and his minions is more like a witch hunt than scientific inquiry, and the grisly ending with a wounded Burt Reynolds dragging himself through an empty factory while the monsters greedily pursue him is worthy of Germany's most sinister days.

Less horrific but probably more compelling, *Forms of Things Unknown* was, like *The Invisibles,* intended as the first of a series, to be called *The Unknown.* Again, however, nothing came of it and this oddity, one of Gerd Oswald's most curious works, was released to a baffled public as an episode of *The Outer Limits*. Weird and elegaic, shot mostly with vaseline-smeared lenses to achieve a soft and delicate effect, *The Forms of Things Unknown* is an odd mixture of horror film and fantasy. In the opening shot, a Rolls-Royce sweeps up a mountain road, driven by a maniacally grinning Adonis (Scott Marlowe), attended by his two mistresses (Vera Miles and Barbara Rush). Stopping at a mountain lake, he wades knee deep into the water, then demands a cocktail, forcing the woman in a weirdly erotic scene to wade to him in stockings and high heels to serve it. The drink, however, is poisoned, and their master dies horribly in the water as they look on unmoved.

A storm breaks and they flee to a lonely house to be admitted by a sinister butler. Oswald turns the ludicrously familiar situation into something remarkable by casting in this role the elderly Sir Cedric Hardwicke. Dying of a respiratory disease, Hardwicke barely managed to complete the role, and by making the character blind Oswald created an appalling grotesque. Hardwicke's master is a scientific experimenter (David McCallum) glimpsed only briefly in his laboratory, where he has constructed a strange machine from hundreds of clocks, all connected to a central shaft by shimmering strings. "My Mister Hobart tinkers with Time," the butler says, "as Time has tinkered with Mister Hobart." As in other programmes in this series, outside locations are intelligently combined with Gothic interiors to achieve effects both beautiful and faintly horrible.

The Outer Limits was not a perfect series, but for consistency of imagination it had few equals. Although shot on film, it used cinematic effects in a television manner, avoiding solid blacks for vaguer, softer tones, relying on pace of direction rather than clever editing to tell the story. While it indulged directors like Oswald and John Brahm in their penchant for low Gothic angles, this technique was never allowed to control the visual style of the series. Perhaps the main cause of its success was the intelligent overall control of Joseph Stefano, whose knowledge of and interest in the cinema and fantasy show through continually. Again, as in the case of Fritz

Lang and Jack Arnold, a coherent personal vision has been impressed on a body of work; the result is something of which both science fiction and television should be proud.

16. New Bottles, Old Wine

Modern sf presents a confused face to the world, wearing a robe of rags and tatters. The films made in America generally adhere to traditional concepts and approaches, but often mixed with those of other fields, especially the horror film and the teenage comedy. In other countries, especially those from which American fantasy borrowed its basic ideas in the Twenties and Thirties, the scene is complicated by a curious feed-back process by which the originators of elements much altered and extended by American artists are now attempting to re-adopt them in their new guise. This process ignores the fact that Italian and French fantasies have gone on developing these ideas in their own way, enriching them just as much as American artists have done. The tension between the two traditionals is apparent in the work of Italian directors like Antonio Margheriti, Mario Bava and Paolo Heusch, whose fantasy and sf films often prove hopelessly confused as American mock-Gothic and Italianate richness conflict in both style and plot.

In some countries, however, original work is being done, with new and imaginative film-makers discarding the irrelevant patterns of American film in favour of new ones based on their own national inclinations, and able, in the same way as American sf film does, to express truths about their own countries. One such film-maker is the English director Peter Watkins, whose *The War Game* and earlier *Culloden*, both for B.B.C. TV, showed a mind easily adaptable to the imaginative necessities of sf and happy to use this form as a vehicle for visionary ideas. His Swedish-made feature *The Gladiators* (1969) shows international political problems of the future settled by representatives competing in sporting events, a slightly faded sf idea from the Fifties but informed by him with a cynical

The imitation of crucifixion: PRIVILEGE

bite. Probably more impressive, however, was his feature which followed *The War Game*, a glossy parable called *Privilege* (1967).

Presented in semi-documentary style, with a detached voice-over and intelligent recreation of events, *Privilege* tells the story of pop star Steve Shorter, whose immense popularity is used by a future British government to subdue and then mould youthful opinion. Shorter, played with melancholy ineptitude by ex-"Manfred Mann" lead singer Paul Jones, suffers manipulation in the name of national expediency, changing his image from that of a tortured rebel confined by unfeeling society to a repentant prodigal begging for forgiveness, but, goaded by his own conscience and the independent views of his girl friend, a portrait painter played by ravishingly beautiful model Jean Shrimpton, he eventually rejects the role and is destroyed by the society he has helped.

As documentary, future or otherwise, the film is often inaccurate. Jones himself points out that individual singers are not popular enough to be followed as Steve Shorter is, and that the film should have been about a group. He himself has written a play called *They Put You Where You Are* in which the mechanics of a pop group were exposed, and portions of *Privilege* reflect his vision of the pop scene's confused and sinister nature. Despite this, Jones calls the film "a marvellous, noble failure," and was unsurprised at its total box-office collapse after the art cinema patrons found it wasn't art and the teenage market discovered that, despite a prominent music score, it wasn't a pop musical.

Generally Watkins creates the near future well. Clothing is consistently designed to feature a tight high collar, usually secured at the throat by a chain or metal clasp, symbolic of Steve's prison background and of youth's confinement. Materials are brocaded, metallic, bright, blending in with the Steve Shorter Discos and "Dream Palaces," the latter quasi-temples featuring posters for selected Shorter-endorsed products and hard sell ad. tapes blaring constantly. Underlining the image is a music score of liturgical inexorability by Mike Leander, with choirs sweeping over the pulse of an electric bass. Unsubtly, Watkins draws a parallel between Shorter and a second-coming Christ, climaxing at an outdoor rally when the star, exposed before a giant image of himself, opens his arms in an imitation of crucifixion and demands "Please Forgive Me" to the tune of his hitherto rebellious big hit.

Jones, horsey and shambling, fits the part ideally in appearance. Early scenes have him welcomed in a provincial city—Liverpool?— and perform on stage at the local town hall, with a looming organ in the background. His stage props are elaborate: a metal cage, four burly men dressed as prison warders. Dragged on stage and bludgeoned by their truncheons, he is flung into the cell. As he howls "Release Me," the warders clash their keys against the bars and beat at his outstretched manacled hands. The predominantly female audience howls orgiastically. The real Steve, however, is revealed in the dressing room later when he cringes exhausted in the corner, and in the gloomy self-pity of the song "I've Been a Bad, Bad Boy," which becomes a *motif*, best used when Steve hears it on his wrist-watch radio, then idly flips from station to station, all of which are playing the same song. Score one for Watkins and his cynical eye.

Watkins is one of many creators who have found sf a suitable vehicle, though his commitment to the medium is more complete than that of most others. Joseph Losey is too personal a film-maker to be concerned excessively with the popular cinema, but in *The Damned* (1961) he found it a convenient mode in which to express his views about the world at large. Set in a small English seaside resort, it told with obsessive clarity the story of a scientist who, determined to save the world despite itself, raised a group of children who could resist radiation. The price, however, of their ability to survive after the anticipated atomic war was total irradiation, and the impossibility of their existing anywhere except in the atomic poisoned bunker under the sea cliffs in which the scientist (Alexander Knox) has confined them.

Into the situation stumbles American tourist Macdonald Carey, his lover (Shirley Anne Field) and a sculptress (Viveca Lindfors) who, in her clifftop studio, creates works ominously like the charred corpses of beasts and men. Penetrating the bunker, where television screens instruct the children daily and by night a silver-suited creature circulates to observe them, the couple release the prisoners, but in doing so hopelessly poison themselves. At the climax, a lumbering helicopter follows the lovers out to sea as they sail away in a launch, hovering like an angel of doom above them, while in the caves the lost children wander, crying out for help which will never come.

Butchered by the producers when they saw whatever commercial appeal the story had removed by Losey's adroit symbolism, *The Damned* remains alarmingly prophetic sf. Although the plot no longer shows the technological society as the blind, ruthless force of his original script—in the film, Knox unaccountably shoots Lind-fors for "romantic" reasons; in the original, the helicopter, symbol of authority, killed her before setting out after the only two other people in the film with any human feeling—there are still some fine moments, and a sense of social relevance which only Losey can attain.

Like *The Damned*, Peter Brook's *Lord of the Flies* (1963), from William Golding's allegoric novel, used sf as a vehicle for social comment, though with infinitely less cinematic skill than in Losey's case. While the story of a children's choir rotting into savagery after they have been stranded on a post-atomic war island sustains itself for much of its length, the sketchy characterisation, rough editing and often repellent visual style make concentration difficult. The Kevin Brownlow-Andrew Mollo *It Happened Here* (1963) counts as sf more by chance than by choice, but in its documentary realism deserves more serious consideration than most films. Related to the *genre* created by Watkins with his chilling *Culloden*, it is an arrest-ing indication of a path that sf may conceivably take in the future when British film-makers are more certain of their views.

Outside Britain, France is the greatest bastion of fantastic film, part of the reason being the devotion French *cinéastes* have always had to American popular culture. The comic strip—*bande dessinée*—is now a French institution, the detective thriller—*roman policier*—equally familiar to French audiences. Directors like Resnais are comic strip buffs, drawing on the stock characterisation and blunt action of the strips for ideas and inspiration. However, the pattern is one of feed-back rather than genuine originality. The comic strips from which many European film-makers derive their ideas are not only American originals, but French or Italian imitations of them. One such strip is the lush space fantasy *Barbarella*, drawn by Jean-Claude Forest and used by Roger Vadim as the basis of his 1968 fantasy of the same name.

Barbarella suffers substantially in the transition from print to film. Impersonated with wide-eyed adaptability by a delightful Jane Fonda, Forest's sexually emancipated space woman becomes less independent and erotically acquisitive than the original, though gaining a sense of humour with which her creator never imbued her. Based on only a handful of the stories drawn by Forest, *Barbarella* has the heroine in conflict with the evil city of Sogo, where a new sin is invented every hour, and in whose streets she encounters such objects as the Excessive Machine, a genuine sex organ on which an accomplished artist of the keyboard, in this case Milo O'Shea, can drive a victim to death by pleasure, a lesbian queen who, in her dream chamber, can make her fantasies take form, and a group of ladies smoking a giant hookah which, via a poor victim struggling in its glass globe, dispenses Essence of Man.

Vadim's version of Forest is always an inadequate one, its designs occasionally reminding one of the original but lacking their free fantasy and spring-tight composition. Fonda, whether writhing in a free-fall striptease under the credits, cuddling lasciviously on furs or twitching in agony as mechanical dolls nibble at her thighs is unfailingly delectable, but this is not enough to rescue the film from tedium. A far better rendering of European comic-strip panache can be found in Mario Bava's *Diabolik* (1968), where John Phillip Law, limbering up for his role as the blind angel Pygar in *Barbarella,* performs a dazzling characterisation of the master criminal Diabolik, pitted against a world for which he has a profound and amused contempt.

Lithe and black, Diabolik loots the world of its riches. Ten million dollars in notes are plucked from the middle of its escort by crane and cargo net, a truck-sized ingot of pure gold blown off a high bridge by an explosion that wrecks the train carrying it. When capitalism begins to bore him, Diabolik destroys every tax office in Britain, forcing the comic Minister of Finance (Terry-Thomas) to go on television begging citizens to pay their tax voluntarily. Meanwhile, in his underground hideout surrounded by Twenty-first century architecture and gadgets to out-Bond Bond, Diabolik makes love to voluptuous Marisa Mell, his sole assistant and companion, while ten million in notes showers down on their naked bodies.

John Phillip Law as the master criminal in DIABOLIK

Mario Bava, brilliant cinematographer and one of Italy's finest fantasy film-makers, gives *Diabolik* the visual pace of a stream-lined juggernaut. Crime follows crime, escape escape. Trapped by his enemies with a priceless necklace in his possession, Diabolik shoots his way out, waits until his enemy is cremated, then recovers from the ashes the jewels he has used for bullets. Returning to the hideout, he finds Mell swimming in a clear stone-floored pool, pastes the gems on her ample breasts, then plunges with her into the water for a well-earned consummation. Bava reserves his best for the final scenes, the lovers surprised in the act of melting down the giant ingot of gold, the machine blowing up as Diabolik fights off the police. A flood of molten gold streams over him, embedding the man and his glistening fire-proof suit in a clot of the congealing metal. For days he stands there, a frozen golden trophy invisible except for one leg, one arm and a blank eye glimpsed through the face plate. Mell returns in widow's furs, weeps for her dead lover—and is rewarded with a conspiratorial wink! As she turns to go, planning his rescue, a maniacal laugh echoes around the cave, Judex is alive and living at Cinecittà.

One would have been happy if François Truffant's *Fahrenheit 451* (1966), the long-awaited film version of Ray Bradbury's novel, had shown a little of *Diabolik's* panache, but the film is a less than courageous failure. Some things remain from Bradbury's vision of a future where books are banned and a group of Firemen burn with flamethrowers those volumes which survive; the awakening interest of Fireman Montag (Oskar Werner) as he stumbles through the beginnings of literacy; his relationship with drug-addled wife and sexily aware underground *littérateuse* Clarisse (Julie Christie in a muffled double role); the tension of Montag's conflict with the chief Fireman (Cyril Cusack). Unfortunately Truffaut has been truer to his spiritual father Alfred Hitchcock than to Bradbury, and his *hommages* to the master—a fascination with the colour red, scenes directed more for tension than point, a black and cynical humour—leave little room for any but a vague retelling of the original story.

The shadow of the comic strip looms over Jean-Luc Godard's *Alphaville* (1965), admixed with a variety of influences from blue movies to pop art, but the basic ambience is of science fiction. There is little difference between the perfunctory establishment of space travel in the average sf film—a stock shot of a rocket taking off; dissolve to pilot's cabin—and Godard's Lemmy Caution (Eddie Constantine) driving his late-model American car through "intersidereal space" to the alternate universe of Alphaville. Godard has paid lip service to the traditions with the same cynicism Hitchcock used in *The Birds*. The rest of the film is similarly viable as sf. One has merely to remove the incongruous characterisation of Caution to expose a routine sf plot, with a mysterious computer ruling a city state where execution is carried out by bikini girls with knives, women are chattels made available to anybody who asks, and the daughter of the ruling authority falls in love with the handsome stranger and runs away with him.

But of course to expose this story by removing the ideas and words of Caution is to neutralise what universality the film has. For Godard as for Losey, Frankenheimer and Arnold, sf film is a vehicle, not the whole point. Godard's reason for using sf is, like all his motives, obscure. Clearly he is talking about the mechanical world in which we live and for which the cramped and asceptic corridors of Alphaville are an apt symbol: Godard demonstrates, as Arnold and others have done, that sf in the cinema is little more than a matter of making a frame for reality. *Alphaville* was shot in and around Paris with no attempt to disguise familiar buildings or locations. As in *Robinson Crusoe on Mars* and Arnold's desert films,

Memorising books: Oskar Werner and Julie Christie in FAHRENHEIT 451

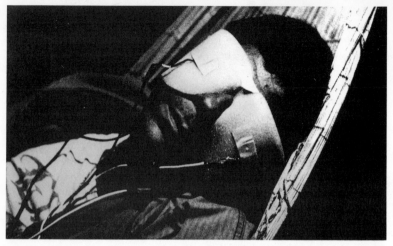

Journeying in time: Marker's LA JETÉE

an alien mood is established merely by placing in familiar locations the elements of a fantasy plot. For Haskin, a tumble of wreckage and a human hand turns Death Valley into Mars, for Arnold, the cold desert wind ruffling a girl's hair makes her alien and the desert a place of menace. And for Godard a naked girl in a glass case makes some suburban hotel the Alphaville Hilton and Eddie Constantine an intergalactic agent.

Just as early experimenters like Delluc and Clair used sf and fantasy as vehicles for experimental film-making techniques, so modern French film-makers have carried on the tradition of introducing unconventional ideas in a fantasy framework. Chris Marker's *La Jetée* (1962), undoubtedly the most distinguished of a group of shorts that included many of the films of Walerian Borowczyk, used stills to tell the story of a man whose vivid memory of a childhood experience allows him to journey back and forward in time from a ruined post-atomic France. Subtly disturbing, Marker's film is in its way a perfect literary sf piece, developed like a short story with a detached narration and brevity of expression most writers would envy. Moody locations—a zoological museum inhabited by stuffed birds and fish, catacombs under a shattered city in which grim scientists work on their human time machine—contrive, however, to make the film a unique combination of literature and cinema.

Despite triumphs like *La Jetée*, short film sf is seldom satisfactory. The necessity for special effects often puts this form beyond the resources of financially limited production teams, while sf plots tend to demand more of actors and technicians than most are prepared to give. Exceptions are rare: allegoric works like Richard Williams' animated *The Little Island* (1958) probably count as sf, though the distinction is difficult. *Neighbours* (1952), Norman McLaren's pixilated fantasy of war on a tiny scale is at most associational. Of all short films in the field, perhaps the best is *Universe*

Small scale war: McLaren's NEIGHBOURS

Left, IKARIE X.B.1.; right, the dance of
THE DAY THE FISH CAME OUT

(1960), a National Film Board of Canada production which, in the process of showing the life of an astronomer at a Canadian observatory, opens up the universe. "The ground beneath our feet is the surface of a planet," the narrator begins, and we are immediately aware of our unimportance in the immensity of space. There are some perfect moments; the dot of Mercury inching across the blazing disc of the sun, re-creations of Saturn's moons and the deeps of Jupiter. The regular pulse of piano chords over planetary scenes echoes the ticking observatory clock, the slow passing of calibrations and the telescope's tracking. Finally, the dawn departure of the astronomer across quiet lawns ends the film on a perfect note of content and rest, of dignity and restraint.

Of the other countries which have attempted sf, most have produced at most a handful of films. Czechoslovakia's *Ikarie X.B.I.* (1964) was an imaginative excursion into future space travel, given novelty by its clever extrapolation of familiar customs. For the first time, life on an exploratory space ship is examined, concepts like entertainment analysed and given a futuristic twist. People on this ship go to dances, have parties, wash themselves, make love. Especially impressive is a dark, sinister and horrific scene in which a derelict space ship they discover is found to be the victim of an ancient dissension, the rotted corpses on board remains of people who succumbed to the familiar scourge of atomic war. The images and bleak playing recall the best of Fritz Lang, an impression which survives even the brutal shortening of the American version.

Atomic war also raises its head in Michael Cacoyannis's *The Day the Fish Came Out* (1967), produced in Greece but with an international cast led, if that is the word, by Tom Courtenay and Candice Bergen. Garish, noisy, aggressively "camp," the film shows a Greek island plagued by the results of a bomber crash which deposits a radioactive device there. Press, spies and hangers-on besiege the place while the pilots, flung into the sea with only their underwear on, lurk in the rocks, not daring to reveal themselves. Homosexual jokes are rife, most of the characters, with the exception of a toothsome Candice Bergen, showing alarming symptoms of sexual confusion. Aside from a frantic dance called "The Jet" in which all indulge at the slightest suggestion, the film lacks sf interest, though its fascination for students of modern sexual mores is unlimited.

His face burned in an industrial accident, a man has a mask made from a flesh-like plastic to cover his scars. Assuming a new identity, he meets and makes love to his wife under the impression that she does not recognise him. Later, however, she claims that she knew of his ruse all along, and the man turns on the doctor who made the mask and murders him. Meanwhile, in another and apparently unrelated situation, a girl whose face has been burned at Hiroshima commits suicide after having allowed her brother to make love to her. This alarming film, *The Face of Another* (1967) is one

207

of the oddest to come out of Japan, and an apt example of science fiction in the service of a superior cinematic intelligence, in this case that of director Hiroshi Teshigahara.

Visually the film is a pastiche of *outré* German elements. The doctor's surgery is a timeless limbo where artificial limbs and organs lie on slickly antiseptic shelves surrounded by Leonardo's anatomical drawings and medical sketches of the human face and limbs. The special plastic is greasy and obscene, but the doctor handles it with professional relish, extolling its virtues. Meanwhile his nurse lurks in the background, kneading indeterminate lumps into shape with a miniature rolling mill or abstractedly moulding a prosthetic breast.

One's first thought is of Edgar Ulmer, and especially of his Thirties masterpiece *The Black Cat*. Both films have the same glossy surface and perspex *décor*. The scene of the brother caressing his sister's horribly scarred cheek is a direct expression of a typically German predilection, while the final murder by carving knife belongs to the same era. One notes too the "Invisible Man" motif of white bandaged face and black hat, the "mad scientist" figure direct from a Karloff vehicle. A *House of Wax* with moral overtones, *The Face of Another* sits uneasily in the Japanese cinema, a strange example of how sf and horror elements can be transplanted to other *genres*. Most countries have attempted sf, some have succeeded to an extent, but the form remains aggressively American, an expression of a national impulse that, like the Western, lies too deep under the American skin ever to be revealed by any but a native son.

★   ★   ★

Decades ago, Stephen Vincent Benet recorded his unsuccessful search for some national impulse, the "American thing" that set the art of the United States apart from that of other nations. One knows what he means; the stretching and athletic music of Copland, the apocalyptic fiction of Melville and the "treasurable dreadful-ness" of John Updike share a common spirit which, despite a pal-pable flavour and hue, defies distillation.

Perhaps he looked too closely at works too clearly intentioned as art. Had to examine the less thoughtful aspects of American culture, he may have found there, as other more recent critics have done, a more definable quality of nationalism and a more truly American spirit. The Western, the Musical, the Hobbies Magazine, the Pop Song; these seem to betray more accurately the qualities that set America apart from other countries of the world.

Science fiction film offers us an extension of these characteristic phenomena. It is the soul of American technology, the modern shadow of the Western, the hobbies magazine made flesh, or at least celluloid. If it seems to disregard the established rules of cinema, and especially the modern visual techniques of the field, it is because these are irrelevant to a form of art which issues direct from the emotions, from the basic spirit rather than the thinking mind.

To the person studying cinema, sf film, like the Western, is less a series of linked works than a diffuse and ill-defined plain, a land-scape with figures which changes as one moves, assumes new shapes depending on viewpoint and perspective. Tracing its ante-cedents does not make it any easier to understand why it exer-cises such an influence over modern man. We can see intellectually that Jack Arnold draws his impulse from Lang and Whale, but it is inexplicable that his work and that of his contemporaries should have acted so substantially on the minds of an entire generation. The response of mankind to alien creatures, his concept of alien surroundings and of his own future is more likely to reflect the traditions of sf film than those of space-age documentary. Like a nightmare glimpsed in childhood, these echoes will linger until doomsday.

Bibliography

1 Amis, Kingsley. *New Maps of Hell*. London: Gollancz, 1961.
2 Houston, Penelope. "Glimpses of the Moon," *Sight and Sound* (Spring 1953).
3 Knight, Damon. *In Search of Wonder*. Chicago: Advent, 1956.
4 Perry, George and Alan Aldridge. *The Penguin Book of Comics*. London: Penguin Books, 1967.
5 Cook, Olive. "A Pioneer of the Cinema," *The Saturday Book 25*. London: Hutchinson, 1965.
6 Sadoul, Georges. *The French Cinema*. London: The Falcon Press, 1953.
7 Scheffauer, Herman G. "The Vivifying of Space," *Introduction to the Movies*. New York: Noonday Press, 1960.
8 Kracauer, Siegfried. *From Caligari to Hitler*. Princeton, N.J.: Princeton University Press, 1947.
9 Bartlett, Nicholas. "The Dark Struggle," *Film* (Summer 1962).
10 Bardèche, Maurice and Robert Brasillach. *History of the Film*. London: George Allen and Unwin, 1945.
11 Durgnat, Raymond. *Films and Feelings*. London: Faber and Faber, 1967.
12 Fielding, Raymond. *The Technique of Special Effects Cinematography*. London: Focal Press, 1965.
13 Von Harbou, Thea. *Metropolis*. London: Readers Library, 1927.
14 Weinberg, Herman G. (comp.). *An Index to the Creative Work of Fritz Lang*. Supplement to *Sight and Sound* (February 1946).
15 *The Scientific Romances of H. G. Wells*. London: Gollancz, 1933.
16 Wells, H. G. *The King Who Was a King*. London: Ernest Benn Ltd., 1929.
17 Wells, H. G. *Two Film Stories: Things To Come* and *The Man Who Could Work Miracles*. London: The Cresset Press, 1940.
18 Bergonzi, Bernard. *The Early H. G. Wells*. Manchester: Manchester University Press, 1961.

19 Graves, Robert and Alan Hodge. *The Long Weekend*. London: Faber and Faber, 1940.

20 Tabori, Paul. *Alexander Korda*. London: Oldbourne, 1959.

21 Hardy, Forsyth (ed.). *Grierson on Documentary*. London: Collins, 1946. Chapter Three, "The Cinema of Ideas," deals extensively with *Things To Come*.

22 Lahue, Kalton H. *Continued Next Week*. University of Oklahoma Press, 1964.

23 Hagner, John G. *Falling for Stars*. Los Angeles: John G. Hagner, 1964.

24 Whitehall, Richard and others. "Four Epics," *Motion*, number 6.

25 *Midi-Minuit Fantastique*, number 3 (1962). Special issue on *King Kong* and *The Lost World*.

26 ———, number 6 (1963). Special issue on Merian C. Cooper and Ernest B. Schoedsack.

27 Behlmer, Rudy. "Merian C. Cooper," *Films in Review* (January 1966).

28 Aubry, Yves and Jacques Petat. *G. W. Pabst. Anthologie du Cinéma*, number 37 (July 1968).

29 Tyler, Parker. *Classics of the Foreign Film*. New York: Citadel Press, 1962.

30 Arnold, Francis. "Out of this World," *Films and Filming* (June 1963).

31 Bogdanovich, Peter. "Working within the System," *Movie*, number 15 (1968). Interview with Don Siegel.

32 Lourié, Gene. "A Background to Horror," *Films and Filming* (February 1960).

33 "Inside *2001*: An Interview with Wally Gentleman." *Take One* (Montreal), number 11 (May/June 1968).

34 *American Cinematographer* (June 1968). Special issue devoted to effects and photography of *2001: A Space Odyssey*.

35 Kneale, Nigel. "Not Quite So Intimate," *Sight and Sound* (Spring 1959).

36 ———. *The Quatermass Experiment*. London: Penguin Books, 1959.

37 ———. *Quatermass II*. London: Penguin Books, 1960.
38 Truffaut, François. "Journal of *Fahrenheit 451*," *Cashiers du Cinéma in English*, numbers 5, 6 and 7 (1967).
39 Godard, Jean-Luc. *Alphaville*. London: Lorrimer, 1967.

Select Filmography

THE ABOMINABLE SNOWMAN (OF THE HIMALAYAS). G. B. 1957. *Director:* Val Guest. *Screenplay:* Nigel Kneale. *Based on the T.V. play* The Creature *by:* Nigel Kneale. *Photography:* Arthur Grant. *Designer:* Ted Marshall. *Producer:* Aubrey Baring. *Production:* Hammer.

Players: Forrest Tucker, Peter Cushing, Maureen Connell, Richard Wattis.

THE ABSENT-MINDED PROFESSOR. U.S.A. 1961. *Director:* Robert Stevenson. *Screenplay:* Bill Walsh. *Based on stories by:* Samuel W. Taylor. *Photography:* Edward Colman. *Designer:* Carroll Clark. *Producer:* Bill Walsh. *Production:* Walt Disney.

Players: Fred MacMurray, Nancy Olson, Keenan Wynn, Tommy Kirk. (*See p. 175*)

AELITA. U.S.S.R. 1924. *Director:* Jacob Protazanov. *Screenplay:* Yuri Zhelyobuzhky, E. Schoenmann. *Designers:* Victor Simon, Isaac Rabinovitch, Alexandra Exter, Sergei Koslonsky. *Production:* Mezhrobpom.

Players: Igor Ilinsky, Yulia Salontsena, Nikolai Tseretelly. (*See p. 20*)

THE AIRSHIP DESTROYER (also known as AERIAL WARFARE, AERIAL TORPEDO and BATTLE IN THE CLOUDS) G.B. 1909. *Director:* Walter Booth. *Based on ideas of:* Rudyard Kipling, H. G. Wells, Jules Verne. *Producer/Production:* Charles Urban. (*See p. 16*)

ALPHAVILLE. France. 1965. *Director:* Jean-Luc Godard. *Screenplay:* Jean-Luc Godard. *Photography:* Raoul Coutard. *Editor:* Agnès Guillemot. *Producer:* André Michelin.

Players: Eddie Constantine, Anna Karina, Howard Vernon, Akim Tamiroff, Laszlo Szabo. (*See p.* 202)

THE AMAZING COLOSSAL MAN. U.S.A. 1957. *Director:* Bert I. Gordon. *Screenplay:* Mark Hanna, Bert I. Gordon. *Photography:* Joe Biroc. *Producer:* Bert I. Gordon. *Production:* American International.

Players: Glenn Langan, Cathy Downs, William Hudson.

ANIMAL FARM. G.B. 1955. *Directors:* John Halas, Joy Batchelor. *Screenplay:* Lothar Wolff, Borden Mace, Philip Stapp, John Halas, Joy Batchelor. *Based on the novel by:* George Orwell. *Photography:* S. G. Griffiths, J. Gurr, W. Traylor, R. Turk. *Animation Director:* John Reed. *Music:* Matyas Sieber. *Producers:* John Halas, Joy Batchelor.

Voices of all the animals: Maurice Denham. *Narrator:* Gordon Heath. (*See* p. 99)

L'ATLANTIDE (ATLANTIS). Germany. 1932. *Director:* G. W. Pabst. *Screenplay:* Herbert Rappoport, Laszlo Vajda, Pierre Ichac. *Based on the novel by:* Pierre Benoit. *Designer:* Erno Metzner. *Production:* Nero-Film.

Players (German version): Brigitte Helm, Gustav Diessl, Florelle, Tela Tchai, Heinz Klingenberg.

Players (French version): Brigitte Helm, Pierre Blanchar, Tela Tchai, Jean Angelo, Florelle.

Players (English version): Brigitte Helm, John Stuart, Gibb McLaughlin, Gustav Diessl, Florelle. (*See p.* 82)

BARBARELLA. France/Italy. 1967. *Director:* Roger Vadim. *Screenplay:* Terry Southern, Roger Vadim, Claude Brule, Vittorio Bonicelli, Clement Biddle Wood, Brian Degas, Tudor Gates, Jean-Claude Forest. *Based on the comic strip by:* Jean-Claude Forest. *Photography:* Claude Renoir. *Special Effects:* August Lohman. *Designer:* Mario Garbuglia. *Artistic Consultant:* Jean-Claude Forest. *Producer:* Dino de Laurentiis.

Players: Jane Fonda, John Phillip Law, Anita Pallenberg, Milo O'Shea, David Hemmings. (*See p.* 199)

BATMAN. U.S.A. 1943. *Director:* Lambert Hillyer. *Screenplay:* Victor McLeod, Leslie Swabacker, Harry Fraser. *Based on the comic strip by:* Bob Kane. *Photography:* James S. Brown. *Producer:* Rudolph Flothow. *Production:* Columbia. Serial in fifteen episodes.

Players: Lewis Wilson, Douglas Croft, J. Carrol Naish, Shirley Patterson. (*See p. 74*)

BATMAN AND ROBIN. U.S.A. 1949. *Director:* Spencer Bennett. *Screenplay:* George H. Plympton, Joseph P. Poland, Royal K. Cole. *Based on the comic strip by:* Bob Kane. *Producer:* Sam Katzman. *Production:* Columbia. Serial in fifteen episodes.

Players: Robert Lowery, John Duncan. (*See p. 74*)

THE BEAST FROM 20,000 FATHOMS. U.S.A. 1953. *Director:* Eugene Lourié. *Screenplay:* Lou Morheim, Fred Frieberger. *Based on the story* The Fog Horn *by:* Ray Bradbury. *Photography:* Jack Russell. *Special Effects:* Ray Harryhausen. *Designer:* Eugene Lourié. *Producer:* Hal Chester. *Production:* Warner Brothers.

Players: Paul Christian, Paula Raymond, Cecil Kellaway, Kenneth Tobey. (*See p. 99, 131*)

THE BEAST WITH A MILLION EYES. U.S.A. 1955. *Director:* David Kramarsky. *Screenplay:* Tom Filer. *Photography:* Everett Baker. *Producer:* Roger Corman.

Players: Paul Birch, Lorna Thayer, Dona Cole. (*See p. 150*)

THE BEGINNING OR THE END. U.S.A. 1947. *Director:* Norman Taurog. *Screenplay:* Frank Wead. *Based on a story by:* Robert Considine. *Producer:* Samuel Marx. *Production:* M-G-M.

Players: Brian Donlevy, Robert Walker, Tom Drake, Joseph Calleia. (*See p. 156*)

BEHEMOTH, THE SEA MONSTER (U.S. title THE GIANT BEHEMOTH). G.B. 1958. *Directors:* Douglas Hickox, Eugene Lourié. *Screenplay:* Eugene Lourié. *Based on a story by:* Robert Abel, Allen Adler. *Photography:* Ken Hodges. *Special Effects:* Jack Rabin, Louis DeWitt, Irving Block, Willis O'Brien, Pete Robinson. *Designer:* Harry White.

Players: Gene Evans, Andre Morell, Leigh Madison. (*See p. 99*)

THE BIRDS. U.S.A. 1963. *Director:* Alfred Hitchcock. *Screenplay:* Evan Hunter. *Based on the story by:* Daphne du Maurier. *Photography:* Robert Burks. *Special Effects:* Lawrence A. Hampton. *Designer:* Robert Boyle. *Sound Consultant:* Bernard Herrmann. *Production:* Universal.

Players: Rod Taylor, Tippi Hedren, Jessica Tandy, Suzanne Pleshette. (*See p.* 151)

THE BLACK SCORPION. U.S.A. 1957. *Director:* Edward Ludwig. *Screenplay:* David Duncan, Robert Blees. *Based on a story by:* Paul Yawitz. *Photography:* Lionel Lindon. *Designer:* Edward Fitzgerald. *Producers:* Frank Melford, Jack Dietz. *Production:* Warner Brothers.

Players: Richard Denning, Mara Corday, Carlos Rivas. (*See p.* 134)

THE BLOB. U.S.A. 1958. *Director:* Irvin S. Yeaworth, Jr. *Screenplay:* Theodore Simonson, Kate Philips. *Photography:* Thomas Spalding. *Designers:* William Jersey, Karl Karlson. *Production:* Tonylyn/Paramount.

Players: Steve McQueen, Aneta Corseaut, Earl Rowe.

BUCK ROGERS. U.S.A. 1939. *Directors:* Ford Beebe, Saul A. Goodkin. *Screenplay:* Norman S. Hall, Ray Trampe. *Based on the comic strip by:* Phil Nowlan, Lt. Dick Calkins. *Photography:* Jerry Ash. *Production:* Universal. Serial in twelve episodes.

Players: Larry "Buster" Crabbe, Constance Moore, Jackie Moran, Henry Brandon.

CHILDREN OF THE DAMNED. G.B. 1963. *Director:* Anton M. Leader. *Screenplay:* John Briley. *Suggested by* The Midwich Cuckoos *by:* John Wyndham. *Photography:* Davis Boulton. *Designer:* Elliot Scott. *Producer:* Ben Arbeid. *Production:* M-G-M.

Players: Ian Hendry, Alan Badel, Barbara Ferris, Alfred Burke. (*See p.* 100)

CITY UNDER THE SEA. G.B. 1965. *Director:* Jacques Tourneur. *Screenplay:* Charles Bennett, Louis M. Heyward. *Based on the poem by:* Edgar Allan Poe. *Photography:* Stephen Dade. *Special Effects:* Frank George, Les Bowie. *Designer:* Frank White. *Producer:* Daniel Haller. *Production:* American International.

Players: Vincent Price, David Tomlinson, Tab Hunter, Susan Hart.

THE COLOSSUS OF NEW YORK. U.S.A. 1958. *Director:* Eugene Lourié. *Screenplay:* Thelma Schnee. *Based on a story by:* Willis Goldbeck. *Photography:* John F. Warren. *Special Effects:* John P. Fulton. *Designers:* Hal Pereira, John Goodman. *Producer:* William Alland.

Players: Ross Martin, Mala Powers, Charles Herbert.

THE CONQUEST OF SPACE. U.S.A. 1955. *Director:* Byron Haskin. *Screenplay:* James O'Hanlon. *Adaptation by:* Philip Yordan, Barré Lyndon, George Worthing Yates. *Based on the book* Mars Project *by:* Wernher von Braun. *Title taken from book by:* Chesley Bonestell, Willy Ley. *Photography:* Lionel Lindon. *Designers:* Hal Pereira, J. McMillan Johnson. *Producer:* George Pal. *Production:* Paramount.

Players: Walter Brooke, Eric Fleming, William Hopper, Ross Martin. (*See p.* 108)

CREATURE FROM THE BLACK LAGOON. U.S.A. 1954. *Director:* Jack Arnold. *Screenplay:* Harry Essex, Arthur Ross. *Based on a story by:* Maurice Zimm. *Photography:* William E. Snyder. *Underwater Photography:* James C. Havens. *Designers:* Bernard Herzbrun, Hilyard Brown. *Producer:* William Alland. *Production:* Universal.

Players: Richard Carlson, Julie Adams, Richard Denning, Antonio Moreno. (*See p.* 119)

THE CREATURE WALKS AMONG US. U.S.A. 1956. *Director:* John Sherwood. *Screenplay:* Arthur Ross. *Photography:* Maury Gertsman. *Designers:* Alexander Golitzen, Robert E. Smith. *Producer:* William Alland. *Production:* Universal.

Players: Jeff Morrow, Rex Reason, Leigh Snowden. (*See ill.* p. 136)

THE DAMNED (U.S. title THESE ARE THE DAMNED). G.B. 1961. *Director:* Joseph Losey. *Screenplay:* Evan Jones. *Based on the novel* The Children of Light *by:* H. L. Lawrence. *Photography:* Arthur Grant. *Designer:* Don Mingaye. *Production Layout:* Richard

MacDonald. *Production Designer:* Bernard Robinson. *Producers:* Anthony Nelson-Keys, Anthony Hinds. *Production:* Hammer.

Players: Macdonald Carey, Shirley Anne Field, Oliver Reed, Viveca Lindfors, Alexander Knox. (*See p.* 198)

THE DAY OF THE TRIFFIDS. G.B. 1963. *Director:* Steve Sekely. *Screenplay:* Philip Yordan. *Based on the novel by:* John Wyndham. *Photography:* Ted Moore. *Special Effects:* Wally Veevers. *Designer:* Cedric Dawe. *Producer:* George Pitcher.

Players: Howard Keel, Nicole Maurey, Janette Scott, Kieron Moore.

THE DAY THE EARTH STOOD STILL. U.S.A. 1951. *Director:* Robert Wise. *Screenplay:* Edmund H. North. *Based on the short story* Farewell to the Master *by:* Harry Bates. *Photography:* Leo Tover. *Designers:* Lyle Wheeler, Addison Hehr. *Music:* Bernard Herrmann. *Production:* 20th Century-Fox.

Players: Michael Rennie, Patricia Neal, Hugh Marlowe, Sam Jaffe. (*See p.* 104)

THE DAY THE WORLD ENDED. U.S.A. 1955. *Director:* Roger Corman. *Screenplay:* Lou Rusoff. *Photography:* Jock Feindel. *Producer:* Roger Corman.

Players: Richard Denning, Lori Nelson, Adele Jergens.

THE DEADLY MANTIS (Also known as THE INCREDIBLE PREYING MANTIS). U.S.A. 1957. *Director:* Nathan Juran. *Screenplay:* Martin Berkeley. *Based on a story by:* William Alland. *Photography:* Ellis W. Carter. *Designers:* Alexander Golitzen, Robert Clatworthy. *Producer:* William Alland. *Production:* Universal.

Players: Craig Stevens, Alix Talton, William Hopper. (*See p.* 135)

THE DEATH RAY (LUCH SMERTI). U.S.S.R. 1925. *Director:* Leo Kuleshov. *Screenplay:* Vsevelod Pudovkin. *Photography:* Alexander Levitsky. *Designer:* Vsevelod Pudovkin. *Production:* Goskino.

Players: Sergei Komarov, Piotr Galadzhev, Alexandra Khokhlova. (*See p.* 20)

DESTINATION MOON. U.S.A. 1950. *Director:* Irving Pichel. *Screenplay:* Robert A. Heinlein, Rip van Ronkel, James O'Hanlon. *Based on the novel* Rocketship Galileo *by:* Robert A. Heinlein.

Photography: Lionel Lindon. *Designer:* Ernst Fegté. *Producer:* George Pal. *Production:* Eagle-Lion.

Players: John Archer, Warner Anderson, Erin O'Brien-Moore, Tom Powers. (*See p.* 103)

THE DEVIL DOLL. U.S.A. 1936. *Director:* Tod Browning. *Screenplay:* Tod Browning, Garrett Fort, Guy Endore, Erich von Stroheim. *Based on the novel* Burn, Witch, Burn *by:* A. A. Merritt. *Photography:* Leonard Smith. *Designer:* Cedric Gibbons. *Production:* M-G-M.

Players: Lionel Barrymore, Maureen O'Sullivan, Frank Lawton, Henry B. Walthall, Rafaela Ottiano. (*See p.* 49)

DIABOLIK (Also known as DANGER: DIABOLIK). Italy/France. 1967. *Director:* Mario Bava. *Screenplay:* Dino Maiuri, Adriano Baracco, Mario Bava. *Based on the comic strip by:* Angela and Luciana Giussani. *Photography:* Antonio Rinaldi. *Designer:* Flavio Mogherini. *Music:* Ennio Morricone. *Production:* Dino de Laurentiis Cinematografica (Rome)/Marianne Productions (Paris).

Players: John Phillip Law, Marisa Mell, Michel Piccoli, Adolfo Celi, Terry-Thomas. (*See p.* 200)

DOCTOR CYCLOPS. U.S.A. 1940. *Director:* Ernest B. Schoedsack. *Screenplay:* Tom Kilpatrick. *Photography:* Henry Sharp, Winton Hoch. *Special Effects:* Farciot Edouart, Wallace Kelly. *Designers:* Hans Dreier, Earl Hedrick. *Producer:* Dale van Every. *Production:* Paramount.

Players: Albert Dekker, Janice Logan, Thomas Coley. (*See p.* 50)

DOCTOR MABUSE DER SPIELER. Part One: DER SPIELER (THE GREAT GAMBLER). Part Two. MENSCHEN DER ZEIT (INFERNO). Germany. 1922. *Director:* Fritz Lang. *Screenplay:* Fritz Lang, Thea von Harbou. *Based on the novel by:* Norbert Jacques. *Photography:* Carl Hoffmann. *Designers:* Otto Hunte, Stahl-Ubach. *Production:* Ullstein-UCO/Ufa.

Players: Rudolf Klein-Rogge, Alfred Abel, Aud Egede Nissen, Gertrude Welcker, Bernhard Goetzke. (*See p.* 26)

DOCTOR STRANGELOVE OR HOW I LEARNED TO STOP WORRYING AND LOVE THE BOMB. G.B. 1964. *Director:*

Stanley Kubrick. *Screenplay:* Stanley Kubrick, Terry Southern, Peter George. *Based on the novel* Red Alert *by:* Peter George. *Photography:* Gilbert Taylor. *Designer:* Ken Adam. *Producer:* Stanley Kubrick.

Players: Peter Sellers, George C. Scott, Sterling Hayden, Keenan Wynn, Slim Pickens. (*See p.* 166)

DOCTOR X. U.S.A. 1932. *Director:* Michael Curtiz. *Screenplay:* Earl Baldwin, Robert Tasker. *Based on a play by:* Howard W. Comstock, Allen C. Miller. *Photography:* Richard Tower, Ray Rennahan. *Production:* Warner Brothers.

Players: Lionel Atwill, Fay Wray, Lee Tracy, Preston Foster. (*See p.* 46)

DONOVAN'S BRAIN. U.S.A. 1953. *Director:* Felix Feist. *Screenplay:* Felix Feist. *Based on the novel by:* Curt Siodmak. *Adapted by:* Hugh Brooke. *Photography:* Joseph Biroc. *Producer:* Tom Gries.

Players: Lew Ayres, Gene Evans, Nancy Davis.

EARTH VERSUS THE FLYING SAUCERS. U.S.A. 1956. *Director:* Fred F. Sears. *Screenplay:* George Worthing Yates, Raymond T. Marcus. *Story by:* Curt Siodmak. *Suggested by the book* Flying Saucers from Outer Space *by:* Maj. Donald Keyhoe. *Photography:* Fred Jackman Jr. *Special Effects:* Ray Harryhausen. *Producer:* Charles H. Schneer. *Production:* Columbia.

Players: Hugh Marlowe, Joan Taylor, Morris Ankrum, John Zaremba. (*See p.* 154)

THE FACE OF ANOTHER (TANIN NO KAO). Japan. 1967. *Director:* Hiroshi Teshigahara. *Screenplay:* Kobo Abe. *Photography:* Hiroshi Sekawa. *Designers:* Arata Isozaki, Masao Yamazaki. *Music:* Toru Takemitsu. *Producer:* Hiroshi Teshigahara.

Players: Tatsuya Nakadai, Mikijiro Hira, Kyoko Kishida, Machiko Kyo, Eiji Okada, Miki Irie. (*See p.* 207)

FANTASTIC VOYAGE. U.S.A. 1966. *Director:* Richard Fleischer. *Screenplay:* Harry Kleiner. *Based on a story by:* Otto Klement, Jerome Bixby. *Adapted by:* David Duncan. *Photography:* Ernest Laszlo. *Special Effects:* L. B. Abbott, Art Cruickshank, Emil Kosa

Jr. *Designers:* Jack Martin Smith, Dale Hennesy. *Production:* 20th Century-Fox.

Players: Stephen Boyd, Raquel Welch, Edmond O'Brien, Donald Pleasence. (*See p.* 173)

FAHRENHEIT 451. G.B./France. 1966. *Director:* François Truffaut. *Screenplay:* François Truffaut, Jean-Louis Richard. *Based on the novel by:* Ray Bradbury. *Photography:* Nicholas Roeg. *Designer:* Syd Cain. *Music:* Bernard Herrmann. *Design and Costume Consultant:* Tony Walton.

Players: Oskar Werner, Julie Christie, Cyril Cusack, Anton Diffring. (*See p.* 202)

FIRST MAN INTO SPACE. G.B. 1958. *Director:* Robert Day. *Screenplay:* John C. Cooper, Lance Z. Hargreaves. *Based on a story by:* Wyott Ordung. *Photography:* Geoffrey Faithfull.

Players: Marshall Thompson, Marla Landi, Bill Edwards, Robert Ayres. (*See p.* 99)

FIRST MEN ON THE MOON. G.B. 1964. *Director:* Nathan Juran. *Screenplay:* Nigel Kneale, Jan Reed. *Based on the novel by:* H. G. Wells. *Photography:* Wilkie Cooper. *Special Effects:* Ray Harryhausen. *Designer:* John Blezard. *Producer:* Charles Schneer.

Players: Edward Judd, Martha Hyer, Lionel Jeffries.

FIVE. U.S.A. 1951. *Producer/Director/Screenplay/Production Designer:* Arch Oboler. *Photography/Editor/Production Assistant:* Sid Lubow, Ed Speigel, Lou Stoumen, Arthur Swerdloff. *Cinematographic Consultant:* Louis Clyde Stoumen. *Production:* Columbia.

Players: William Phipps, Susan Douglas, James Anderson, Charles Lampkin, Earl Lee.

FLASH GORDON. U.S.A. 1936. *Director:* Frederick Stephani. *Screenplay:* Frederick Stephani, George Plympton, Basil Dickey, Ella O'Neill. *Based on the comic strip by:* Alex Raymond. *Photography:* Jerry Ash, Richard Fryer. *Production:* Universal. Serial in thirteen episodes.

Players: Larry "Buster" Crabbe, Jean Rogers, Charles Middleton. (*See p.* 73)

FLASH GORDON CONQUERS THE UNIVERSE. U.S.A. 1940.

Directors: Ford Beebe, Ray Taylor. *Screenplay:* George H. Plympton, Basil Dickey, Barry Shipman. *Based on the comic strip by:* Alex Raymond. *Production:* Universal. Serial in twelve episodes.

Players: Larry "Buster" Crabbe, Carol Hughes, Frank Shannon, Charles Middleton. (*See p.* 73)

FLASH GORDON'S TRIP TO MARS. U.S.A. 1938. *Directors:* Ford Beebe, Robert Hill. *Screenplay:* Wyndham Gittens, Norman S. Hall, Ray Trampe, Herbert Dalmas. *Based on the comic strip by:* Alex Raymond. *Production:* Universal. Serial in fifteen epsodes.

Players: Larry "Buster" Crabbe, Carol Hughes, Charles Middleton. (*See p.* 73)

THE FLY. U.S.A. 1958. *Director:* Kurt Neumann. *Screenplay:* James Clavell. *Based on the story by:* George Langelaan. *Photography:* Karl Struss. *Special Effects:* L. B. Abbott. *Designers:* Lyle Wheeler, Theobald Holsopple. *Production:* 20th Century-Fox.

Players: Al Hedison, Patricia Owens, Vincent Price. (*See p.* 138)

THE FLYING TORPEDO. U.S.A. 1916. *Director:* Jack O'Brien. *Screenplay:* D. W. Griffith. *Producer:* D. W. Griffith. *Production:* Triangle.

Players: John Emerson, Bessie Love, Spottiswoode Aitken. (*See p.* 20)

LA FOLIE DU DOCTEUR TUBE (THE MADNESS OF DR. TUBE). France. 1915. *Director/Screenplay:* Abel Gance. *Photography:* Wentzel. *Producer:* Louis Nalpas. *Production:* Les Films d'Art.

Players: Albert Dieudonné. (*See p.* 18)

FORBIDDEN PLANET. U.S.A. 1956. *Director:* Fred McLeod Wilcox. *Screenplay:* Cyril Hume. *Based on a story by:* Irving Block, Allen Adler. *Photography:* George Folsey. *Special Effects:* A. Arnold Gillespie, Warren Newcombe, Irving G. Ries, Joshua Meador. *Electronic Tonalities by:* Louis and Bebe Barron. *Designers:* Cedric Gibbons, Arthur Lonergan. *Producer:* Nicholas Nayfack. *Production:* M-G-M.

Players: Walter Pidgeon, Anne Francis, Leslie Nielsen, Warren Stevens. (*See p.* 112)

F.P.I. ANTWORTET NICHT (F.P.I. FAILS TO REPLY). G.B./France/Germany. 1933. *Director:* Karl Hartl. *Screenplay:* Walter Reisch, Curt Siodmak. *Photography:* Gunther Rittau, Konstantin Tschet. *Producer:* Erich Pommer. *Production:* Gaumont/Fox/Ufa.

Players: Hans Albers, Peter Lorre, Sybille Schmitz, Paul Hartmann, Herman Speelmans. (*See p. 37*)

DIE FRAU IM MOND (WOMAN IN THE MOON) (Also known as BY ROCKET TO THE MOON). Germany. 1928. *Director:* Fritz Lang. *Screenplay:* Fritz Lang, Thea von Harbou. *Photography:* Kurt Kourant, Oskar Fischinger, Otto Kanturek. *Designers:* Otto Hunte, Emil Hasler, Karl Vollbrecht. *Production:* Fritz Lang Film/G.M.B.H. Ufa.

Players: Gerda Maurus, Willy Fritsch, Fritz Rasp. (*See* p. 35)

FROM THE EARTH TO THE MOON. U.S.A. 1964. *Director:* Byron Haskin. *Screenplay:* Robert Blees, James Leicester. *Based on the novel by:* Jules Verne. *Photography:* Edwin B. DuPar. *Special Effects:* Lee Zavitz. *Designer:* Hal Wilson Cox. *Producer:* Benedict Bogeaus.

Players: Joseph Cotton, George Sanders, Debra Paget.

GABRIEL OVER THE WHITE HOUSE. U.S.A. 1933. *Director:* Gregory La Cava. *Screenplay:* Carey Wilson. *Based on the novel by:* Thomas Frederic Tweed. *Production:* M-G-M.

Players: Walter Huston. (*See p. 147*)

THE GIANT CLAW. U.S.A. 1957. *Director:* Fred F. Sears. *Screenplay:* Samuel Newman, Paul Gargelin. *Photograph:* Benjamin H. Kline. *Designer:* Paul Palmentola. *Producer:* Sam Katzman.

Players: Jeff Morrow, Mara Corday, Morris Ankrum.

GODZILLA (GOJIRA in Japan). Japan. 1955. *Director:* Inoshiro Honda. *Screenplay:* Takeo Murata, Inoshiro Honda. *Based on a story by:* Shigeru Kayama. *Photography:* Maseo Tamai, Guy Roe. *Special Effects:* Eiji Tsuburuya. *Designer:* Satoshi Chuko. *Production:* Toho.

Players: Raymond Burr, Takashi Shimura, Momoko Kochi. (*See p. 136*)

GOLD. Germany. 1934. *Director:* Karl Hartl. *Screenplay:* Rolf E.

Vanloo. *Photography:* Gunther Rittau, Otto Beacker, Werner Bohne. *Designer:* Otto Hunte. *Production:* Ufa.

Players: Brigitte Helm, Hans Albers, Michael Bohnen. (*See p.* 38)

HEAVEN SHIP (HIMMELSKIBET). Denmark. 1917. *Director:* Forest Holger-Madsen. *Screenplay:* Sophus Michaelis, Ole Olsen. *Photography:* Louis Larsen, Frederik Fuglsang. *Designer:* Axel Bruun.

Players: Nicolai Neiiendam, Gunnar Tolnas, Zanny Petersen, Nils Asther. (*See p.* 18)

HIGH TREASON. G.B. 1929. *Director:* Maurice Elvey. *Screenplay:* L'Estrange Fawcett. *Based on the play by:* Pemberton Billing. *Production:* Gaumont.

Players: Benita Hume, Jameson Thomas, Basil Gill. (*See p.* 90)

HIS PREHISTORIC PAST (Also known as A DREAM). U.S.A. 1914. *Director/Screenplay:* Charles Chaplin. *Production:* Keystone.

Players: Charles Chaplin, Mack Swain, Gene Marsh. (*See p.* 21)

HOMUNCULUS (Also known as HOMUNCULUS DER FUHRER). Germany. 1916. *Director:* Otto Rippert. *Screenplay:* Otto Rippert, Robert Neuss. *Photography:* Carl Hoffmann. *Production:* Bioscop.

Players: Olaf Föns, Fredrick Kuhn, Maria Carmi. (*See p.* 21)

HOUSE OF DRACULA. U.S.A. 1945. *Director:* Erle C. Kenton. *Screenplay:* Edward T. Lowe. *Based on a story by:* George Bricker, Dwight V. Babcock. *Photography:* George Robinson. *Designers:* John B. Goodman, Martin Obzina. *Producer:* Paul Malvern. *Production:* Universal.

Players: Lon Chaney Jr., Martha O'Driscoll, Jane Adams, John Carradine, Lionel Atwill, Glenn Strange. (*See p.* 48)

I BURY THE LIVING. U.S.A. 1957. *Director:* Albert Band. *Screenplay:* Louis Garfinkle. *Photography:* Frederick Gately. *Designer:* E. Vorkapich. *Producers:* Albert Band, Louis Garfinkle.

Players: Richard Boone, Theodore Bikel, Peggy Maurer.

I MARRIED A MONSTER FROM OUTER SPACE. U.S.A. 1958. *Director:* Gene Fowler Jr. *Screenplay:* Louis Vittes. *Photography:*

Haskell Boggs. *Special Effects:* John P. Fulton. *Designers:* Hal Pereira, Henry Bumstead. *Producer:* Gene Fowler Jr.

Players: Tom Tryon, Gloria Talbott, Peter Baldwin, Robert Ivers. (*See p.* 142)

IKARIE X.B.I. (Also known as VOYAGE TO THE END OF THE UNIVERSE). Czechoslovakia. 1964. *Director:* Jindrich Polak. *Screenplay:* Pavel Juracek, Jindrich Polak. *Photography:* Jan Kalis. *Designer:* Jan Zazvorka.

Players: Sdenek Stepanek, Radovan Lukavsky, Dana Medricka. (*See p.* 207)

THE INCREDIBLE SHRINKING MAN. U.S.A. 1957. *Director:* Jack Arnold. *Screenplay:* Richard Matheson. *Based on the novel* The Shrinking Man *by:* Richard Matheson. *Photography:* Ellis W. Carter. *Special Effects:* Clifford Stine. *Optical Effects:* Roswell A. Hoffman, Everett A. Broussard. *Designers:* Alexander Golitzen, Robert Clatworthy. *Producer:* Albert Zugsmith. *Production:* Universal.

Players: Grant Williams, Randy Stuart, April Kent. (*See p.* 126)

L'INHUMAINE (THE INHUMAN ONE). France. 1923/24. *Director:* Marcel L'Herbier. *Screenplay:* Georgette Leblanc, Marcel L'Herbier. *Photography:* Specht, Roche. *Designers:* Mallet-Stevens, Alberto Cavalcanti, Claude Autant-Lara, Fernand Léger. *Production:* Cinegraphic.

Players: Georgette Leblanc, Philippe Hériat. (*See p.* 18)

INVADERS FROM MARS. U.S.A. 1953. *Director/Production Designer:* William Cameron Menzies. *Screenplay:* Richard Blake. *Photography:* John Seitz. *Designer:* Boris Leven. *Music:* Raoul Kraushaar. *Producer:* Edward L. Alperson.

Players: Helena Carter, Arthur Franz, Jimmy Hunt, Leif Erickson. (*See p.* 67)

INVASION U.S.A. U.S.A. 1952. *Director:* Alfred E. Green. *Screenplay:* Robert Smith. *Based on a story by:* Robert Smith, Franz Spencer. *Photography:* John L. Russell. *Designer:* James Sullivan. *Producers:* Albert Zugsmith, Robert Smith.

Players: Gerald Mohr, Peggie Castle, Dan O'Herlihy, Robert Bice.

(*See p.* 157)
INVASION OF THE BODY SNATCHERS. U.S.A. 1956. *Director:* Don Siegel. *Screenplay:* Daniel Mainwaring. *Based on a novel by:* Jack Finney. *Photography:* Ellsworth Fredericks. *Designer:* Edward Haworth. *Producer:* Walter Wanger. *Production:* Allied Artists.

Players: Kevin McCarthy, Dana Wynter, Carolyn Jones, King Donovan. (*See p.* 139)

AN INVENTION FOR DESTRUCTION (Also known as THE FABULOUS WORLD OF JULES VERNE). Czechoslovakia. 1957. *Director:* Karel Zeman. *Screenplay:* Karel Zeman, Francis Gross. *Based on works by:* Jules Verne. *Photography:* George Taran, B. S. Piccard, Anthony Hora. *Designer:* Zdenek Rozkopal. *Animation:* Ernest Marchand, Henry Liss, Francis Kramm.

Players: Louis Tock, Ernest Navara, Milo Holl.

THE INVISIBLE MAN. U.S.A. 1933. *Director:* James Whale. *Screenplay:* R. C. Sherriff, Philip Wylie. *Based on the novel by:* H. G. Wells. *Photography:* Arthur Edeson, John Mescall. *Special Effects:* John P. Fulton. *Production:* Universal.

Players: Claude Rains, Gloria Stuart, William Harrigan, Henry Travers. (*See p.* 51)

THE INVISIBLE MAN RETURNS. U.S.A. 1940. *Director:* Joe May. *Screenplay:* Curt Siodmak. *Based on a story by:* Joe May and Curt Siodmak. *Photography:* Milton Krasner. *Production:* Universal.

Players: Sir Cedric Hardwicke, Vincent Price, Nan Grey, John Sutton. (*See p.* 52)

THE INVISIBLE RAY. U.S.A. 1936. *Director:* Lambert Hillyer. *Screenplay:* John Colton. *Based on a story by:* Howard Higgins, Douglas Hedges. *Photography:* George Robinson, John P. Fulton. *Producer:* Edmund Grainger. *Production:* Universal.

Players: Boris Karloff, Bela Lugosi, Frances Drake, Frank Lawton. (See *p.* 43)

THE INVISIBLE WOMAN. U.S.A. 1940. *Director:* A. Edward Sutherland. *Screenplay:* Robert Lees, Fred Rinaldo, Gertrude Purcell. *Based on a story by:* Curt Siodmak, Joe May. *Photography:* Elwood Bredell. *Production:* Universal.

Players: John Barrymore, Virginia Bruce, Margaret Hamilton. (*See p. 52*)

ISLAND OF LOST SOULS. U.S.A. 1932. *Director:* Erle C. Kenton. *Screenplay:* Waldemar Young, Philip Wylie. *Based on the novel* The Island of Dr. Moreau *by:* H. G. Wells. *Photography:* Karl Struss. *Production:* Paramount.

Players: Charles Laughton, Richard Arlen, Leila Hyams, Kathleen Burke, Arthur Hohl. (*See p. 47*)

IT CAME FROM BENEATH THE SEA. U.S.A. 1955. *Director:* Richard Gordon. *Screenplay:* George Worthing Yates, Hal Smith. *Photography:* Harry Freulich. *Special Effects:* Ray Harryhausen. *Designer:* Paul Palmentola. *Production:* Columbia.

Players: Kenneth Tobey, Faith Domergue, Ian Keith.

IT CAME FROM OUTER SPACE. U.S.A. 1953. *Director:* Jack Arnold. *Screenplay:* Harry Essex. *Based on a treatment by:* Ray Bradbury. *Photography:* Clifford Stine. *Designers:* Bernard Herzbrun, Robert Boyle. *Producer:* William Alland. *Production:* Universal.

Players: Richard Carlson, Barbara Rush, Charles Drake. (*See p. 117*)

IT HAPPENED HERE. G.B. 1963. *Producer/Director/Screenplay:* Kevin Brownlow, Andrew Mollo. *Based on an original story by:* Kevin Brownlow. *Photography:* Peter Suschitzky. *Additional Photography/Editor:* Kevin Brownlow. *Designer/Military Adviser:* Andrew Mollo.

Players: Pauline Murray, Sebastian Shaw, Fiona Leland, Honor Fehrson. (*See p. 199*)

LA JETÉE (THE PIER). France. 1962. *Director/Screenplay:* Chris Marker. *Photography:* Jean Chiabaud. *Music:* Trevor Duncan. *Production:* Argos Films.

Players: Helene Chatelain, Davos Hanich, Jacques Ledoux. (*See p. 204*)

KING KONG. U.S.A. 1933. *Directors:* Merian C. Cooper, Ernest B. Schoedsack. *Screenplay:* James Creelman, Ruth Rose. *Based on a story by:* Edgar Wallace, Merian Cooper. *Photography:* Edward

Lindon. *Special Effects:* Willis O'Brien. *Designers:* Carroll Clark, Al Herman. *Music:* Max Steiner. *Production:* RKO.

Players: Fay Wray, Robert Armstrong, Frank Reicher. (*See p.* 85)

KONGA. G.B. 1960. D*irector:* John Lemont. *Screenplay:* Aben Kandel, Herman Cohen. *Photography:* Desmond Dickinson. *Designer:* Wilfred Arnold. *Producer:* Herman Cohen.

Players: Michael Gough, Margo Johns, Jess Conrad, Claire Gordon. (*See p.* 135)

KRONOS. U.S.A. 1957. *Director:* Kurt Neumann. *Screenplay:* Lawrence Louis Goldman. *Based on a story by:* Irving Block. *Photography:* Karl Struss. *Designer:* Theobald Holsopple. *Producer:* Kurt Neumann. *Production:* 20th Century-Fox.

Players: Jeff Morrow, Barbara Lawrence, John Emery, George O'Hanlon. (*See p.* 138)

THE LADY AND THE MONSTER. U.S.A. 1944. *Director:* George Sherman. *Screenplay:* Dane Lussier, Frederick Kohner. *Based on the novel* Donovan's Brain *by:* Curt Siodmak. *Photography:* John Alton. *Production:* Republic.

Players: Richard Arlen, Erich von Stroheim, Sidney Blackmer. (*See p.* 48)

THE LAND UNKNOWN. U.S.A. 1957. *Director:* Virgil Vogel. *Screenplay:* Laslo Gorog. *Based on the story by:* Charles Palmer. *Photography:* Ellis Carter. *Special Effects:* Roswell A. Hoffman, Fred Knoth, Orien Ernest, Jack Kevan. *Designers:* Alexander Golitzen, Richard Riedel. *Producer:* William Alland. *Production:* Universal.

Players: Jock Mahoney, Shawn Smith, William Reynolds.

LOST HORIZON. U.S.A. 1937. *Director:* Frank Capra. *Screenplay:* Robert Riskin. *Based on the novel by:* James Hilton. *Designer:* Stephen Goosson. *Editors:* Gene Milford, Gene Havlick. *Music:* Dmitri Tiomkin. *Production:* Columbia.

Players: Ronald Colman, Jane Wyatt, Sam Jaffe, Margo, H. B. Warner. (*See p.* 82)

THE LOST WORLD. U.S.A. 1925. *Director:* Harry Hoyt. *Screenplay:* Marion Fairfax. *Based on the novel by:* Sir Arthur Conan

Doyle. *Photography:* Arthur Edeson. *Special Effects:* Willis H. O'Brien. *Producer:* Watterson R. Rothacker. *Production:* First National.

Players: Wallace Beery, Bessie Love, Lewis Stone, Lloyd Hughes. (*See* p. 84)

THE MAGNETIC MONSTER. U.S.A. 1953. *Director:* Curt Siodmak. *Screenplay:* Curt Siodmak, Ivan Tors. *Photography:* Charles Van Enger. *Designer:* George Van Marten. *Producer:* Ivan Tors.

Players: Richard Carlson, King Donovan, Jean Byron, Jarma Lewis. (*See* p. 39)

THE MANCHURIAN CANDIDATE. U.S.A. 1962. *Director:* John Frankenheimer. *Screenplay:* George Axelrod. *Based on the novel by:* Richard Condon. *Photography:* Lionel Lindon. *Music:* David Amram. *Producers:* John Frankenheimer, George Axelrod. *Production:* United Artists.

Players: Frank Sinatra, Laurence Harvey, Janet Leigh, Angela Lansbury, James Gregory. (*See* p. 176)

THE MAN IN THE WHITE SUIT. G.B. 1951. *Director:* Alexander Mackendrick. *Screenplay:* Roger MacDougall, John Dighton, Alexander Mackendrick. *Photography:* Douglas Slocombe. *Designer:* Jim Morahan. *Production:* Ealing.

Players: Alec Guinness, Joan Greenwood, Ernest Thesiger. (*See* p. 93)

THE MAN THEY COULD NOT HANG. U.S.A. 1939. *Director:* Nick Grinde. *Screenplay:* Karl Brown. *Based on a story by:* Leslie T. White, George W. Sayre. *Photography:* Benjamin Kline. *Producer:* Wallace MacDonald. *Production:* Columbia.

Players: Boris Karloff, Loran Gray, Robert Wilcox. (*See* p. 45)

THE MAN WHO COULD CHEAT DEATH. G.B. 1959. *Director:* Terence Fisher. *Screenplay:* Jimmy Sangster. *Based on the play* The Man in Half Moon Street *by:* Barré Lyndon. *Photography:* Jack Asher. *Designer:* Bernard Robinson. *Producer:* Anthony Hinds. *Production:* Hammer.

Players: Anton Diffring, Hazel Court, Christopher Lee, Arnold Marle. (*See* p. 91)

THE MAN WITH X-RAY EYES (Also known as X-THE MAN WITH X-RAY EYES). U.S.A. 1963. *Director:* Roger Corman. *Screenplay:* Ray Russell, Robert Dillon. *Based on the story by:* Ray Russell. *Photography:* Floyd Crosby. *Producer:* Roger Corman. *Production:* American International.

Players: Ray Milland, Diane van der Vlis, Harold J. Stone, John Hoyt. (*See p. 179*)

THE MASK OF FU MANCHU. U.S.A. 1932. *Director:* Charles Brabin. *Screenplay:* Irene Kuhn, Edgar Woolf, John Willard. *Based on the novel by:* Sax Rohmer. *Photography:* Tony Gaudio. *Production:* M-G-M.

Players: Boris Karloff, Lewis Stone, Myrna Loy, Charles Starrett. (*See p. 46*)

THE MAZE. U.S.A. 1953. *Director/Designer:* William Cameron Menzies. *Screenplay:* Dan Ullman. *Based on the story by:* Maurice Sandoz. *Photography:* Harry Neumann. *Producer:* Walter Mirisch. *Production:* Allied Artists.

Players: Richard Carlson, Veronica Hurst, Katherine Emery, Michael Pate. (*See p. 66*)

METROPOLIS. Germany. 1926. *Director:* Fritz Lang. *Screenplay:* Fritz Lang, Thea von Harbou. *Based on the novel by:* Thea von Harbou. *Photography:* Karl Freund, Günther Rittau. *Designers:* Otto Hunte, Erich Kettelhut, Karl Vollbrecht. *Production:* Ufa.

Players: Brigitte Helm, Alfred Abel, Gustav Froehlich, Rudolf Klein-Rogge, Heinrich George, Fritz Rasp. (*See p. 25*)

MIGHTY JOE YOUNG (Also known as MR. JOSEPH YOUNG OF AFRICA). U.S.A. 1949. *Director:* Ernest B. Schoedsack. *Screenplay:* Ruth Rose. *Based on a story by:* Merian C. Cooper. *Photography:* J. Roy Hunt. *Special Effects:* Willis H. O'Brien, Ray Harryhausen. *Designer:* James Basevi. *Producers:* John Ford, Merian C. Cooper. *Production:* RKO.

Players: Terry Moore, Ben Johnson, Robert Armstrong, Frank McHugh, Regis Toomey. (*See p. 86*)

THE MONOLITH MONSTERS. U.S.A. 1957. *Director:* John Sherwood. *Screenplay:* Norman Jolley, Robert M. Fresco. *Based on a story by:* Jack Arnold, Robert M. Fresco. *Photography:* Ellis Carter. *Designers:* Alexander Golitzen, Bob Smith. *Producer:* Howard Christie. *Production:* Universal.

Players: Grant Williams, Lola Albright, Les Tremayne. (*See p.* 154)

THE MOST DANGEROUS MAN ALIVE. U.S.A. 1961. *Director:* Allan Dwan. *Screenplay:* James Leicester, Phillip Rock. *Based on the story* The Steel Monster *by:* Phillip Rock, Michael Pate. *Photography:* Carl Carvahal. *Producer:* Benedict Bogeaus. *Production:* Columbia.

Players: Ron Randell, Debra Paget, Elaine Stewart, Anthony Caruso. (*See p.* 143)

MOTHRA. Japan. 1962. *Director:* Inoshiro Honda. *Screenplay:* Shinichi Sekizawa. *Photography:* Hajime Koizumi. *Special Effects:* Eiji Tsuburaya. *Production:* Toho.

Players: Franky Sakai, Horishi Koizumi, Kyoko Kagawa. (*See p.* 136)

THE ? MOTORIST. G.B. 1906. *Director:* Walter Booth. *Producer:* R. W. Paul. (*See p.* 16)

THE MYSTERIES OF MYRA. U.S.A. 1916. *Directors:* Theodore and Leo Wharton. *Production:* Pathé. Serial in fifteen episodes.

Players: Jean Sothern, Howard Estabrook, Allen Murnane, M. W. Rale. (*See p.* 70)

MYSTERIOUS ISLAND. U.S.A. 1961. *Director:* Cy Endfield. *Screenplay:* John Prebble, Daniel Ullman, Crane Wilbur. *Based on the novel by:* Jules Verne. *Photography:* Wilkie Cooper. *Special Effects:* Ray Harryhausen. *Designer:* Bill Andrews. *Producer:* Charles H. Schneer. *Production:* Columbia/B.L.C.

Players: Michael Craig, Joan Greenwood, Michael Callan, Herbert Lom.

THE NAKED JUNGLE. U.S.A. 1953. *Director:* Byron Haskin. *Screenplay:* Philip Yordan, Ranald MacDougall. *Based on the story* Leiningen versus the Ants *by:* Carl Stephenson. *Photography:* Ernest Laszlo. *Designers:* Hal Pereira, Franz Bachelin. *Producer:* George Pal. *Production:* Paramount.

Players: Charlton Heston, Eleanor Parker, William Conrad, Abraham Sofaer. (*See p.* 108)

THE NEXT VOICE YOU HEAR. U.S.A. 1950. *Director:* William Wellman. *Screenplay:* Charles Schnee. *Based on the story by:* George Sumner Albee. *Photography:* William Mellor. *Designers:* Cedric Gibbons, Eddie Imazu. *Producer:* Dore Schary. *Production:* M-G-M.

Players: James Whitmore, Nancy Davis, Gary Gray, William Bronson. (*See p.* 147)

NINE DAYS IN ONE YEAR (DEVYAT'DNEY ODNOGO GODA). U.S.S.R. 1961. *Director:* Mikhail Romm. *Screenplay:* Mikhail Romm, Danily Khrabovitsky. *Photography:* German Lavrov. *Designer:* G. Koltchanov. *Producer:* Mikhail Romm.

Players: Alexei Batalov, Innokenty Smoktunovsky, Tamara Lavrova. (*See p.* 163)

1984. G.B. 1956. *Director:* Michael Anderson. *Screenplay:* William P. Templeton, Ralph Bettinson. *Based on the novel by:* George Orwell. *Photography:* C. Pennington Richards. *Designer:* Terence Verity. *Producer:* N. Peter Rathvon. *Production:* A.B.P.C.

Players: Edmond O'Brien, Jan Sterling, Michael Redgrave, David Kossoff. (*See p.* 99)

NOAH'S ARK. U.S.A. 1929. *Director:* Michael Curtiz. *Screenplay:* Darryl F. Zanuck. *Adaptation:* Anthony Coldeway. *Photography:* Hal Mohr, Barney McGill.

Players: Dolores Costello, George O'Brien, Noah Beery, Louise Fazenda. (*See p.* 146)

ONE MILLION B.C., (Also known as MAN AND HIS MATE). U.S.A. 1940. *Directors:* Hal Roach, Hal Roach Jr., D. W. Griffith. *Screenplay:* Mikell Novak, George Baker. *Photography:* Norbert Brodine. *Special Effects:* Roy Seawright. *Designer:* Charles D. Hall. *Production:* United Artists.

Players: Victor Mature, Carole Landis, Lon Chaney Jr., Mamo Clarke. (*See p.* 87)

ONE MILLION YEARS B.C. G.B. 1966. *Director:* Don Chaffey. *Screenplay:* Michael Carreras. *Based on the story by:* Mikell Novak, George Baker, Joseph Frickert. *Photography:* Wilkie Cooper. *Special*

Effects: Ray Harryhausen. *Producer:* Michael Carreras. *Production:* Hammer.

Players: John Richardson, Raquel Welch, Percy Herbert, Robert Brown. (*See p.* 87)

ON THE BEACH. U.S.A. 1959. *Director:* Stanley Kramer. *Screenplay:* John Paxton. *Based on the novel by:* Nevil Shute. *Photography:* Giuseppe Rotunno. *Designer:* Rudolph Sternad. *Producer:* Stanley Kramer.

Players: Gregory Peck, Ava Gardner, Fred Astaire, Anthony Perkins, John Meillon. (*See p.* 159)

ORLACS HÄNDE (THE HANDS OF ORLAC). Austria. 1925. *Director:* Robert Weine. *Screenplay:* Ludwig Nerz. *Based on the novel by:* Maurice Renard. *Photography:* Gunther Krampf, Hans Andreschlin. *Designer:* Stevan Wessely.

Players: Conrad Veidt, Alexandra Sorina, Carmen Cartellierei, Fritz Kortner. (*See p.* 40)

PANIC IN YEAR ZERO. U.S.A. 1962. *Director:* Ray Milland. *Screenplay:* Jay Simms, John Morton. *Based on a story by:* Jay Simms (*adapted uncredited from* Lot *and* Lot's Daughter *by:* Ward Moore.) *Photography:* Gil Warrenton. *Designer:* Daniel Haller. *Producers:* Arnold Hoagland, Lou Rusoff. *Production:* American International.

Players: Ray Milland, Jean Hagen, Frankie Avalon. (*See p.* 162)

PARIS QUI DORT (PARIS ASLEEP, also known as THE CRAZY RAY). France. 1923. *Director/Screenplay:* René Clair. *Photography:* Maurice Desfassiaux, Paul Guichard. *Designer:* André Foy. *Producer:* Henri Diamant-Berger.

Players: Henri Rolland, Madeleine Rodrigue, Albert Préjean, Martinelli, Marcel Vallee. (*See p.* 24)

THE PERFECT WOMAN. G.B. 1949. *Director:* Bernard Knowles. *Adapted by:* George Black, Bernard Knowles. *Based on the play by:* Wallace Geoffrey, Basil John Mitchell. *Dialogue:* J. B. Boothroyd. *Photography:* Jack Hildyard. *Designer:* J. Elder Wills. *Producers:* George and Alfred Black.

Players: Nigel Patrick, Stanley Holloway, Patricia Roc. (*See p.* 92)

THE PHANTOM EMPIRE. U.S.A. 1935. *Directors:* B. Reeves Eason, Otto Brower. *Screenplay:* Wallace MacDonald, Gerald Geraghty, H. Freedman. *Producer:* Armand Schaefer. *Production:* Mascot. Serial in twelve episodes.
Players: Gene Autry, Smiley Burnette. (*See p.* 72)
THE PIRATES OF 1920. G.B. 1911. *Directors:* Dave Aylott, A. E. Coleby. *Photography:* J. H. Martin. *Production:* Cricks and Martin. (*See p.* 17)
PLANET OF THE APES. U.S.A. 1967. *Director:* Franklin J. Schaffner. *Screenplay:* Rod Serling, Michael Wilson. *Based on the novel* Monkey Planet *by:* Pierre Boulle. *Photography:* Leon Shamroy. *Special Effects:* L. B. Abbott, Art Cruickshank, Emil Kosa Jr. *Designers:* Jack Martin Smith, William Creber. *Music:* Jerry Goldsmith. *Makeup:* John Chambers. *Producer:* Arthur P. Jacobs. *Production:* 20th Century-Fox.
Players: Charlton Heston, Roddy McDowall, Kim Hunter, Maurice Evans, James Whitmore. (*See p.* 172)
THE POWER. U.S.A. 1967. *Director:* Byron Haskin. *Screenplay:* John Gay. *Based on the novel by:* Frank M. Robinson. *Photography:* Ellsworth Fredericks. *Special Effects:* J. McMillan Johnson, Gene Warren. *Designers:* George W. Davis, Merrill Pye. *Music:* Miklos Rozsa. *Producer:* George Pal. *Production:* M-G-M.
Players: George Hamilton, Suzanne Pleshette, Michael Rennie, Nehemiah Persoff. (*See p.* 102, 173)
PRIVILEGE. G.B. 1967. *Director:* Peter Watkins. *Screenplay:* Norman Bogner. *Based on the story by:* Johnny Speight. *Photography:* Peter Suschitsky. *Designer:* Bill Brodie. *Music:* Mike Leander. *Producer:* John Heyman.
Players: Paul Jones, Jean Shrimpton, Mark London, Max Bacon, Jeremy Child, William Job. (*See p.* 196)
QUATERMASS AND THE PIT (also known as FIVE MILLION YEARS TO EARTH). G.B. 1967. *Director:* Roy Ward Baker. *Screenplay:* Nigel Kneale. *Based on the T.V. serial by:* Nigel Kneale. *Photography:* Arthur Grant. *Special Effects:* Bowie Films. *Production Designer:* Bernard Robinson. *Music:* Tristram Cary. *Producer:*

Anthony Nelson-Keys. *Production:* Hammer.

Players: James Donald, Andrew Keir, Barbara Shelley, Julian Glover. (*See p.* 97)

THE QUATERMASS EXPERIMENT (also known as THE CREEP-ING UNKNOWN). G.B. 1955. *Director:* Val Guest. *Screenplay:* Val Guest, Richard Landau. *Based on the T.V. serial by:* Nigel Kneale. *Photography:* Jimmy Harvey. *Special Effects:* Leslie Bowie. *Designer:* J. Elder Wills. *Production:* Hammer.

Players: Brian Donlevy, Richard Wordsworth, Jack Warner, Margia Dean. (*See p.* 96)

QUATERMASS II. G.B. 1957. *Director:* Val Guest. *Screenplay:* Nigel Kneale, Val Guest. *Based on the T.V. serial by:* Nigel Kneale. *Photography:* Gerald Gibbs. *Designer:* Bernard Robinson. *Producer:* Anthony Hinds.

Players: Brian Donlevy, John Longden, Sidney James, Bryan Forbes. (*See p.* 96)

RED PLANET MARS. U.S.A. 1952. *Director:* Harry Horner. *Screenplay:* John L. Balderston, Anthony Veiller. *Based on a play by:* John L. Balderston, John Hoare. *Photography:* Joseph Biroc. *Designer:* Charles D. Hall. *Production:* United Artists/Veiller/Hyde.

Players: Peter Graves, Andrea King, Herbert Berghof, Orley Lindgren. (*See p.* 147)

REPTILICUS. Denmark. 1961. *Director:* Poul Bang. *Screenplay:* Ib Melchior, Sidney Pink. *Photography:* Aage Wiltrup. *Designers:* Otto Lund, Helge Hansen, Kai Koed. *Production:* Saga.

Players: Asbjorn Anderson, Ann Smyrner, Mimi Heinrich, Carl Ottosen. (*See p.* 135)

REVENGE OF THE CREATURE. U.S.A. 1955. *Director:* Jack Arnold. *Screenplay:* Martin Berkeley. *Photography:* Charles S. Welbourne. *Designers:* Alexander Golitzen, Alfred Sweeney. *Producer:* William Alland. *Production:* Universal.

Players: John Agar, Lori Nelson, John Bromfield, Robert B. Williams, Nestor Paiva. (*See p.* 124)

RIDERS TO THE STARS. U.S.A. 1954. *Director:* Richard Carlson.

Screenplay: Curt Siodmak. *Photography:* Stanley Cortez. *Producer:* Ivan Tors.

Players: William Lundigan, Richard Carlson, Herbert Marshall, Martha Hyer. (*See ill. p.* 6)

ROBINSON CRUSOE ON MARS. U.S.A. 1964. *Director:* Byron Haskin. *Screenplay:* Ib Melchior, John C. Higgins. *Based on the novel* Robinson Crusoe *by:* Daniel Defoe. *Photography:* Winton Hoch. *Designers:* Hal Pereira, Arthur Lonergan. *Producer:* George Pal. *Production:* Paramount.

Players: Paul Mantee, Vic Lundin, Adam West. (*See p.* 171)

RODAN. Japan. 1956. *Director:* Inoshiro Honda. *Screenplay:* Tameshi Kimura, Takeo Murata. *Based on a story by:* Takashi Kuronuma. *Photography:* Isamu Ashida. *Special Effects:* Eiji Tsuburaya. *Designer:* Tatsuo Kita. *Production:* Toho.

Players: Kenji Sawar, Yumi Shirakawa, Akihiko Hirata. (*See p.* 136)

SATELLITE IN THE SKY. G.B. 1956. *Director:* Paul Dickson. *Screenplay:* John Mather, J. T. McIntosh, Edith Dell. *Photography:* Georges Périnal. *Designer:* Erik Blakemore. *Producers:* Edward J. and Harry Lee Danziger.

Players: Kieron Moore, Lois Maxwell, Donald Wolfit, Bryan Forbes, Jimmy Hanley.

SECONDS. U.S.A. 1966. *Director:* John Frankenheimer. *Screenplay:* Lewis John Carlino. *Based on the novel by:* David Ely. *Photography:* James Wong Howe. *Designer:* Ted Haworth. *Music:* Jerry Goldsmith. *Producer:* Edward Lewis. *Production:* Paramount/Joel/ Gibraltar.

Players: Rock Hudson, John Randolph, Salome Jens, Will Geer, Jeff Corey, Richard Anderson, Murray Hamilton. (*See p.* 176)

THE SECRET OF THE SUBMARINE. U.S.A. 1916. *Director:* George Sargent. *Production:* Mutual. Serial in fifteen episodes.

Players: Juanita Hansen, Tom Chatterton, William Tedmarsh. (*See p.* 70)

SEVEN DAYS IN MAY. U.S.A. 1964. *Director:* John Frankenheimer. *Screenplay:* Rod Serling. *Based on the novel by:* Fletcher

Knebel, Charles W. Bailey II. *Photography:* Ellsworth Fredericks. *Music:* Jerry Goldsmith. *Producer:* Edward Lewis. *Production:* Seven Arts/Joel/John Frankenheimer Productions.

Players: Burt Lancaster, Kirk Douglas, Fredric March, Ava Gardner, Edmond O'Brien, Martin Balsam. (*See p.* 176)

SON OF KONG. U.S.A. 1933. *Director:* Ernest B. Schoedsack. *Screenplay:* Ruth Rose. *Photography:* Eddie Linden, Vernon Walker, J. O. Taylor. *Special Effects:* Willis H. O'Brien. *Production:* RKO.

Players: Robert Armstrong, Helen Mack, Frank Reicher, John Marston. (*See p.* 85)

THE SOUND BARRIER (Also known as BREAKING THE SOUND BARRIER). G.B. 1951. *Director:* David Lean. *Screenplay:* Terence Rattigan. *Photography:* Jack Hildyard. *Designers:* Joseph Bato, John Hawkesworth. *Music:* Malcolm Arnold. *Producer:* Alexander Korda. *Production:* British Lion.

Players: Ralph Richardson, Nigel Patrick, Ann Todd, John Justin, Denholm Elliot, Joseph Tomelty. (*See p.* 94)

THE SPACE CHILDREN. U.S.A. 1958. *Director:* Jack Arnold. *Screenplay:* Bernard C. Schoenfeld. *Based on a story by:* Tom Filer. *Photography:* Ernest Laszlo. *Special Effects:* John P. Fulton. *Designers:* Hal Pereira, Roland Anderson. *Producer:* William Alland. *Production:* Universal.

Players: Adam Williams, Peggy Webber, Michel Ray, John Crawford. (*See p.* 129)

THE SPIDER RETURNS. U.S.A. 1941. *Director:* James W. Horne. *Screenplay:* Jesse A. Duffy, George Plympton. *Based on a story by:* Margan B. Cox, Lawrence E. Taylor, John Cutting, Harry Fraser. *Photography:* James S. Brown. *Producer:* Larry Darmour. *Production:* Columbia. Serial in fifteen episodes. (*See p.* 75)

THE STRANGE WORLD OF PLANET X. G.B. 1958. *Director:* Gilbert Gunn. *Screenplay:* Paul Ryder, Joe Ambor. *Based on the novel by:* René Ray. *Photography:* Joe Ambor. *Designer:* Bernard Sarron. *Producer:* George Maynard.

Players: Forrest Tucker, Gaby Andre, Martin Benson. (*See p.* 99)

TARANTULA. U.S.A. 1955. *Director:* Jack Arnold. *Screenplay:* Martin Berkeley, Robert M. Fresco. *Based on a story by:* Jack Arnold, Robert M. Fresco. *Photography:* George Robinson. *Designers:* Alexander Golitzen, Alfred Sweeney. *Producer:* William Alland. *Production:* Universal.

Players: John Agar, Mara Corday, Leo G. Carroll, Nestor Paiva. (*See p. 122*)

TEENAGE CAVEMAN (also known as OUT OF THE DARKNESS). U.S.A. 1958. *Director:* Roger Corman. *Screenplay:* R. Wright Campbell. *Photography:* Floyd Crosby. *Producer:* Roger Corman.

Players: Robert Vaughn, Leslie Bradley, Darrah Marshall, Frank de Kova. (*See p. 88*)

THEM! U.S.A. 1954. *Director:* Gordon Douglas. *Screenplay:* Ted Sherdeman. *Based on a story by:* George Worthing Yates. *Photography:* Sid Hickox. *Designer:* Stanley Fleischer. *Production:* Warner Brothers.

Players: James Whitmore, Edmund Gwenn, Joan Weldon, James Arness, Onslow Stevens. (*See p. 132*)

THE THING (Also known as THE THING FROM ANOTHER WORLD). U.S.A. 1951. *Director:* Christian Nyby. *Screenplay:* Charles Lederer. *Based on the story* Who Goes There? *by:* Don A. Stuart (John Campbell Jr.). *Photography:* Russell Harlan. *Designers:* Albert D'Agostino, John J. Hughes. *Producer:* Howard Hawks. *Production:* RKO.

Players: Kenneth Tobey, Margaret Sheridan, Robert Cornthwaite, James Arness. (*See p. 105*)

THINGS TO COME (Also known as THE SHAPE OF THINGS TO COME). G.B. 1936. *Director:* William Cameron Menzies. *Screenplay:* H. G. Wells. *Based on the writings of:* H. G. Wells. *Photography:* Georges Périnal. *Special Effects:* Ned Mann, (Harry Zech, uncredited) *Designer:* Vincent Korda. *Music:* Arthur Bliss. *Costumes:* René Hubert, John Armstrong. *Producer:* Alexander Korda.

Players: Raymond Massey, Ralph Richardson, Sophie Stewart,

Marguretta Scott, Edward Chapman, Maurice Bradell. (*See p.* 53)
THIS ISLAND EARTH. U.S.A. 1955. *Director:* Joseph Newman. *Screenplay:* Franklin Coen, Edward O'Callaghan. *Based on the novel by:* Raymond F. Jones. *Photography:* Clifford Stine. *Designers:* Alexander Golitzen, Richard H. Riedel. *Producer:* William Alland. *Production:* Universal.

Players: Jeff Morrow, Rex Reason, Faith Domergue, Lance Fuller, Russell Johnson. (*See p.* 110)

THE TIME MACHINE. U.S.A. 1960. *Director:* George Pal. *Screenplay:* David Duncan. *Based on the novel by:* H. G. Wells. *Photography:* Paul C. Vogel. *Special Effects:* Gene Warren, Tim Barr. *Producer:* George Pal. *Production:* M-G-M.

Players: Rod Taylor, Yvette Mimieux, Alan Young, Sebastian Cabot. (*See p.* 109)

TWENTY MILLION MILES TO EARTH. U.S.A. 1957. *Director:* Nathan Juran. *Screenplay:* Bob Williams, Christopher Knopf. *Based on a story by:* Charlott Knight. *Photography:* Irving Lippman, Carlos Ventimiglia. *Special Effects:* Ray Harryhausen. *Designer:* Cary Odell. *Production:* Columbia.

Players: William Hopper, Joan Taylor, Frank Puglia, John Zaremba.

THE 27th DAY. U.S.A. 1957. *Director:* William Asher. *Screenplay:* John Mantley. *Based on the novel by:* John Mantley. *Photography:* Harry Freulich. *Designer:* Ross Bellah. *Producer:* Helen Ainsworth. *Production:* Columbia.

Players: Gene Barry, Valerie French, George Voskovec. (*See p.* 157)

20,000 LEAGUES UNDER THE SEA. U.S.A. 1955. *Director:* Richard Fleischer. *Screenplay:* Earl Felton. *Based on the novel by:* Jules Verne. *Photography:* Franz Planer. *Special Effects:* Ub Iwerks. *Production:* Walt Disney.

Players: James Mason, Paul Lukas, Peter Lorre, Kirk Douglas.

THE TWONKY. U.S.A. 1953. *Producer/Director/Screenplay:* Arch Oboler. *Based on the story by:* Henry Kuttner. *Photography:* Joseph Biroc.

Players: Hans Conreid, Billy Lynn, Gloria Blondell, Janet Warren.
2001: A SPACE ODYSSEY. G.B. 1968. *Director:* Stanley Kubrick.
Screenplay: Stanley Kubrick, Arthur C. Clarke. *Based on the story*
The Sentinel *by:* Arthur C. Clarke. *Photography:* Geoffrey Unsworth. *Additional Photography:* John Alcott. *Special Photographic Effects designed and directed by:* Stanley Kubrick. *Special Effects:* Wally Veevers, Douglas Trumbull, Con Pederson, Tom Howard. *Production Designers:* Tony Masters, Harry Lange, Ernie Archer. *Art Director:* John Hoesli. *Producer:* Stanley Kubrick. *Production:* M-G-M.

Players: Keir Dullea, Gary Lockwood, William Sylvester. (*See* p. 181)

UNDERSEA KINGDOM. U.S.A. 1936. *Directors:* B. Reeves Eason, Joseph Kane. *Screenplay:* John Rathmell, Maurice Geraghty, Oliver Drake. *Based on a story by:* John Rathmell, Tracy Knight. *Producer:* Barney Sarecky. *Production:* Republic. Serial in twelve episodes.

Players: Ray Corrigan, Monte Blue.(*See* p. 72)

LE VOYAGE DANS LA LUNE (A TRIP TO THE MOON). France. 1902. *Producer/Director/Screenplay:* Georges Méliès. (*See* p. 15)

LE VOYAGE Á TRAVERS L'IMPOSSIBLE (AN IMPOSSIBLE VOYAGE). France. 1904. *Producer/Director/Screenplay:* Georges Méliès. (*See* p. 15)

VILLAGE OF THE DAMNED. G.B. 1960. *Director:* Wolf Rilla. *Screenplay:* Stirling Silliphant, Wolf Rilla, George Barclay. *Based on the novel* The Midwich Cuckoos *by:* John Wyndham. *Photography:* Geoffrey Faithfull. *Special Effects:* Tom Howard. *Designer:* Ivan King. *Production:* M-G-M.

Players: George Sanders, Barbara Shelley, Michael Gwenn, Laurence Naismith. (*See* p. 100)

WAR OF THE WORLDS. U.S.A. 1953. *Director:* Byron Haskin. *Screenplay:* Barré Lyndon. *Based on the novel by:* H. G. Wells. *Photography:* George Barnes. *Special Effects:* Gordon Jennings, Wallace Kelley, Paul Lerpae, Ivyl Burts, Jan Donela, Irmin Roberts, *Designers:* Hal Pereira, Albert Nozaki. *Producer:* George Pal.

Production: Paramount.

Players: Gene Barry, Ann Robinson, Henry Brandon, Les Tremayne, Jack Kruschen. (*See p.* 148)

WHEN WORLDS COLLIDE. U.S.A. 1951. *Director:* Rudolph Maté. *Screenplay:* Sydney Boehm. *Based on a story by:* Edwin Balmer, Philip Wylie. *Photography:* John F. Seitz. *Designers:* Hal Pereira, Albert Nozaki. *Producer:* George Pal. *Production:* Paramount.

Players: Richard Derr, Barbara Rush, Peter Hanson, Judith Ames. (*See p.* 152)

WILD IN THE STREETS. U.S.A. 1968. *Director:* Barry Shear. *Screenplay:* Robert Thom. *Based on the story* The Day It All Happened, Baby *by:* Robert Thom. *Photography:* Richard Moore. *Designer:* Paul Sylos. *Songs:* Barry Mann, Cynthia Weil. *Producers:* James H. Nicholson, Samuel Z. Arkoff. *Production:* American International.

Players: Christopher Jones, Shelley Winters, Diane Varsi, Hal Holbrook, Bert Freed, Ed Begley. (*See p.* 178)

THE WORLD, THE FLESH AND THE DEVIL. U.S.A. 1959. *Director/Screenplay:* Ranald MacDougall. *Story:* Ferdinand Reyher. *Based on the novel* The Purple Cloud *by:* Matthew Phipps Shiel. *Photography:* Harold J. Mazorati. *Designers:* William A. Horning, Paul Groesse. *Music:* Miklos Rozsa. *Producer:* George Englund. *Production:* M-G-M.

Players: Harry Belafonte, Inger Stevens, Mel Ferrer. (*See p.* 161)

X, THE UNKNOWN. G.B. 1956. *Director:* Leslie Norman. *Screenplay:* Jimmy Sangster. *Photography:* Gerald Gibbs. *Producer:* Anthony Hinds. *Production:* Hammer.

Players: Dean Jagger, Edward Chapman, Leo McKern, William Lucas.